MACHADO
DE ASSIS

MACHADO
DE ASSIS

THE BRAZILIAN MASTER AND HIS NOVELS

HELEN CALDWELL

UNIVERSITY OF CALIFORNIA PRESS
BERKELEY • LOS ANGELES • LONDON • 1970

UNIVERSITY OF CALIFORNIA PRESS
BERKELEY AND LOS ANGELES, CALIFORNIA

UNIVERSITY OF CALIFORNIA PRESS, LTD.
LONDON, ENGLAND

Copyright © 1970 by The Regents of the University of California
SBN 520–01608–4
Library of Congress Catalog Card Number: 76–89891
Printed in the United States of America

ACKNOWLEDGMENTS

I thank the poet Ann Stanford for her translation of Machado de Assis's sonnet to his wife—"To Caroline," which appears in chapter 17 of this book.

My gratitude also goes to the American Association of University Women for its grant of a fellowship that made it possible for me to devote much needed time to research.

CONTENTS

INTRODUCTORY—
BEFORE THE NOVELS

THE WIDTH OF THE
RUA DO OUVIDOR

Machado de Assis is no longer unknown among us. Four of his novels and some fifteen or so short stories have now appeared in English and have been greeted with a kind of indignant wonder that this Brazilian author who was born in 1839 and died in 1908 was not even a name to us. As his readers increase in our Northern Hemisphere, there has sprung up some curiosity about the man as well as about his writings.[1]

Assis himself did not consider a knowledge of his life necessary to an understanding of his fiction. He stated more than once that his writing constituted the true Machado de Assis—that he lived for and in the literary art and had no true existence outside it.[2]

Indeed, with one exception, the facts of his life, so far as we know them, shed little, if any, light upon his narrative genius or upon any of his major works. Attempts to relate the two, life and works, have served only to obscure the meaning of the works. And this, no doubt, is what he feared as he became increasingly reticent about the details of his private life, though some critics have suggested other, less flattering motives. Be that as it may, there is no overwhelming evidence that any circumstance of his life had a direct bearing on a major work of fiction—with the exception of his last novel, *Ayres's Memorial* (*Memorial de Ayres*). In that book, the influence of his wife—or perhaps one should say of her death—is indisputable. We have Assis's word on it. And, beyond his word, there is a strange testimony in the novel's manuscript, which is written in Assis's own hand.

This one exception, then, of *Ayres's Memorial* perhaps justifies a concession to idle curiosity, because to properly appreciate *Ayres's Memorial* one needs to know how his wife's influence may have worked through him to make that novel what it is. To study the problem one must go back over his life, to a certain extent at least.

Some readers will be gratified to learn that Machado de Assis was an intellectual; a courteous gentleman; a patriot; a devoted husband; a hard working, steady, law-abiding citizen and public servant; drank tea instead of something stronger; an honest man in every sense of the word; a great reader but also gregarious; a "joiner" of both political and literary societies; a man given to warm friendships, fond of animals, children, whist, chess, dancing, music, theater, and conversation; and above all a man of infinite good taste.[3] Others, no doubt, will be repelled by this array of bourgeois charm. Let these take comfort in the legend, for there is, or was, a legend that Machado de Assis was a cold, churlish, self-centered eccentric, quick to take offense, given to biting sarcasm;[4] a prude,[5] a social climber,[6] indifferent to the welfare of his country and his fellowmen;[7] timid and withdrawn because of a feeling of inferiority over his Negro blood and impoverished childhood as son of a Negro laborer and Negro washerwoman;[8] that he was gloomy and sickly, stammered unmercifully, and staggered from epileptic fit to epileptic fit;[9] that he abandoned his stepmother and had affairs with actresses—not very good actresses.[10]

He was and still is accused of being secretive because he was not very expansive about his parents, his childhood, early struggles with poverty, his wife, other women, and his illnesses—in particular his epilepsy—and because he seldom mentioned to anyone a work he might have in hand, but preferred to keep the matter to himself and let the book come upon the stands with a certain fresh éclat.[11] In the face of the legend mentioned above, his "secretiveness" is surely not to be wondered at. And the indications are that he was not born secretive: secretiveness apparently was forced upon him. When Machado de Assis was fifteen years old there appeared in the January 12, 1855, issue of the magazine *Marmota*, his second published literary effort, a poem, "The Palm Tree" (*A Palmeira*).[12] It was dedicated to a fellow poet and friend Francisco Gonçalves Braga. During the following months of that year twenty more poems appeared over his signature: of these, three were dedicated to friends, a fourth "to my cousin Sr. Henrique José Moreira," a fifth to the Emperor Pedro II, and still another, "An Angel" (*Um Anjo*), "to the memory of my sister." His first volume of verse, *Chrysalides (Chrysalidas)*, published nine years later in 1864, bore the dedication "To the memory of Francisco José de Assis and Maria Leopoldina Machado de Assis, my father and mother." This volume of 1864 was the last of Assis's books to carry a dedication to anyone until 1906, when he published a volume of collected pieces, *Relics from an Old House (Relíquias de Casa Velha)*, which opened with a hitherto unpublished sonnet, "To Caroline" (*A Carolina*).

Although his writings and his acts tend to show that he thought he best served the literary art and his own works by removing the author's physical presence from the scene, still there is reason to suppose that he came to have a healthy fear of a certain proclivity in late-nineteenth-century Brazilians—especially in his fellow Cariocas, that is, inhabitants of Rio de Janeiro. It seems that during the last half of the nineteenth century there was a tendency, in and about downtown Rio, toward idle gossip.

In the very center of the city was a rather long, very narrow street named Rua do Ouvidor, which means in Portuguese, "street of the hearer" or "listener." In Colonial Brazil, Ouvidor was the title of a sort of district judge, or justice of the peace, who had his office on this street: hence the name "hearer," or "listener," so appropriate to the nature of the street in Assis's own time. Its narrowness, he wrote, gave it an aspect and a feeling of intimacy. It was "a street made for rumor," because "Rumor demands ear on mouth in order to whisper fast and low, and then leap from side to side."[13] In its narrowness the Rua do Ouvidor was "condensed whisper," the "vivarium" of the city's rumors, and one rumor (as he reminded his readers) has more effect than ten leading articles.[14]

In 1860, when most of the city's streets were still lighted by oil lamps, the Rua do Ouvidor was piped for gas and its much frequented, brilliantly lighted, fashionable shops and restaurants kept open to late night, so that there was little interruption in the generating and dispatching of gossip.[15] One could dine, he wrote, in a restaurant on one side of the street and take a glass of wine in an establishment across the way almost without leaving one's table.[16]

By the time he was twenty-two years of age, Assis had begun to manifest an interest in the phenomena of gossip and rumor. In his column of January 7, 1862, in the *Diário do Rio de Janeiro*, he wrote: "Rumor is an invisible, an impalpable being that speaks with the voice of a man. It is everywhere and nowhere. No one knows whence it comes nor where it hides itself. It carries with it the celebrated lamp of Aladdin, by virtue of which it surpasses in power and magical potency all that is magically potent and powerful."[17] Two years later, he wrote in the same column, November 14, 1864, "[Rumor] is one of the handiest of human inventions because it has all the advantages of malicious gossip with none of the inconveniences of responsibility. . . . It is falsehood's telegraph system."[18]

For Machado de Assis, Rua do Ouvidor was the symbol par excellence for "rumor." As such it appears frequently in his journalistic columns and also in his fiction. Those who have read the novel *Esau and Jacob* (*Esaú e Jacob*) will recall that it was on Rua do Ouvidor that Ayres first learned of the "revolution." In the short story "Who Tells a Tale . . ." (*Quem Conta um Conto . . .*) (1873), the rumor that causes such comic devastation starts on this street.[19] In the novel *Resurrection* (*Resurreição*) (1872), the rumor of Felix's engagement to Livia started "on the Rua do Ouvidor at the corner of the Rua Direita. In ten minutes it reached the Rua da Quitanda, traveling so fast that in a quarter of an hour it was a subject of conversation at the corner of Rua dos Ourives. One hour was all it took to run the entire length of our main public artery. From there it spread over the whole city."[20] Referring to this street as a "hatchery" of political rumors, Machado de Assis proposed in his column, "The Week" (*A Semana*), (December 6, 1896), that the Rua do Ouvidor be widened: "If I had a voice on the City Council, rather than concern myself about the city's sanitation, I would propose the widening of the Rua do Ouvidor. When this alley is a broad avenue so that a person can hardly recognize someone on the other side of the street, one thousand political difficulties will cease."[21]

The Rua do Ouvidor was not widened. And it is still there, as Machado de Assis foresaw. In the same column (June 7, 1896), discussing the proposal to move the capital from Rio de Janeiro, he named over the things that would not be taken from Rio—"the bay, the Rua do Ouvidor, the women . . ."

Although much of the legend that has gathered about Assis no doubt circulated as anecdote and gossip during his lifetime, it appeared in print, for the most part, only after his death. Then, like Virgil's Rumor, it walked erect with its head in the clouds.

Two months to the day after his death there appeared in the *Gazeta de Notícias,* Rio, November 29, 1908, an article on Machado de Assis, the man and his work, written by one Hemetério dos Santos—a schoolteacher and writer of sorts, and a Negro. This article not only attacked Assis's prose as having no form, no style, no grammar, no psychological depth, and for being banal, obscure, monotonous, feeble, unoriginal, false, and passionless, it also attacked Assis's character.

The head and front of his offending (according to Santos) was a repudiation, a betrayal, of his Negro blood: Although his father was a Negro, a house painter of some artistic talent, Assis (said Santos) was a heartless snob who had abandoned his stepmother, a lovely mulatto lady who had been an affectionate mother to him, taught him all she knew when he was a small child, arranged for him to be taught French by a French baker in the establishment where she worked, et cetera, et cetera. And he (Assis) had refused to serve his "suffering colored brothers" with his talents, even refused to take an interest in emancipation and in other social and political problems of Brazil, "that glorious creation of Portuguese and Negro," that is, of the mulatto, "a society without compare in the New World, without peer in all history!"

This spontaneous effusion by a rather obscure elementary schoolteacher, strangely enough, was given a kind of immortality by being reprinted in the *Almanaque Brasileiro* for 1910, an annual put out by Assis's publisher and edited by Assis's friend and colleague João Ribeiro.[22]

Items from this article were repeated so many times, in so many books and articles,[23] that until rather recently they passed for truth in most quarters, and like the rumor in Assis's own "Who Tells a Tale . . ." those who repeated them "added a tittle." For example, there was a third- or fourth-hand report that Coelho Netto once went with Machado de

Assis to a poor old woman's funeral, which was interpreted by one of those who repeated the story as that of Assis's stepmother. Thus the famous author and friend of Assis was made to confirm Santos's charge of ingratitude.[24]

Machado de Assis, as mentioned above, wrote nothing about his childhood or family, but his patriotism and concern over slavery are written large throughout his works for all to read who will. In recent years Brazilian writers, in particular R. Magalhães Júnior,[25] have completed the picture of Assis's social and political concern by pointing up pertinent passages in his less read works and by revealing records of his public actions and speeches; the recovery of additional correspondence has also helped to dispel much of this myth.[26]

During his lifetime, it is true, he was attacked in his public life by political enemies; and his writings were assailed—by one influential critic in particular, Sylvio Romero. But these men could be answered and were when Assis deemed it necessary or advisable.[27] Not all the rumors that began to envelop the writer and his works were malicious in intent. Some were simple errors; besides, friends and colleagues exaggerated, and embroidered upon, the facts of his lowly origin and early struggles in order to make his accomplishments appear the greater.[28] After his death, it was not merely the envious who rushed into print; admirers in the writing profession also hastened to publish pious testimonials to the greatness and goodness of the master. For example, within a month, two younger writers whom he had encouraged, Mário de Alencar and José Veríssimo, set on paper their reminiscences and evaluations of their famous friend.[29] These two men had been in almost daily contact with him in the years preceding his death—Veríssimo for seventeen years, Alencar for four. Veríssimo's discussion of Assis's art is excellent. Both men undoubtedly admired Machado de Assis, as man and as writer, and valued his friendship, but both acknowledged that they did not understand him—Alencar frankly, Veríssimo by implication. Indeed Veríssimo here, as elsewhere in his criticism, betrays beneath his measured and admiring judgments on Assis's art a certain antipathy to it. In spite of an admitted inability to understand either the man or his genius, both writers make statements about his feelings and opinions, which may with reason be questioned. Alencar tells us, for example, that Assis had no religion of any sort, and yet he goes on to describe his "cult" of his dead wife Carolina. Veríssimo interprets a final utterance (which he claims to have made out in Assis's rambling talk as he lay dying), reports and amplifies an opinion on writing for money (which he says he heard from Assis's lips), and he gives his own explanation for Assis's dislike of angry political argument—as stemming from his fear that it would bring on an epileptic attack, and so on. In addition, *his* article, as well as Santos's, became a source of dubious biographical items that were repeated in later biographies, for example, that his father was a poor bricklayer or carpenter, and that both parents were colored and illiterate. Veríssimo is also a source of the fiction that Machado de Assis's parents died "as he was entering puberty."[30] For all his seventeen years' association, it is plain that he was not in Assis's confidence. And it was Veríssimo who belabored Assis's "immoderate" secretiveness about his life and about his work, stating that Assis would not discuss his books even after they were published.

Both these articles have inadvertently contributed, if not given rise, to what would seem to be a certain misconception of Machado de Assis's nature: they stress his *timidez*. And Veríssimo, whose article is much the longer, constantly makes use of the adjective *timido*; but, as in Alencar's article also, the word is usually coupled with the adjective *delicado*, which means "courteous and considerate." *Timido* they seem to use in the sense of "reticent"; they also make it abundantly clear that Assis was a man of character and strong will and, although modest in manner, aware of his own worth. Unfortunately, this adjective *tímido* has since been liberally applied to Assis in the sense of "timid," and a great luxuriant "inferiority complex" of tremendous proportions has grown out of it.[31] Springing from the roots of this giant exotic is a whole wonderful psychological legend, or myth if you prefer, in which Assis has been identified with protagonists in his novels—Braz Cubas, Quincas Borba, Dom Casmurro, and the retired diplomat Ayres, and with Luiz Garcia of the novel *Yayá Garcia*. The man, Assis, has been identified with these characters variously, and with all of them at once as if they were one character under different names. And he has been identified with his heroines, Estella of *Yayá Garcia*, Helena of the novel of the same name, with Guiomar of *Hand and Glove* (*A Mão e a Luva*), and with Flora, the lovely heroine of *Esau and Jacob*. The natures and vagaries of these personages have been accounted for by Machado de Assis's epilepsy, stammering, humble origin . . . and by the emotional states and drives that were supposed to arise from such "afflictions."[32] Heroic attempts have been made to create love affairs to account for the heroines Capitu and Fidelia.[33]

Even within his lifetime, Assis was subjected to this kind of criticism. In 1897 the Brazilian critic Sylvio Romero, taking exception to his condensed, impressionistic style, wrote that Machado de Assis's style was the exact photograph of his mind, of his indecisive psychological nature; that he stuttered in his style as the result of a *lacuna* in his organs of speech.[34] It was no doubt such use of biographical material that Machado de Assis feared when he refused to publish his correspondence, or write memoirs,[35] or disclose his methods of composition, or discuss his books before or after publication—in short, why he did everything in his power to make a biography difficult if not impossible.

Since his writing was paramount in his life, his fear of personal publicity was no doubt fear of the harm it would do his published works. And he foresaw that the Rua do Ouvidor would not be widened. Indeed, the Rua do Ouvidor is still there, physically and spiritually, as Agrippino Grieco, writing one hundred years after the street was piped for gas, confirms. In his book *Machado de Assis* (Rio, 1960) Grieco tells how he and his confrères preferred to sit in their comfortable bookstore-club and chew over old gossip generated by Hemetério dos Santos rather than journey up the street and consult living witnesses.[36]

But these, too, would probably have been regarded with skepticism by Machado de Assis. Such testimony did exist until recently, perhaps still does exist, handed down in a long oral tradition; and alongside it are the blown-up recollections of persons who knew, or saw, or heard tell of him when they were children, finally published after the lapse of many years. It is not impossible that the comment by Ayres, the fictional narrator of the novel *Esau and Jacob*, reflected some of Assis's own feeling in the matter. In that novel, after the political-minded Senhora Baptista (who is likened by Ayres to Lady Macbeth) had badgered her poor politician of a husband into obtaining an interview with the President of the Republic, had coined some telling expressions for him to use at the interview, had sent him off, and had anxiously awaited his return, which for some reason was unnaturally delayed, then, when he did appear, "She ran to greet him, excitedly grasped his hand, and led him to their bedroom." Dona Perpetua, a lady who collected worthless objects for sentimental reasons, saw it all and "exclaimed tenderly, 'They are like two turtledoves.' " Ayres comment: "See what eyewitnesses to history are worth!"[37]

CHAPTER TWO

VITAL STATISTICS

A hundred years after Machado de Assis's birth, the record of his baptism was discovered in a church registry of the Rio de Janeiro parish in which he was born. It stated that on November 13, 1839, in Senhora do Livramento, a branch chapel of Santa Rita Church, the Reverend Narcizo Jozé de Moraes baptized and anointed the baby Joaquim, legitimate son of Francisco Jozé de Assis and Maria Leopoldina Machado de Assis, he a native of Rio de Janeiro and she of the Island of São Miguel; that the godparents were his Excellency Chamberlain Joaquim Alberto de Souza da Silveira and Dona Maria Jozé de Mendonça Barrozo; and that the baby was born June 21, 1839.[1]

Since it was learned by this that his mother was Portuguese, a native of one of the Azores, it was presumed that she was a white woman and not of Negro blood as stated in biographies up to that time. The godparents proved to be of high social category: the godfather a twice decorated chamberlain of the imperial palace; the godmother a Portuguese by birth, and widow of a brigadier general and senator of the Brazilian Empire. (Tradition already had it that Assis's father and mother were dependents living on this lady's estate, Quinta do Livramento.)[2]

Within the next twenty years, 1939–1959, further certificates pertaining to the Assis family were found in this and two other parish registries of the city. These documents also bring into question a number of items in the legend of Machado de Assis's origin and early life. There were:

> Baptismal certification of Machado's father, which stated that he, Francisco, was the legitimate son of Francisco de Assis, mulatto, freed slave, and native of Rio de Janeiro, and of Ignacia Maria Rosa, mulatto, freed slave, and native of Rio de Janeiro, and that he was baptized on October 11, 1806.
>
> Marriage certificate of Machado's parents (August 19, 1838). From this document were learned the names of Machado's maternal grandparents and the city and parish of his mother's origin in Portugal.
>
> Baptismal certificate of Machado's sister, born May 3, 1841, and christened Maria.
>
> Death certificate of Maria who died of measles, July 4, 1845.
>
> Death certificate of Machado's mother, stating that she died of tuberculosis, January 18, 1849, at the age of thirty-four.
>
> Certificate of marriage of Machado's father Francisco José de Assis to Maria Ignez da Silva, June 18, 1854.

These last two certificates cast some doubt on Hemetério dos Santos's story that Machado's stepmother taught him to read when he was a child, since his mother did not die until he was nearly ten years old, and his father did not remarry until the boy was fifteen and already out in the world earning a living. In addition, Gondin da Fonseca, who discovered these last four records, informs us that he was able to deduce from his research: (1) that Machado de Assis's mother arrived in Brazil two years before her marriage; (2) that her full maiden name was Maria Leopoldina Machado da Câmara; (3) that she could read and write and wrote her own name in a firm, well-formed, flowing hand; (4) that there exist certain similarities between her hand and her son's. It may very well be that she taught him to read and write. It is most unlikely that she was ever the washer-woman of the legend.[3]

In short, all these documents indicate that Machado de Assis was born into a humble but not uncultured milieu—which might help account for his early, unswerving devotion to letters, and explain his refined manners, remarked by many of his contemporaries, manners that made one of them say of him, "He was born well brought up."[4]

Fonseca also discovered through announcements appearing in the *Jornal do Commercio*, April 27 and May 22 and 23, 1864, that the father, Francisco José de Assis, died April 22, 1864—that is, when Machado de Assis was nearly twenty-five years old. This discovery not only contradicts José Veríssimo's "information," it also casts doubt on Hemetério dos Santos's contention that the boy Machado had been cared for by his stepmother. Further, the notices of separate masses to be held for the deceased by the widow, her mother and brothers, and by Machado de Assis, indicate by their wording and tone, that the latter was not on good terms with his stepmother and her family.[5] In any event, by the time of his father's marriage in 1854, the fifteen-year old Machado was out in the publishing world, and, like Hop-o'-my-Thumb, marking which way he went with his own literary pebbles.

CHAPTER THREE

MAN OF LETTERS

At fifteen Machado de Assis was a literary man, and a literary man he remained the rest of his sixty-nine years. We in the world outside Brazil know him for his fiction, but he did not begin his writing career with fiction. His first piece in that medium was not published until January 5, 1858, when he was eighteen years old. It was a comic short-short story entitled, "Lost: Three Treasures" (*Três Tesouros Perdidos*)—the three treasures being the protagonist's wife, his best friend, and two-thousand milreis—the price he paid for a ticket to Minas Gerais for the man whom he supposed to be his wife's lover, the wrong man naturally. By the time Assis wrote this story at the age of eighteen, he had already tried his literary hand in five other media: poetry, biographical sketch, polemic, opera libretto, and translation from French into Portuguese.

Within the next six months he had added to those fields: political criticism and invective, comic literary sketches, literary criticism, theatrical reviews, and discussion of the philosophy of the theater.

During his first fifteen years of professional writing, that is, between the ages of fifteen and thirty (January, 1855 to January, 1870), Machado de Assis composed some 6,000 lines of poetry, 19 plays and opera librettos, 24 short stories, 182 columns and articles, and 17 translations into Portuguese from French and Spanish.[1]

Much of the above appeared in periodicals; some items were published in book form—ten volumes in all. An essay, "The Weakness Women have for Fools" (*Queda Que as Mulheres Tem Para os Tolos*), based on Champcenetz's "Petit Traité de l'Amour des Femmes pour les Sots," and labeled "A Translation," was his first published book, in 1861.[2] There followed within the next five years a volume of two one-act comedies, three more comedies published in single volumes, a collection of verse, *Chrysalides* (*Chrysalidas*), and a translation of Victor Hugo's novel *Les Travailleurs de la Mer* in three volumes.

All these forms of literary endeavor Machado de Assis was to pursue in later years, along with the novel, in which he was destined to surpass not only his Brazilian contemporaries but a good many novelists of other countries as well.

None of this early writing was what one could call remunerative. When he was nineteen he wrote enthusiastically of journalism—that it would set the writer free from economic worries by giving him the means of earning a living by his pen.[3] In later columns he commented on the low pay of letters, comparing the wealth of tenors and chorus girls with the poverty of Balzac and George Sand.[4] In the years before 1874, the date he entered government service, he too it would appear had led a hand-to-mouth existence working at various more regular occupations as he pursued the Muses on his own time. Researchers are not in complete agreement on the periods and exact capacities in which Machado de Assis served during those early years; but in general, there is reasonable evidence that he was, at various times between the ages of fifteen and thirty, typesetter, proofreader, editor, staff writer, and possibly even clerk in a book or stationery store.[5]

Besides his writing, besides his working at other occupations, he engaged in extensive artistic ventures and social activities. A few records taken from programs, official reports, and notices in the public press will give an idea of such pursuits. First, in the theatrical world:

On November 24, 1859, his three-act opera *Pipelet*, an adaptation of Eugène Sue's novel *Les Mystères de Paris*, was presented at the Theatro de São Pedro de Alcântara. On July 8, 1861, an original one-act opera *Joaninha's Wedding (As Bodas de Joaninha)*, music by Luiz Olona, was presented in the Gymnásio Dramático.

On January 31, 1862, Machado de Assis was admitted by vote of the entire membership in full session to membership in the Conservatório Dramático Brasileiro—a government-sponsored group to promote the theater. From 1862 to 1864 he exercised the office of censor for the Conservatório. (In 1952 Eugenio Gomes discovered in a heap of papers in the National Library sixteen manuscripts written and signed by Machado de Assis in his capacity of censor, "opinions" on plays submitted to the Conservatório.)[6] In the same year, 1862, two of his one-act comedies, *The Way Out (O Caminho da Porta)* and *Protocol (O Protocolo)*, were acted at the Atheneu Dramático in Rio de Janeiro; and on September 12 a two-act drama, *Gabriela* was produced in the city of São Paulo.

On March 18, 1864, he submitted his comedy, *The Apple of Discord (O Pomo de Discórdia)*, to the Conservatório Dramático Brasileiro. The outcome is not known. On August 11, *O Caminho da Porta* was produced in São Paulo. On October 12, his translation of a French comedy by O. Feuillet, *Montjoye*, was presented in the Theatro Gymnásio.

September 30, 1865, his translation of *Suplice d'une Femme*, a three-act drama by Girardin and Dumas fils, was presented in the Gymnásio Dramático.

On July 5, 1866, Machado de Assis's translation of a five-act French drama, by Barrière and Plouvier, was presented in the Theatro Gymnásio, and, September 7, in the same theater, his translation of the *Barber of Seville*.

In 1867 he collaborated with the poet Joaquim Serra and the musician Arthur Napoleão, on a musical extravaganza *O Remorso Vivo* in four acts and eight tableaux, which was first presented on February 21, 1867 at the Theatro Gymnásio. In the same theater, on May 4 of that year, his translation of a comedy by Sardou, *La Famille Benoiton*, had its first showing. It had other performances during the same year.

From Assis's numerous theatrical reviews during these years and from his remarks in later columns of journalism, it may be judged as certain that his own attendance at the theater was regular and serious. The evidence points to frequent attendance at the opera as well. In later years he often poked fun at the Carioca's craze for Italian opera, but admitted that he too had a weakness that way. In a column written when he was thirty-eight, he openly confessed:

> Another event of some interest is the resurrection of Candiani.
>
> Candiani is not known to the present generation, but the old fellows like me still remember what she was, because I myself (*me, me adsum*), I myself was one of the temporary horses of the prima donna's chariot on the nights of the beautiful *Norma!*
>
> O tempora! O nostalgia! I was twenty, full blown moustache, the blood bursting in my veins, and an enthusiasm, an enthusiasm capable of pulling all the chariots, from the chariot of State to the Sun's chariot—two metaphors that have grown old along with me.
>
> Those were the days!
>
> Candiani did not sing, she put heaven in her mouth, and her mouth in the world. When she sighed forth *Norma* it would twist the heart out of a body. The Rio folk, who are as crazy for melody as a monkey for a ba-

nana, were then in their lyric dawn. They listened to Candiani and lost all notion of reality. Every man about town became a Pindar.

And today Candiani returns after this great silence, to awake the echoes of those days. The old fellows like me will go, to recall a bit of their youth—the best thing in life, and perhaps the only thing.[7]

Paralleling and intermingling with Assis's activity in the theater were other activities of a literary and social nature.

In 1862–1863 he was librarian of the literary Sociedade Arcádia Brasileira.

July 19, 1862, at a soirée in another club, O Retiro Literário Português, he recited his poem "Charity" (*A Caridade*).

On September 7, 1863, at the Brazilian Independence Day celebration in the Sociedade Ensaios Literários (Literary Essays Society), he read his translation of a poem by Dumas fils and recited a poem of his own composition, "The Lost Maiden" (*A Menina que se Perde*). On November 23, 1863, in a "literary and artistic" farewell party for the Portuguese pianist Arthur Napoleão, held in an amateur theatrical club, his comedy *Almost a Minister* (*Quase Ministro*) was performed, and he recited his poem "Mexico's Epitaph" (*Epitáphio do Mexico*).

On April 4, 1864, at a farewell party given for João Cardoso de Menezes e Sousa by a group of literary men, Machado de Assis recited his satirical poem "The Clowns" (*Os Arlequins*).

On September 15, 1865, at a celebration of the hundredth anniversary of Bocage's birth in the Clube Fluminense, the poetry club Arcádia Fluminense was founded. Among the founding members was Machado de Assis, who recited poems on the occasion. At the first soirée of this society, held on October 14, Assis recited his poem, "In Space" (*No Espaço*); and the next meeting opened with the singing of the society's newly composed hymn, words by Machado de Assis, music by José Amat. At the third meeting, December 28, 1865, Assis read Bittencourt Sampaio's translation of Longfellow's "The Old Clock on the Stairs"; and his own comedy, *The Gods in Frock Coat*, (*Os Deuses de Casaca*), was presented.[8]

February 27, 1866, Assis published a poem, "Os Polacos Exilados," to help raise money for exiled Poles. And on September 28, 1866, a poem of his, now lost, was recited by the actress Antonina Marquelou at a benefit for a charitable society, A Real Sociedade Amante de Monarquia e Beneficente.

In 1867 he was decorated by the Emperor, with the Order of the Rose.

In this gregarious life it is not to be wondered at that Machado de Assis had many friends, nor that most of them were men of letters. To name his friends and associates of those days is to name over all the writers then resident in Rio de Janeiro, and they were legion. Some of them are still known in these northern climes: like José de Alencar, author of *The Guarani*, the lyric poets Gonçalves de Magalhães, Gonçalves Dias, and Castro Alves. Many of Assis's early literary friends were immigrants from Portugal. As mentioned above, he dedicated his second published poem, "The Palm Tree," to a youthful Portuguese poet-friend, Francisco Gonçalves Braga. From 1860 to 1869 he shared living quarters with another young Portuguese, Francisco Ramos Paz.[9] And there was in this colony of Portuguese writers a particular friend and collaborator, Faustino Xavier de Novaes, whose sister Carolina was to play a major part in Machado de Assis's life. Through Novaes, Assis became known to the almost fabulous giant of nineteenth-century Portuguese letters, Camillo Castello Branco, who consented to contribute stories to a magazine edited by Novaes and Assis, *O Futuro*.[10]

Most of the friends of Assis's youthful years died early; a few remained to be friends in old age, like Paz, Salvador and Lúcio de Mendonça, and Joaquim Nabuco whose friendship dated from 1865 when the old man of letters Assis (aet. 25) noticed the young poet (aet. 15), in his column.[11] Some of his friends strayed from poetry to politics, like the two men with whom he had worked closely on the newspaper: Quintino Bocayuva, who became a key figure in the formation of the Republic in 1889, and Pedro Luiz Pereira de Souza, later head of the Ministry of Agriculture, in which Assis was an employee. Assis had edited the *Diário do Rio de Janeiro* with Bocayuva; and he and Pedro Luiz had been reporters together taking notes on the debates in the Imperial Senate.[12] Although Machado de Assis's name appeared as candidate for deputy from Minas Gerais to the legislature of 1867–1868, he evidently did not actually run for office.[13] And although he wrote many columns of political comment and some even of invective, he was never drawn into what might be called active participation in politics.

Besides the more formal literary and social life described above, Machado de Assis and his friends used to gather informally, first in the bookstore of Paula Brito, who published Assis's first poems in his *Marmota Fluminense* in 1855, and his first book in 1861. Later, after Brito's death, the bookshop of the publisher Baptiste L. Garnier, located on the Rua do Ouvidor, became a popular gathering place. In such "Mermaid taverns" Machado de Assis and his confrères planned literary ventures—magazines, prefaces and dedications, puffs and defenses for themselves and for others—and discussed literature and other things. In a column of 1865, Machado de Assis recalls conversations at Paula Brito's:

Where we all went, politicians, poets, dramatists, artists ... where we talked of everything—from the fall of a minister to the pirouette of the dancer in vogue; where we discussed everything from the pain in Tamerlick's chest to speeches by the Marquis of Paraná. . . .

Suppose you wanted to know the latest parliamentary happening . . . of the new Italian soprano . . . of the publication of our book . . . of E***'s last party . . . of Macedo's or Alencar's latest play . . . of the state of the exchange . . . rumors of any sort whatsoever. . . . One needed go no further.[14]

There is reason to believe that Machado de Assis was not silent in such gatherings, for we have more than one testimonial to his conversational style.[15]

A literary critic to whom he had given favorable notices, Araripe Júnior, in a rather witty attempt to explain Assis's feeling for, and treatment of, women in his novels, alludes to his art of conversation.

It is necessary to know Machado in his most curious aspect, that of *causeur*.

We Brazilians, as a rule, prefer to cultivate conversation of the pornographic school. Ninety per cent of the remarks uttered daily on the Rua do Ouvidor are either out-and-out Bocage or underscored with the vermillion of lubricity: climate, indolence, or upbringing—any explanation will do. What is absolutely certain is that we are rarely disposed to make up a duet on philosophy or a literary olla podrida over a stein of German beer.

If sensuality does not take complete possession of us, we fall into political personalities and libelous gossip that everyone listens to, everyone knows, and all the world repeats.

Machado de Assis is a crying exception to this rule. Woman for him, constitutes one of the cabalistic formulas of the occult sciences. In *his* discourse, Adam's companion passes like a shadow; the desperate longings of the flesh, transports of Poppaea's secret sins, Canidia's deadly philtres, do not provoke him to indiscreet curiosity, nor to allusions that go beyond purely literary pleasure.

"Ovid thought thus in his *Metamorphoses*; Catullus was a great cultivator of the art of women; Balzac uttered such-and-such paradoxes on woman and prescribed the manner in which husbands should enter the house!"

But, he concludes, Machado de Assis is an "incomparable *causeur*."[16]

How Machado de Assis who, most likely, did not finish the eighth grade of elementary school, acquired the familiarity with literature, art, and philosophy evinced, as here, in conversation, and in all his writing, has long puzzled critics and biographers. Even in his very first writings there are so many allusions to Portuguese classics, to Greek, Roman, French, and English literature, and to philosophy, that one is tempted to amplify Cybrão's remark and say that Machado de Assis was not only born well bred but that he was also born well read.

This, then, was the youth of the poor, frail, timid, stammering, epileptic, inferiority-ridden, neurotic mulatto of Machadean myth!

But we have not quite done. In those first years, before he was thirty, he also found time to make love to two women and to fall in love with a third. Even here, however, letters predominated. He composed no less than three hundred and eighty-five verses to the first woman;[17] the third came out of his literary life and was absorbed back into it. As he wrote many years later to his young literary friend Magalhães de Azeredo, who had complained of the exhausting hours a career diplomat had to put in, "One way or another, the main thing is not to neglect *letters*. Do not take this as advice. A true call to letters does not need such admonitions, it goes of itself whichever way it must go, and finds in actual practice its own best exhortations."[18]

CHAPTER FOUR

THE THIRD WOMAN

If there is no evidence that Machado de Assis's life influenced his works, it is probably fair to say his literary work influenced his life. One of his close friends, as mentioned above, was Faustino Xavier de Novaes. This satiric poet, born February 17, 1820, was the son of a jeweler in the Portuguese city Porto (Oporto), eldest of six children—Faustino, Miguel, Henrique, Adelaide, Emilia, and Carolina—all of whom eventually came to Brazil, although Henrique, after a failure in the jewelry business in Rio de Janeiro, returned to Portugal in 1864.[1]

In 1855, while still in Portugal, Faustino de Novaes married, with high hopes (as he wrote a friend) that his wife would understand him and, since she was a woman of extreme sensibility, would repay his devotion with her tenderness. In 1858, the couple came to Rio de Janeiro where Novaes's poems had had some popularity. With the help of his wife's uncle, Baron de Ivay, a prominent Rio de Janeiro merchant, he started a book and stationery store. Not only was his business venture disastrous, but it seems he had greatly overrated his wife's "sensibility." According to his biographer, Sanches de Frias, his home life became "hell" because his wife insisted on having their black slaves beaten, and on very slight provocation. Novaes refused to consent to these whims of hers; he had to leave home. Finally he persuaded her to go back to Portugal. All the while he kept up a literary career, writing articles and poetry, and founding a literary magazine to which Machado de Assis, Camillo Castello Branco, and others contributed. None of these efforts, however, proved sufficient for his economic needs. A wealthy widow, the Baroness of Taquary, had taken him into her home (in 1861) where he was treated as a son. When she died in 1866, her daughter Rita de Cássia Rodrigues, continued to look after him. But the baroness's death sent him into a state of shock: his sister Carolina was sent for. She arrived, from Oporto, accompanied by the pianist Arthur Napoleão, who had grown up in the Novaes household. As Napoleão wrote later, they found Faustino in a nervous breakdown, with deranged mind. Dona Rita received Carolina into her house and urged Faustino's friends to visit and cheer the brother and sister with evenings of music and recitation. Faustino's mental health at least must have improved, because he continued with his writing and was still publishing articles as late as April, 1868.

It was another friend, the Count de São Mamede, who had given Novaes financial assistance with his bookstore and eventually liquidated it and paid the creditors. This man was a Brazilian banker and a count and viscount of the Brazilian Empire but, like Novaes, his birthplace was Oporto, from which he had emigrated to Brazil at an early age. During this time of Novaes's illness the count and countess were on a European trip, and while entertained by Novaes's relatives in Oporto they invited Miguel and Adelaide to visit them in Rio de Janeiro. Emilia was already in Brazil, married to a chancellor in the Portuguese consulate in Pernambuco.

In 1868, then, Miguel and Adelaide came to Rio de Janeiro where they were lodged in the São Mamede mansion. Toward the end of that year Faustino's health grew much worse. His brothers and sisters took him to Petropolis, a mountain resort city near Rio de Janeiro, for a change of air, but as his health continued to worsen they soon returned to Rio de Janeiro where he died the following year, August 16, 1869.

It was perhaps during the Novaeses' sojourn in Petropolis that Machado de Assis wrote Carolina the two love letters that are given below: they are supposed to be the only remnants of correspondence between Assis and his Carolina. The end of the second letter is missing.

[Tuesday] March 2 [1869][2]

My darling C.

Yesterday I received your two letters after two days of waiting. You can imagine my pleasure as I read them, reread them, and kissed them—all my sadness turned to sudden joy. I was so anxious for word from you that I left the *Diário* at one o'clock and went home: there I found your two letters, one of which should have arrived before but was probably delayed in the mail. You too must have received two letters from me yesterday. The one written Saturday, I took to the postoffice on Sunday at eight o'clock without remembering (Forgive me!) that on Sunday the ferryboat leaves at six in the morning. At four o'clock I posted the other and both must have gone on yesterday's two-o'clock boat. Thus I was not the only one to suffer from delayed letters. I can judge of your disappointment by my own, and I trust it will be the last.

I had already heard here that M. had rented the house in Larangeiras, but what I did not know was that the trip to Juiz de Fora had been planned. Like you I believe the change of air will do nothing for F. but I also know of course that one cannot say so. You are quite right in reminding me that the move to another house here in Rio would be excellent for all of us. F. once spoke to me of it and that is sufficient reason to consider it. The house *will* be found because my heart is set on it. I believe, however, it will be best to speak to F. again on Saturday and be

definitely authorized by him. Even so, we have time and
to spare, twenty-three days—time enough for love to perform a miracle, and this is no miracle at all.

You will probably say that I am always indulging your
wishes. Why shouldn't I? You have endured so much that
you have lost the sense of your own *imperium*. Always
ready to obey others, you are surprised that you are
obeyed. Do not be surprised; it is only natural. You are as
gentle and amenable to reason as I. Reason speaks out
clear in both of us. You ask of me things that are so right
and just that I could have no excuse for refusing you if I
wanted to, and I don't want to.

The move from Petropolis back here is an absolute
necessity. The change of air is not doing F. any good, and
the house there is a real danger for anyone who lives in it.
If you were here you would not be so afraid of thunder
storms; you are not yet a true Brazilian girl but I trust
God you *will* be.

You accuse me of not confiding in you? It is true and yet
it is not true. I do confide in you; if there is anything I
have not told you, it is something not worth the telling.
The history of my heart may be summed up in two chapters: one, a love not reciprocated; the other, a love that was
reciprocated. Of the first there is nothing to say. Of the second I do not complain; it was I who broke it off. Do not
blame me; there are situations that cannot be continued
without causing pain. A lady who is my good friend convinced me that I should tear that melancholy page out
of my life. I did it with regret but without remorse. There
is the whole story.

Your question naturally is this: which of the two chapters was Corinna? Inquisitive girl! The first. And I will
confess that of the two the most loved was the second.

But neither the first nor the second has any resemblance
to my heart's third and last chapter. Mme. de Staël says
that first loves are not the strongest because they are born
of a simple necessity to love. So it was with me, but, be-

sides, there is another, major factor, and it is this: you do not resemble in any respect the other women I have known. Mind and heart like yours are rare gifts; a soul so good and noble, a sensibility so delicate, reason so straight and true, are not treasures that nature scatters generously among the members of your sex. You belong to the very small number of women who have the ability to both love and feel, and think. How should I not love you? Besides, you have one quality that enhances all the others: you have suffered. I long to say to your great, despondent soul, "Rise, believe, and love. Here is a soul that understands you and loves you in return."

The responsibility of making you happy *is* frightening, but I accept it with joy and am sure I shall find a way to accomplish the pleasant task. Look, darling, I too have anxious thoughts about my future happiness, but what is this but the natural fear of one who has not yet known complete happiness.

Thank you for the flower you sent me. I gave it two kisses as if it had been you, for, although dry and its fragrance gone, it brought me a bit of your soul.

Saturday is the day of my departure. Only a few days, and yet it seems so far away. Patience! One who is at heaven's gate must be resigned. Let us not tempt fate, which has been so kind to us.

To return to the matter of the house, write and tell me if you approve what I said above, that is, if *you* think it better to speak to F. again and be authorized by him, so that it will not appear to M. that I am making an unwarranted intrusion into the affairs of his family. For the present we must take these precautions. Soon . . . soon, darling, we'll send the world to the devil. He alone is master of the world who is above its empty pomp and sterile ambitions. We are both of this sort and we love each other, and I live and die in you. Write me, and believe in the true heart of your

Machadinho.

[Tuesday] March 2nd.

My Carola,

You must already have to hand the letter I sent you this very day in answer to the two I received yesterday. In it I explained the reason you did not receive a letter on Sunday. You must have received two on Monday.

Would you like to know what I did on Sunday? I worked and then went home, lonely and filled with longing for my C. You can imagine how lonely and with what longing! and, besides, I was depressed, as I told you, at not receiving letters from you for two whole days. I give you my word, it was one of the saddest days I have yet passed. To comprehend my state of depression, it is enough to know that I even began to suspect opposition from F. as I implied in one of my last letters. It was more than unjust of me, it was ridiculous. Just think, at the very time I was building these castles out of air, our dear F. was talking to A. about me and apparently expressing his approbation of my intentions (Forgive me, of our intentions!). What else would you expect of F.? He has always been my friend, my true friend, one of the few who have survived time and circumstance and remained close to my heart. May God keep him and restore his health so that he live to share our happiness, yours and mine.

Araújo informed me today that he met Miguel in one of the coaches that go to Botafogo and Laranjeiras, and that the latter said he was looking for a house because he had let the other one. I do not know whether the house he is looking for is just for himself or for the whole family. I thought it best to mention this to you. Perhaps you already know something about it. Meanwhile, I am also waiting for your reply to what I asked in yesterday's letter, about moving.

You say that when you read a book you hear only my words and that I appear to you in everything and everywhere? Is it then really true that I occupy your thoughts and your life? You have already told me this so many

times, and I keep asking you the same thing over and over
—so great a piece of good fortune does it seem to me. Look,
I would like you to read a book I just finished reading a
few days ago: its title is *The Family*. I am going to buy a
copy for us to read in our house, as a kind of Holy Bible.
It is a serious book, inspiring and profound; just reading
it gives one a desire to marry.

Only four days more. Four days from now you will
have the best letter that I could possibly send you, that is,
me, and at the same time I shall read the best.

Beyond the words of these two letters, nothing is known
of their courtship nor of how they met. On November 12,
1869, they were married in Santa Rita Church, with the
Count of São Mamede and Arthur Napoleão as witnesses.
Assis was thirty; Carolina, thirty-five.

A copy of the marriage certificate is preserved in the Instituto Histórico e Geográfico Brasileiro in Rio de Janeiro.[3]
With this marriage certificate, Carolina drops from sight
for thirty-five years, or at least she is relegated to the close of
letters to intimate friends—"my wife sends her compli-
ments," and of the replies, "remember me to your gracious
wife."[4] The one exception is: Assis, in a letter to Azeredo
(April 2, 1895), mentions that some years before when he
was having trouble with his eyes, his wife read everything to
him, and served as his secretary—he even dictated some half-
dozen chapters of *Posthumous Memoirs of Braz Cubas (Memórias Posthumas de Braz Cubas)* to her.[5] Miguel de Novaes
in letters to Machado from Lisbon does complain of his
sister's not writing and expends some sarcasm on her lazi-
ness, on how busy she must be with one husband and a dog
to take care of.[6]

Critics have fancied that a few poems such as "When She
Speaks" *(Quando Ela Fala)* refer to Carolina, but this, although not at all improbable, is surmise.

A week after the wedding, Assis sent a letter to his close

friend Francisco Ramos Paz which seems to indicate that the newly married couple were short of cash.

[Rio de Janeiro]
[Friday] November 19 [1869].

My dear Paz,

I am very, very glad that you are better, and truly sorry not to have been able to visit you before you left for Tijuca. I thank you for your congratulations on my marriage. Here we are on the Rua dos Andradas, where you will be received as a true friend and one eagerly expected.

Unfortunately I cannot send you any further material on the drama. In your letter of the 8th you informed me of your illness and asked me to get the thing ready for the following Monday. To be sure, you did not realize the impossibility of this. I was counting on the postponement and your letter cancelled all my hopes. You cannot imagine what I had to do between Monday night and Friday morning. Ordinarily the time just before a man's wedding is all roses; for me it was all thorns. Fortunately my courage was equal to my responsibilities and I was able to obtain through other means the resources necessary to the occasion. Even so, I could do no more than just that, so that even now I am working for the bare necessities from one day to the next, since I will not be able to put my life on an orderly basis until after the first of the month.

These are the reasons I could not go on with our work. I will go on with it as soon as I get a bit of free time. It is necessary to me and you know that I do not spare any effort. I hope then you will forgive me if, at the moment, I concern myself with the solution of difficulties that I did not foresee nor expect.

If Tijuca were not so far away, I would go to see you. The minute you come back home let me know, in order that I may pay you the visit I owe you and we can talk about the conclusion of the work on the play.

Your
Machado de Assis.

A note written not long after shows the ebullience and resilience of the young husband in those difficulties.

[Rio de Janeiro, 1869.]

Paz,

Sunday I pounded and re-pounded on your door. Not a living soul. I wanted to tell you what the situation was in respect to the tickets, and at the same time talk with you about a *superb* idea!!! Send me word when you can see me. In the event you receive this letter after the messenger has left, write to my house (Andradas, 119) naming the hour and place today.

The thing is urgent.

Your
Machado de Assis.

Four more notes written to Paz in the next few months are in a similar vein.

Aside from the implications of these letters and the compliments-to-your-wife sort of thing, there is no mention, during a period of thirty-five years, either of Carolina or of the couple's life together.

FIRST FOUR NOVELS

FICTION AND THEATER

Carolina aside, "Corinna" and her nameless follower aside, there remain two big romances in Assis's life: Thalia and Melpomene, the Muses of comedy and tragedy respectively, although perhaps Machado de Assis would not have admitted to the second.

One of his earliest pieces of prose was an essay on "Modern Comedy," published when he was seventeen years old.[1] Another of his early literary attempts was a comic libretto entitled *Windows Opera (A Opera das Janelas)*, which he submitted to the Conservatório Dramático when he was eighteen. The censor's opinion read in part: "In my judgment it can be produced without impropriety, I only regret that it does not possess greater purity of language and more vivacity in the dialogue. I believe, however, that it will cause an impression through its originality."[2] The opera was not produced, but Machado de Assis was not discouraged from further attempts at drama by that fact nor by the censor's reflection upon his style. As we have seen, he went on to write a good many comedies and operettas within the next few years. It appears that with one exception he never wrote anything for the stage but comedy.[3] In the preface to his *Theater (Theatro)*, (1863), a volume containing two comedies, he stated his ambitions in the dramatic field: "to progress from such simple groups of scenes as these to comedy of greater compass, in which character study shall be conscientious and accurate, and the observation of society wedded to a practical command of the genre."[4] It is plain that he contemplated only comedies, not melodramas, not tragedies, not problem plays or dramas with a social or political message—although as critic he had reviewed all those types and had translated a number of such plays for presentation on the Brazilian stage. He continued to write comedies, from time to time throughout his life, but his serious interest in the professional theater fell off—a process perhaps hastened by the exigencies of his new life as married man and head of a household. In his review of the state of Brazilian literature, "Instincto de Nacionalidade" (1873), he devotes little space to the theater, stating that "there is at present no Brazilian theater," "no new and original play," nothing but "translations." "Now that public taste has touched the lowest rung of decadence and perversion, no future is held out to a man who feels the call to compose serious works of art. What audience is there to receive them if what dominates the stage is burlesque and the obscene ballad, the cancan, the magician's apparatus, everything that appeals to the lower instincts?" Talented Brazilian authors, he says, have abandoned the stage, which has "little by little sunk into what we have today, that is—nothing."

The tone of the 1863 preface to his *Theater* and that of this article of 1873 are vastly different. It is plain that he too with the other talented authors had "abandoned" the theater. Fiction was taking its place in his career: first the short story, then, along with the short story, the novel.

His debut in the short story, we have seen, was the comic short-short of 1858, "Lost: Three Treasures." In the course of his life he wrote more than two hundred tales and short stories of varying length. Long and short they continued to be cast in the comic mold. Melodramatic and romantic elements are present in some of these stories—in the earlier ones, especially—but none, I believe, properly falls into the class of pure romance or complete melodrama. Many of them contain tragic elements or tragic possibilities; they do not contain heroic characters, however, and so cannot qualify as tragedies—great or small.

CHAPTER SIX

RESURRECTION

The preface to Assis's first novel, *Resurrection*[1] (1872), reminds one of the preface to his 1863 book of theater. After discussing his ambition and his ability to progress in the new field, he states the theme and structure of the present novel:

> My idea in writing this book was to put into action that thought of Shakespeare's:
> "Our doubts are traitors,
> And make us lose the good we oft might win,
> By fearing to attempt."
> I had no intention of composing a novel of manners but only the sketch of a situation and the throwing into contrast of two natures; with these simple ingredients I have sought to create the book's interest.

The preface to his second novel, *Hand and Glove*, published the following year, states the same aim and method for that book and betrays the same questioning attitude toward his ability in the field.

> The portrayal of these characters—especially of Guiomar's —has been my principal, if not my only, object, the action serving as no more than a canvas on which I daubed the outlines of the figures in broad strokes. They are incomplete but have they, by chance, come out natural and true?

Again, in his criticism (1878) of Eça de Queiroz's *Cousin Bazilio* and the Naturalist school of fiction, he put forth as the proper aim of the novel the displaying of action caused by passions and ideas arising from within the natures of the characters. His complaint against the Naturalistic novel was that, playing on the surface, it is false and artificial.

> The substitution of the accessory for the principal, the transferring of the action from the nature and feelings of the characters to the incidental and fortuitous, seems to me incompatible with and contrary to the laws of art . . . . Desdemona's handkerchief plays a big part in her death; but the hot, jealous soul of Othello, the perfidy of Iago, and the innocence of Desdemona—these are the principal elements of the action. The drama exists because it is in the natures, in the passions, in the spiritual condition of the characters: the accessory does not control the absolute; it, like Boileau's *rhyme*, "ne doit qu'obéir."

This concern with "character" might lead one to think that Assis's ambition was to write tragedy rather than comedy, in which the action does not necessarily result from conflicts of emotion or will. One may observe that in the above criticism of *Cousin Bazilio*, Assis uses a tragedy, *Othello*, to illustrate his point. And Felix, the protagonist of *Resurrection*, has in his nature the seeds of tragic conflict: a strain of tenderness and desire to love that warred with a cynical distrust. We find in him the refusal to yield that typifies the Sophoclean hero, even though the essence of Felix's nature was doubt.

The title of the novel explains its action. Felix's dead heart or capacity for love came to life in the warming flame of a woman's love, then sank back into the tomb again, snuffed out by jealousy. The jealousy was engendered and fed by distrust and fear of being deceived by himself and others. His doubt downed all other emotions, all arguments, all reason, all truth. It is a trait common to us all in greater or less degree, so that the fate of Felix has a certain sinister universality.

The other personages of the novel are no match for Felix's tragic nature. They have little of the tragic about them. They are out of other media. Livia, the heroine, is a bundle of womanly virtues topped with a sensuous though queenly physical beauty. Love, perfect, romantic love, was her guiding light. Except for one little show of jealous anger,[2] her lovely character is completely unblemished. Although she did not die an early death from a consumption, there is something about her magnanimous withdrawal and resignation to a prolonged wasting away with age which reminds one of *La Dame aux Camélias*.

All the women in this novel are possessed of a submissiveness (to men and life) that almost passes belief. The abandoned mistress Cecilia and the adoring but unloved Rachel are of an unrelieved magnanimity in their relinquishment of Felix to "another." The resignation of the fourth woman, Clara, wife of a sensuous beast of a philandering villain, Baptista, is different. Assis likens her to Aesop's community of frogs.

> His wife? His wife, dear reader, was a relatively happy girl. She was more than resigned, she was completely habituated to her husband's neglect. . . . She had sought conjugal felicity with a heart that was hungry and thirsty for love. She did not realize her dream. She asked heaven for a king; they gave her a log. She accepted the log and asked for nothing else.[3]

Clara is comic.

The men too, all except Felix, are out of comedy. Menezes, the hero's loyal friend,

> was a good soul, compassionate and generous. All youth's illusions were in full bloom in him. He was enthusiastic and sincere and totally free of the least trace of an ulterior motive. It might be that with time he would lose some of his natural qualities. Not all resist the two terrible acids:

fortune's blows and the wearing away of character. But in those days he had not yet suffered a change.[4]

Vianna, Livia's conniving brother, "was born a parasite as others are born dwarfs. He was a parasite by divine right."[5] Chief among the comedians is Baptista—and this is a name Assis reserved for characters with a Shakespearean flavor. Baptista, a plain-dealing villain like Don John of *Much Ado About Nothing*, mapped a definite campaign of treachery. "Observant and perspicacious," "without feelings or scruples," he "did not adopt Iago's method because it seemed risky and childish to him. He was a model of dissimulation and ulterior motive."[6]

The author and his heroine took a serious view of the problem facing their hero—a life without love. Not all the characters shared their feeling. Needless to say Baptista and Vianna saw everything through eyes distorted by self-interest. Others found it hard to be completely serious about Felix. A newspaper man, "a friend of his, used to compare him to Achilles' shield—a mixture of tin and gold —'but much less solid,' he would add."[7] (One sees here the beginning of the narrative method that Assis brought to such perfection in the later novels *Dom Casmurro and Esau and Jacob*—a method by which the characters push the author aside, write their own lines, and act out their own play.)

Resurrection's odd assortment of personages—from various walks of literature—makes a tragic struggle on the hero's part scarcely worth the trouble, so that the story becomes by turns either comic or sentimental, with only the specter of tragedy peering from the shadow of Felix's soul.

CHAPTER SEVEN

HAND AND GLOVE

Assis's second novel, *Hand and Glove*,[1] published 1874, two years after *Resurrection*, has no hero of tragic proportions, or of tragic possibilities. And yet the novel is concerned with "will"—will in the Stendhalian sense. *Hand and Glove* contains no less than two Julien Sorels: one male, one female. If Stendhal's Sorel was a travesty of the Napoleonic hero, Guiomar and Luiz are little tin Sorels. There is no murder, no seduction, no melodrama, however; *Hand and Glove* is romantic comedy, with more comedy than romance. The protagonist, Guiomar, was a beautiful, intelligent, elegant young lady; she was also poor, orphaned, and the foster daughter of a wealthy widow, a baroness. Although sensitive and affectionate, Guiomar was secretly possessed by strong ambitions and the will to succeed, to be somebody in life. Her nature (the author confides) demanded and loved the heart's flowers but not wild flowers nor stragglers growing round a cottage door, they had to be choice blooms in a Sèvres vase placed on a bit of rare furniture in a tastefully decorated room.[2]

The widow's nephew Jorge, attracted by Guiomar's charms and egged on by his aunt's officious paid companion, Mrs. Oswald, made Guiomar a proposal of marriage. The aunt was in seventh heaven. There was, however, the matter of the second "Sorel" to be dealt with—Luiz Alves, a successful young lawyer with political ambitions, who had a house next door to the widow's estate. Although his will to succeed had led him to exclude romance from his thoughts as a waste of valuable time, he became convinced that Guiomar would furnish him added strength in his ascent to glory. He too made her a proposal of marriage—a lawyer's proposal, a standing offer so couched that it required neither acceptance nor refusal.[3]

These are comic types and they find themselves sooner or later in embarassingly comic predicaments. Guiomar had still another admirer, Estevam, a romantic lover who never had a chance with this female Sorel: he was easily disposed of at the proper time by the male of the species. As far as the plot is concerned this man could be dispensed with; but, for the comedy, he is indispensable: in himself he is a complete satire on romantic love—a lovesick egotist who builds dreams out of air, making an ass of himself before the lady, firing up his melancholy with thousands of pages of *Werther*,[4] and serving as a constant butt for both Assis's and Alves's wit. A companion piece of fatuous love is the nephew Jorge, a vain, idle, empty-headed stuffed shirt. When Guiomar found Jorge's letter of proposal in a novel she had been reading, her first thought was, " 'Another one!' " After reading the letter, "She looked at it for a time and mentally at the man who had written it. Finally she laid it to one side, opened the book again, and went on with her story."[5] Later she analyzed the three men's love as follows: "Estevam offered her the sentimental life, Jorge the vegetative life; in Luiz Alves she saw a warm domestic love combined with the excitement of the world outside."[6] Her author's view is similar, but slightly more cynical. Alves's love, he tells us, was "a little on the calm side, not crazy and blind like Estevam's, not trivial and sensual like Jorge's, a middle term something between one and the other—as we might expect in the heart of an ambitious man."[7]

The title *Hand and Glove*, besides being borrowed from

the English expression, may be an allusion to Shakespeare's *All's Well That Ends Well*. Mrs. Oswald, in urging some rather underhand methods of courtship, quoted the title, "All's well that ends well," with the meaning, the end justifies the means.[8] The perfect love between Guiomar and her foster mother, the baroness, resembles in all points that which existed between Helena and the Countess of Rousillon: the grateful devotion of the daughter; the admiration, and indulgent, protective love of the mother, and her siding with the foster child against the blood-relative—the nephew in one case, the son in the other. The lines of the play's determined heroine:

> Our remedies oft in ourselves do lie,
> Which we ascribe to heaven; the fated sky
> Gives us free scope; only doth backward pull
> Our slow designs when we ourselves are dull.[9]

might be taken as a posy for this novel. Guiomar, like Helena, was capable of bold action. When she was ambushed by Mrs. Oswald and Jorge, she closed with Luiz Alves's standing offer with decisive suddenness. She threw a note in his window—in itself a hardy, unladylike thing to do in the Rio de Janeiro of the 1850's. The note was a command to ask for her hand in marriage, that is, to make the formal demand of her foster mother. This note was more dramatic in Portuguese than it would be in English. It was a single word, "peça-me"—the anguished cry of a girl torn between her determination to repay the baroness's love at all costs with grateful acquiescence, and her ambition—the latter reinforced by revulsion as a woman—mental, moral, and physical—from Jorge, and by her attraction to Alves. The note, landing at Alves's feet, in the presence of the third admirer, Estevam, is dramatic; but the shaky underpinnings of Guiomar's ambitious will and the surprised but complete satisfaction with which Alves received the note are comic. We laugh.

In other words, the story appears to bear out the implications of its title: a pair of strong wills appear to win out. Since the hero and heroine are spiritual twins, their wills do not clash but join forces in a silent entente cordiale. Like Julien Sorels with preconceived ambitions and with a certain amount of sangfroid and detached determination, they exert their wills over other people's. Though not ruthless they get their way because their opponents' wills are flabby and their owners more stupid than not. This is what seems to be the case. Actually, Guiomar and Alves were trapped by their own better natures—by "love"—as happens in romantic comedy. They thought they were attracted to each other by an identity of interest—for the better furthering of their individual ambitions; but this was only partially true, as the author makes apparent on the last page of the novel, where, I believe, he laughs at this delusion of theirs.

Destiny should not lie, nor did she belie Luiz Alves's ambition. Guiomar had judged aright: he was a strong man. A month after the wedding as they were talking about what newlyweds talk about, that is, themselves, and recalling the brief campaign of the courtship, Guiomar confessed to her husband that it was then that she had recognized the full power of his will.

"I saw that you were a resolute man," she told him as he sat listening to her.

"Resolute and ambitious," he added with a smile, "you must have perceived that I was one and the other."

"Ambition is not a defect."

"On the contrary, it is a virtue. I know I have it and that I must realize it. I do not rely on youth alone and on my own moral strength, I rely on you—you will be a new strength to me."

"Oh! yes!" she exclaimed, then continued in a mocking tone, "But what will you give me in return? A seat in the legislature? A minister's post?"

"The luster of my name," he answered.

Guiomar, who had been standing in front of him with her hands held in his, let herself slip gently down on her husband's knees; and the two ambitions exchanged the long kiss of fraternity. For those two ambitions fitted each other as if that glove had been made for that hand.

Undoubtedly there is also an allusion here to *All's Well That Ends Well*, V. iii. 271–272:

This woman's an easy glove, my lord; she goes off and on at pleasure.[10]

but the words and attitude are also reminiscent of *Romeo and Juliet*, II. ii. 23–25:

See, how she leans her cheek upon her hand!
O, that I were a glove upon that hand,
That I might touch that cheek!

Both these quotations, along with Assis's sly manipulation of the scene's gesture and dialogue, cast derisive aspersions on the principals' grand professions, so that the theme of this second novel is seen to be no more than a variation on that of the first. In *Hand and Glove* we have the reverse of the coin: it is will, where the obverse, in *Resurrection*, was doubt. There tragedy demanded the defeat of love, here comedy contrives love's triumph.

As a comedy, *Hand and Glove* is not flawless; still it is a gem—a slight satire on various manifestations of human vanity. Only the baroness is spared: she has no vanity. When Jorge referred to her "saintly qualities," she replied, "Only one, Jorge, only one: that of loving you both—you and her."

CHAPTER EIGHT

HELENA

Whereas *Hand and Glove* is pure comedy, Assis's next novel *Helena*[1] (1876) skirts tragedy and ends in melodrama. It too is shot through with threads of satire on human desires and mental aberrations. And its opening paragraph is out of low comedy:

> Counselor Valle died at seven o'clock in the evening, April 25, 1859. He expired of a thundering stroke of apoplexy . . .

The paragraph goes on to explain that because of the sudden nature of his taking off he was obliged to die without any assistance from the medical profession and even without the consolation of religion. On the other hand, his funeral, the following day, was one of the best attended ever seen in all that neighborhood. (It might be noted that Machado de Assis was partial to apoplexy as a *deus ex machina* to dispose of unwanted and embarrassing persons. In the short story, "The Rod of Justice" (*O Caso da Vara*), he refers to this device as the "apoplectic solution.")

In spite of its almost frivolously macabre opening, this novel marks a big step forward in Assis's early avowed artistic purpose of presenting the drama resulting from the emotional conflicts of his characters. The personages of the novel *Helena* are more true and far more complex, more fully developed, than those of either *Resurrection* or of *Hand and Glove*. In a tragic situation they could have been

tragic characters of heroic stature. But the situation is not
truly tragic: it is, in a sense, false and trivial. As a result, the
whole novel takes on an air of impossible romance. The
characters' emotions are extreme for the ultimate situation.
The theme, which could be tragic, suffers the same disloca-
tion as the characters.

The book starts with a theme not unlike that of Aeschy-
lus's *Oresteia*—the idea that crime begets crime. There is a
curse on the aristocratic and wealthy house of Valle as there
was on the house of Atreus. A wealthy man's caprice and his
extramarital adventures not only brought about the suffering and early death of his wife, but it was also to foster un-
governable passions in his children, destroying his daughter
Helena in the bloom of youth and ruining the happiness of
his only son.

The Counselor's will disclosed that he had a natural
daughter, Helena, a young lady of sixteen whose widowed
mother, now dead, had been his mistress. The girl was in
school in a suburb of Rio de Janeiro. The will directed that
Helena be recognized as a legal heir and brought to live in
the family mansion, where she was to be treated with all the
honor and indulgence of a legitimate daughter. The family,
consisting of Valle's sister, Dona Ursula, who was mistress
of the house, and his son, Estacio, were amazed, and embar-
rassed by the position in which they would be placed in the
eyes of society.

Dona Ursula, in particular, found it hard to reconcile
herself to Helena's presence. But soon even she, like the
rest of the household, was captivated by the girl's beauty
and gentleness. Her intelligence and elegant accomplishments as musician, linguist, and horsewoman commanded
their admiration. Estacio, without being aware of it, began
to fall in love with Helena. His passion for his sister was
revealed to him by the family priest, Melchior. Helena already knew that she was in love with Estacio. She knew also

that she was not the Counselor's daughter but only treated as such from childhood when her mother became Valle's mistress.

Helena's mother, Angela, and father, Salvador, had eloped, been disowned, and lived in Rio de Janeiro in the direst poverty. When Helena was six years old, Salvador at a summons from his dying father went home to Rio Grande do Sul. After burying his father, settling the estate, and finding himself little richer than before, he returned to Rio de Janeiro, where he discovered Angela and Helena in a luxurious establishment provided by Counselor Valle. He proudly withdrew from their lives for the good of Helena's future education. Upon Angela's death his paternal feelings got the better of him and he entered into a regular correspondence with his daughter, who was then twelve years old. After Valle's death, Salvador gained admittance to Helena's presence at the school and persuaded her, against her feelings of pride, honesty, and love for her real father, to accept the inheritance. As he confessed later, he thought only of his daughter's future. He promised to remain always near her, took up residence in a little tumbledown house not far from the Valle estate, and continued the correspondence with her. He was alarmed then when she began to visit the old house in her horseback rides, but her presence was so soothing to all his outraged feelings of paternal love that he made only a feeble protest.

Estacio's possessive love of Helena refined his powers of observation. Suspicion finally led him to the old house that lay in the path of Helena's rides: he thought she was visiting a lover; he found her father. Estacio's first impulse was to throw family reputation to the winds and marry Helena; but all opposed him: his aunt, the priest Melchior, the family physician Camargo, Helena, and even his own ideas of "society's law."

Helena was persuaded to acquiesce in the situation because she was unwilling to add further disgrace to the Valle name, which she felt she had already sullied by initially concealing her true origin and permitting herself to be acknowledged as the Counselor's daughter—and particularly was she unwilling to dishonor the memory of an affectionate and indulgent foster father. Her love for Estacio engendered a desire to avoid interference in *his* life: he had become engaged to Camargo's daughter; Helena urged the marriage, as she had done all along. At the same time, her pride rebelled against receiving an inheritance not rightfully hers, and at exposing herself to pity and, as she supposed, to the contempt of the family. In her despairing struggle to repress her love for Estacio and conquer her feelings of remorse and shattered pride, she died.

That Machado de Assis had wanted to write a novel of real incest is not impossible. If he had done so, the emotions of the novel's personages would probably strike a more sympathetic response in the present-day reader. As it is, Helena's struggle against her passion is motivated primarily by respect for the Valle family's position in society and by her own understandable, but excessive, pride, and this strains our credulity a little, and our patience.

Many years before this novel's publication, Machado de Assis had written a review of a historical novel, *Sombras e Luz* by B. Pinheiro, a Portuguese writer, in which he condemned a brother-sister incest and concluded his condemnation with these words: "This [incestuous] love is a glorification of the animal instincts; feelings of morality do not interpose in any way."[2] If Helena and Estacio had been blood brother and sister, Helena's suppression of her love would have a more powerful effect on us: it would be the action of the "feeling of morality" mentioned by Assis in this early piece of criticism.

That Assis was not uninterested in "incest" is shown elsewhere in this very novel and in other of his writings. In his short story "Brother Simon" (*Frei Simão*), published in 1864, a strong passion exists between Simão and his cousin Helena, an orphan whose parents had left her to the care of Simão's father. The cousins had grown up together "under the same roof." In the short story, "Possible and Impossible" (*Possível e Impossível*) (1867), Theophilo marries his adopted sister Helena. In another story, "Girl With the Light-Brown Eyes" (*A Menina dos Olhos Pardos*) (1873–74), there is a suggestion of a different sort. There exists a kind of father-daughter relationship between Dr. Leandro, the young hero's father, and the heroine, Helena, whose face was lovely as pagan Helen's but whose true heart would never have allowed her to follow Paris. Dr. Leandro falls in love with her also. The son steps aside in favor of his father. Then the father steps aside, marries his son to Helena, and resumes his fatherly feelings toward her. "A Sacristan's Manuscript" (*Manuscrito de um Sacristão*) is a satiric story of the priest Theophilo and his cousin Eulalia, who separate when they are forced to acknowledge that they are in love. "Old Home" (*Casa Velha*), a novelette published 1885–86, tells a story of supposed brother-sister love as in *Helena*. Its heroine, Claudia, like Helena is excessively proud. In 1905, Assis published a short story of the real thing, "Tale of the Cabriolet" (*Anecdota do Cabriolet*): it recounts the elopement of lovers born of the same mother and of a different father and fully aware of their relationship.

One notes in this series, the recurrence of the name Helena, the Portuguese form of our Helen. One recalls also that *All's Well That Ends Well* was apparently in Assis's thoughts when he composed *Hand and Glove*, the novel published two years before *Helena*, and that Shakespeare's play revolves around an accomplished and learned young woman named Helena who was passionately in love with her foster brother, Rousillon, and this Helena had been "bequeathed"[3] to the count's mother by Helena's father.

In his journalistic columns, and even in the novel *Esau and Jacob*, Machado de Assis joked about brother-sister incest, for example, "A Semana," May 20, 1894, which pokes fun at Spiritualism and its "extraordinary revelations," to which Assis adds a few of his own:

> Some day, it is my belief, spirits will be born twins and already married. That will be human perfection—spiritual and social. Worries will be over for families trying to marry off daughters, and for young men who are looking for wives. Couples will come into the world already married and dancing the procreation minuet. . . .[4]

This idea is perhaps reminiscent of the myth surrounding another Helen—Helen of Troy. Leda, Helen's mother, seduced by Zeus in the disguise of a swan, laid two eggs, from one of which were hatched Helen and Pollux, children of Zeus; from the other, Clytemnestra and Castor, children of Leda's husband Tyndareus. Leonardo da Vinci's painting (universally reproduced in mythology books) shows at the feet of Leda and her swan the cracked shells of two rather enormous eggs, and a set of twin babies, male with female, playing in each.

Braz Cubas, narrator of Assis's fifth novel, mentions that Zeus as Leda's swan used insinuation and as Europa's bull, force—"the two approved ways to win a woman's favors."[5] Counselor Valle, as we are emphatically shown, used insinuation.

In his passages on spiritualistically married twins, Assis was perhaps making fun of the Platonic myth (told in the *Symposium*) which defines love as the rejoining of the two halves of a soul that had been parted. In *Helena* there are, I believe, several allusions to this myth. One is in the last chapter when Estacio and Helena finally acknowledge to each other their love.

> At first it was a simple meeting of the eyes, but within a few seconds it was something more. It was the first reve-

lation, tacit but conscious, of the feeling that bound them together. Neither of them had sought this coming together of souls but neither shrank from it. What they said with their eyes alone cannot be written on paper, cannot be repeated for human ears—a secret, mysterious confession made from one heart to the other, heard only in heaven because it was not said in the language of earth, nor did they speak for this earth. Their hands of themselves joined, as their glances had; no shame, no fear, no consideration held back that fusion of two beings born to form a single existence.

A similar idea is expressed earlier in the book, but with respect to the love between brother and sister. Camargo, when trying to persuade Helena to use her influence with Estacio in order to get him to proceed with his avowed intention of marrying Camargo's daughter, says to her, "You have come to complete your brother's soul."[6] This line possesses dramatic irony: Camargo knew that Estacio was not Helena's brother.

Even before he saw Helena, Estacio had anticipatory feelings of love for her.

The thought of having a sister, warmed his heart with a promise of new, unknown adventures. Between his mother and all other women he had known, he felt the want of that intermediary being, whom he already loved though he had never met her, who would be the confidante of his hopes and disappointments. Estacio remained looking at the windows for a long time, but neither did Helena's form appear nor did he see even a fleeting shadow of the new lodger.[7]

And when he did see her, he was soon won over to her side. "It was an easy victory: his heart leaning toward her as none of the others' did."[8]

Estacio's newborn, fraternal love, fostered by his sister's charm and devotion, by the mystery surrounding her, and by the intimacy of their daily life together, grew more and

more jealously possessive until it assumed monstrous proportions, altering a noble and generous nature. He became
willing to commit rash and dishonorable acts to keep Helena his.[9] He refused his consent to her marriage—a marriage
she desired—with his old friend and classmate Mendonça.
His explanation to Mendonça was wild and insulting.

> "It would be an everlasting torment to me if Helena
> should come to endure a life of unhappiness. We did not
> share the same cradle, we passed our childhood under
> different roofs, we did not learn to speak from the lips of
> the same mother. It matters little: not for these reasons
> do I love her any the less."[10]

The dramatic irony of the above speech is matched by
other dialogue in the novel, giving the whole a tragic atmosphere. In this particular instance one thinks of Oedipus
as he unwittingly called down a curse on his own head. The
priest Melchior, who shortly after this scene discloses to
Estacio the nature of his love for Helena, has all the ve-
hemence of a Tiresias, but none of the angry venom: "You
have transgressed God's law and man's, without knowing
it. . . . Estacio, you love your sister." The priest then warns
that it is the Evil One tempting him.

> The deadly seed entered your heart, penetrated its inner-
> most recesses. . . . Cast it out, this is the teaching of the
> Eternal Master. You did not recognize it for what it was.
> You saw lawful affection in what was unlawful love; hence
> your jealousy, suspicion, demanding egotism, your intent
> to draw Helena's soul away from all life's joys for the
> sole purpose of contemplating it yourself, alone, like a
> miser. . . .
> The poisonous plant sent forth a branch into Helena's
> chaste, virgin heart, and the same passion bound you both
> in its invisible tendrils. You did not see it, nor did she; but
> I saw it, I was the sad spectator of your terrible and piti-
> able situation. You are brother and sister, yet you love

each other. Tragic poetry may turn the subject into dramatic action; but what morality and religion condemn must not find refuge in the soul of an honest Christian man.[11]

The priest's private opinion was that a wealthy man's caprice and life of sensuality had passed on a curse to his children. "Might there not be in that house a generation of woes destined to beat down wealth's pride with the pitiless spectacle of human frailty?"[12]

The "tragic poetry" the author had in mind, I believe, was not primarily Greek tragedy, but Jacobean. The situation bears a startling resemblance to John Ford's *'Tis Pity She's a Whore*, not only in the lovers' passion, but also in the character and arguments of father-confessors Melchior and Bonaventura. The incest, in both instances, is not so much a violation of a divine or universal law with dire consequences to family, government, and people, as happened with Sophocles' Oedipus. The main god here is society's opinion. In Ford's play and in this novel the priest's advice is the same, with only a slight change for sex. Bonaventura says in effect, marry the girl with all speed to her unsuspecting suitor; Melchior's advice, let the *boy* marry "immediately," and Helena also. In *'Tis Pity She's a Whore* the incest is real; a child has been conceived. The priest's advice is to save the family honor by concealing the truth; prayers and repentance can be taken care of later. The "incest" in *Helena* is not actual in any sense, but the scenes between Estacio and Melchior are charged with the same mysteriously tense emotion as those between the priest Bonaventura and the youth Giovanni of Ford's tragedy.

Since Helena was not Counselor Valle's daughter, it was necessary to account for the deception. Assis used a romantic solution, with a personage out of romance. When Estacio first saw Helena's father, Salvador (who he thought was her lover), it struck him that the man had "the air of an Italian tenor."[13] And Salvador did have that quality in all his actions, letters, and speeches. They drip with operatic saccharine and tears. He lacks verisimilitude, to put it mildly. But he is necessary in the given situation. Helena and Estacio are in essence tragic characters, but the situation is a matter of nineteenth-century Rio de Janeiro etiquette, and the proper narrative framework would be the comic. If Estacio and Helena had been brother and sister, the outcome could have been tragic; as it is, it is melodramatic. The unhappy ending seems forced, and the characters overacting. Unlike the novel *Resurrection* in which the situation had tragic possibilities but the characters fell short of their destiny, here it is the situation that is meretricious; the characters' struggle could have had universal implications. Indeed, as the book stands, one closes it with that sensation of being in a world fallen apart such as tragedy engenders; but the feeling is momentary, for this little world had no real substance in the first place, and on second thought one perceives that the story was only an exciting series of events with no implications beyond themselves—in short, a melodrama. The author knows it. By way of holding our emotions in subjection he inserts into the ending a poetic burst of romance that might have come out of Goethe—with wind, beating rain, and a hero toiling under the weight of a heroine's almost lifeless body.

As if to offset the tale's romantic improbability, or in revulsion against it, Assis introduced into the narrative an instance of true incestuous love. It is not given tragic treatment, however, but satiric. Camargo, the family physician, is portrayed as a cynical, avaricious, ambitious man who schemed to marry his daughter to Estacio do Valle for the sake of wealth and family aggrandizement. Even his softer side had a somewhat sinister aspect: his feeling for his daughter places him in a class with Mr. Barrett of Wimpole

Street. His daughter was named Eugenia, ironically, for, alas, her circumstances were anything but eugenic.

He loved "the beautiful Eugenia," as he called her, above everything and everyone—his only daughter, the apple of his eye . . . but he loved her with a silent, secret love.[14]

In the first chapter of the story, when he arrived home from Counselor Valle's funeral, with the matrimonial scheme fresh in his head, he looked at Eugenia

with unaccustomed tenderness; his somber visage seemed to be lighted with an inner radiation. The girl felt herself clasped in his arms. She did not resist. But this expansiveness was so new that she was alarmed, and asked in a faltering voice, "Did something happen there?"

"Absolutely nothing," he answered, giving her a kiss on the forehead.

It was the first kiss he had ever given her, at least the first she had any memory of.

His matrimonial plans for his daughter progressed. Later, at Estacio's birthday ball, one of the guests whispered in his ear,

"Your daughter is the queen of the evening."

"She really is, isn't she?" Camargo replied, and his heart flew on the tips of the sash round her waist as she danced.[15]

After he received Estacio's formal demand for Eugenia's hand,

her father imprinted his second kiss on her forehead. The first, as the reader will recall, was given her on the night after the counselor's death.[16]

This man used the diabolical cunning and witty boldness of a Richard III, and like that wicked monarch, he should have ended badly. But he did not. The novel's two final pages are given over to Estacio's grief and Helena's funeral. Just before they left the house, Estacio bent over the open casket, "and the dead girl's forehead received love's first kiss." The final sentence of the book is this:

> At the same time, at home in Rio Comprido, Estacio's fiancée, horrified by Helena's death and depressed by the gloomy and somber ceremony, sadly retired to her bedroom; on the threshold she received her father's third kiss.

Camargo is Assis's caustic comment on the marriage of convenience, which is, in a sense, the subject of this novel. The story ends on a note of fierce comedy. Helena's love was selfless. Estacio's became so, as did Dona Ursula's, Melchior's, and Mendonça's; even Eugenia was affected by Helena's death, but Camargo's love was and remained selfish. As Assis explains more than once, it was himself he loved in his daughter.

> His love for his daughter, though violent, slavish, and blind, was a way this father had of loving himself. . . . He contemplated her with the same pride a goldsmith feels when he admires the jewel in its setting as it goes from beneath his hands.[17]

As tragedy reveals the soul of the individual hero, so comedy reveals the common, the all-too-human beneath the individual mask.[18] Camargo's humanity is ludicrous and we laugh, but our laughter is not hilarious. The comic villain and his marriage of convenience win out. But it is Helena's pride that is the determining factor in the plot of this novel. Without it, the wills of the others—Estacio, Melchior, Ursula—would have given way to their love for her, and Camargo would have been powerless; but pride was a part of the beauty of her nature.

Along with its characters of larger stature and the almost-tragic theme, we suddenly find developing in this novel the symbolism that was to become an integral part of Assis's later novels, with its subtle, poetic, pervasive strength. The symbols are as yet few and barely hinted, but they add their bit to the book's atmosphere of deceit, menace, and love. There is the heart as house—the symbol Assis enlarged to form the main thematic structure of *Dom Casmurro*—the color blue for pure love and unalloyed, present joy; birds for worldly thoughts, memories, and regrets; a white eagle woven in the carpet suggests Camargo's relentless, scheming ambition.

CHAPTER NINE

YAYÁ GARCIA

Symbolism is present in his next novel, *Yayá Garcia*[1] (1878), although for the most part its role does not go beyond that in *Helena*. It was in *Yayá Garcia*, however, that Time with its shifting masks of past, present, and future, came to have a permanent place in Machado de Assis's dramatis personae. It is a great prestidigitator that plays fast and loose with all human things.

> Time, the invisible chemist who dissolves, compounds, extracts, and transforms all spiritual substances, ended by killing in the widower's heart not the memory of his wife, but his pain at losing her.[2]

> One woman [Yayá] was going toward the future, while the other [Estella] had just come out of the past; and if Estella felt the need of tempering her spiritual atmosphere with a ray of the other's adolescence, Yayá instinctively felt that there was in Estella something that would heal and console.[3]

Yayá "wanted to be a barrier between the past and the present."[4] But when the young girl's love of Jorge overwhelmed her she was no longer of the future but of the present, because, for Machado de Assis, love is always the present moment, and eternal love is a series of presents, or a never ending present moment.

> Although the black storm clouds that had gathered above her head were scattered, Yayá still discerned a specter

toward the setting sun [the past], and in the east [the future] a possibility. These two points of blackness troubled the sheer blue of the sky and made it heavy and melancholy. The future's mystery was uniting with the mysterious secret of the past; one and the other could devour the present, and she feared being crushed between them.[5]

Estella's fear was quite different, because she was trying to rid herself of her old love for Jorge.

The future took her to the present, and the present carried her into the past.[6]

That is, with the "force" of her pride she pushed her love back into the past and marched forward with pride alone, but the other force kept dragging her back.

These metaphors tend to give the novel's personages a grandeur of action and gesture that draws us to a spiritual no-man's land where we are at one with them.

Time changes all emotions in this story—all except Estella's love, her love and her pride: the two go battling to the end, with pride barely holding the upper hand as it beats down love and makes of Estella the distant star her name suggests.[7]

From at least the year 1869 and the short story "Miss Dollar,"[8] women's pride was an object of Assis's study and admiration. In this fourth novel it holds the center of the stage: a woman's innate personal pride; a woman's pride of family; and the wounded pride of outraged love. Estella, the central figure, was of a warm, almost passionate nature, but her intense personal pride became a terrible weapon and armor with which she not only subdued her own loving nature but stood up to the inhuman family pride of her foster mother Valeria; and, with this same pride, Estella later conquered the jealousy and suspicion of her stepdaughter Yayá Garcia. Valeria, willing to sacrifice the happiness or even the life of her only son, Jorge, to her family pride, which was nothing more than pride of class, sent him off to the Paraguayan War. She reminds one of another bloodthirsty mother, Shakespeare's Volumnia, who sent her son Coriolanus to fight the Volscians. And this Brazilian mother had a Roman name, Valeria, the name of a third female character in Shakespeare's tragedy, *Coriolanus*. It is the manifestations of pride in these three women which make the plot's complications: at its base is the novel's theme—nature's struggle against artificial restraints of society. The following soliloquy of Jorge's defines the issue.

> "Your mother is right," an inner voice shouted, "you were going to lower yourself to an alliance that was unworthy of you; and if you did not know enough to respect either yourself or your family's name, it is just that you pay for your mistake by casting your lot with the fortunes of war. Life is not a Virgilian eclogue; it is a natural contract which cannot be entered into with reservations nor broken without paying a penalty. There are two *natures*, and society's has as great a right to command as the other. The two do not run counter; they complement each other. They are man's two halves, and you were going to yield to the first, disregarding the laws imposed by the second."
>
> "No, you are the one that is right," said a contrary voice, "because this woman is worth more than a future, and the heart's law is before and above the other laws. You would not have lowered yourself; you would have raised her; you would have corrected fortune's blunder. Listen to the voice of God and leave to men that which is of men."[9]

Fighting on the side of society, Estella and Valeria triumphed over their own hearts, with Pyrrhic victories. Eventually we pity Valeria. We admire Estella. Her pride is of almost tragic proportions, but it is excessive in her human surroundings. It has something of the falsity of Valeria's pride, for it is, in a sense, Valeria's pride in reverse—a kind of snobbishness of the lower classes. It places Estella, like Valeria, beyond the pale of human emotion. As her father said of her, she is a *fera*, a wild female animal, incapable of human weakness. In Jorge and Yayá, the heart triumphed, with happy results. Luiz Garcia, Yayá's father, made a true compromise. There is little doubt where Assis's sympathies lay. This novel, like *Helena*, could be taken as a tract against the marriage of convenience, or rather for marriage based on love.

A character in one of Assis's short stories says, "Most marriages are arranged without regard for love. Well, I am profoundly skeptical about everything else, but I have a kind of inclination to believe in love, even though it is rare, and I want it to be the only reason for my marriage."[10] Opinions of this sort are not uncommon among the more sympathetic personages of Assis's short stories. And Assis himself seemed to have had some such idea—at least in 1878, nine years after his own marriage, and the year in which *Yayá Garcia* was published. In April of that year appeared his famous criticism of Eça de Queiroz's *Primo Bazílio* (*Cousin Bazilio*),[11] in which he castigated the Naturalistic school of fiction for being meretricious and obscene. The main example for his argument is the wife Luiza who betrayed her husband, then suffered—but not from remorse, from fear of discovery. That is, she had no real love for her husband. In her own words, he was a "caprice" of hers. To which Machado de Assis wrote this comment: "Horrors! A caprice for a husband!" Plainly, he was outraged by Queiroz's conception of conjugal love.

We are probably justified in assuming that his own marriage to Carolina was one of mutual attraction. Certainly they were both poor enough; he had little fame and she little more in the way of family importance than he. Shortly before the publication of *Helena*, Salvador de Mendonça, then consul general in New York City, wrote him an ec-

static letter about his bride to be, one Mary Redman of
Boston. The complete approval and unselfconscious enthusiasm of Assis's reply indicate, I think, that he did not
include his own marriage among the usual Brazilian ones.
From his repeated congratulations and from his many as-
surances of the happiness and inspiration (for his work) that
Mendonça will receive from this marriage, one gains the
impression that he feels he and Mendonça are in the same
class, maritally speaking. The following brief excerpt con-
veys the general tone of the letter.

Rio, April 15, 1876.

No, my dear Salvador, even if I sent you a letter of thirty
or forty pages, I could not give you an idea of the surprise
yours of the seventh last caused me: the greatest, most
agreeable of surprises. When I opened it and counted the
twelve sheets in your hand, written close and small, I was
extremely flattered, and I believe I was an object of affectionate envy to those who were with me—Quintino [Bo-
cayuva] and João de Almeida. But, as soon as I started to
read it, I experienced a gentle disillusionment: only love
can be so eloquent, only love can so inspire the most serious of young men and the most jovial of consuls. I reread
the letter, not only because it was from you but also because it would be difficult to find a better portrait of a
young American woman. Everything about her is individual and original. We love and marry here in Brazil, as
they love and marry in Europe. In that country where you
are, it seems as though these things are a kind of compromise between the romantic and the patriarchal. Add the
intellectual gifts of Miss Mary Redman—perhaps even
now Mrs. Mendonça. To marry thus, and with such a
bride, is simply to live in the broadest sense of the word.
. . . There is no need to justify your haste. The best loves
spring into being in a moment. You only followed the
good rule: you were a Yankee among Yankees. . . .

It is notable that the plots of Assis's second, third, and

fourth novels are concerned with the marriage of convenience. In *Hand and Glove* there was the proposed marriage between Guiomar and Jorge and the actual one with Alves, which, one suspects, was after all for love. In *Helena*, aside from the proposed marriages for Estacio and Helena, it is intimated that Counselor Valle's had been an arranged marriage, and his philandering—which caused such tragic consequences—the normal life of husbands of his class. In *Yayá Garcia*, Valeria opposed her son Jorge's marriage to Estella, a lovely girl, but of obscure family. Estella refused to marry Jorge, although she loved him, and married Luiz Garcia whom she respected but did not love; with him she hoped to find surcease from her love of Jorge. Luiz Garcia married Estella for the good of his daughter Yayá. In the end Yayá and Jorge married for love.

Yayá Garcia is the last of Assis's novels in which society and its class distinctions enter the main argument. In the other novels social problems, when they appear, are subordinated to the struggle within the human heart, where their ultimate cause lies—the hatred, cruelty, greed, and indifference of self-love. *Resurrection* told of a battle of life with death, love with self-love. A man tried to resurrect his "dead heart," his ability to love another. Love was the true manifestation of life; self-love of death. In the three novels that followed, the theme is the same but it is obscured and confused by a shift of emphasis: we turn our eyes from the elemental struggle within the heart to watch the heart's response to what seems to be great and immediate pressures from the outside.

The basic life-death, love-self-love theme is resumed, full force, in *Posthumous Memoirs of Braz Cubas*, the fifth novel, and maintains its power through the remaining four. The return to this theme was foreshadowed in *Yayá Garcia*, not so much in love's triumph over the main plot and characters as in the ex-slave Raymundo who had no real exis-

tence apart from that of his master and young mistress.
Raymundo is a kind of phantom or presence, a disembodied
symbol of selfless devotion and of the gentleness in the Brazilian nature—a trait to which Machado de Assis adverted
more than once.[12]

> When Luiz Garcia inherited him from his father . . . he
> immediately gave him his emancipation papers. . . .
>
> "You are free," he said. You may live with me as long as
> you like."
>
> From then on Raymundo was a sort of external spirit of
> his master: he thought for him and reflected his inner
> thought in all his actions, which were no less silent than
> punctual. Luiz Garcia never gave an order; he had every-
> thing at the proper hour and in the proper place. Al-
> though he was the only servant in the house, Raymundo
> had time left over in the evening to converse with his for-
> mer master, in the tiny garden, as night came on. There
> they talked of their little world, of the rare domestic occur-
> rences, of what the weather would be the next day, of one
> thing or another that had happened outside. When dark-
> ness fell and the city opened its gaslight eyes, they with-
> drew to the house, slowly, side by side.
>
> "Raymundo'll sing tonight, shall he?" the Negro would
> sometimes say.
>
> "When you will, old fellow."
>
> Raymundo would light the candles, go fetch his ma-
> rimba, walk out to the garden, and sit there playing and
> singing in a low voice—songs of Africa, faint memories of
> the tribe in which he had been born. They were not songs
> of homesickness and longing; none of the airs were pitched
> in a mournful key; they were joyous, war-like, spirited.
> Finally he would fall silent. His thought, instead of re-
> turning to its African home, leapt through the window of
> the room where Luiz Garcia sat working and hovered over
> the white man's head like a protective spell. Whatever
> social and natural differences there were between the two
> men, their domestic relations had made them friends.[13]

Raymundo, an image of gentle manners, and the simple joys of love, stands as an element of Brazil's true culture in contrast to the unnatural, barbarous restraints imposed by a European civilization. After his conference with Valeria about her son, Luiz Garcia, filled with anxieties that had been induced by the false pride, contention, hypocrisy, and deceit of that house, returned to the loving peace of a simpler, a better society—Raymundo's.

> It was night when Luiz Garcia left Valeria's house. He was annoyed with everything, with the mother and with the son, with his own ties to that house, with the situation in which he saw himself placed. As he hurried up the steep, stone path of the road he stopped from time to time to look below, as if apprehensive of the future, seized with strange, superstitious fears that came and went. It was not long before the light of his own house appeared, and, then, he heard the slave's solitary song and the rude notes of his marimba. They were the voices of peace; he hastened his step and fled into the safety of that solitude.[14]

A further fillip is given the rigidity of an old-world class society in a sarcastic side glance at the deterministic philosophies which Assis was to ridicule in extenso in his next novel. "Raymundo," says the author in describing him, "seemed made for the express purpose of serving Luiz Garcia."[15]

POSTHUMOUS MEMOIRS
OF BRAZ CUBAS

CHAPTER TEN

CUBAS'S LIGHTER SIDE— THE PICARO

With his fifth novel, *Posthumous Memoirs of Braz Cubas* (1880),[1] Machado de Assis returned both to the simple theme sounded in his first novel, *Resurrection*, and to the comic genre of his second, *Hand and Glove*. After tracing the intricacies of the feminine psyche through three novels concerned with social problems, *Hand and Glove*, *Helena*, and *Yayá Garcia*, he abandoned the female protagonist for good and all and resumed his exploration of the male heart and the basic problem of love and self-love, life and death, good and evil. In *Posthumous Memoirs of Braz Cubas* he gave self-love a thorough going-over. Consequently death enters its every page; even life takes on the role of death at times; and death, of life. There is no gentle Raymundo in this narrative—practically nothing in the way of unadulterated love, or of unadulterated good or evil or life or death, although self-love does hold the scene, assuming many masks, as greed, vanity, envy, ambition, and so on.

For all its concern with dead and half-dead souls, *Posthumous Memoirs of Braz Cubas* is cast in the form of a comedy, with comic personages and comic action arising out of their comic natures. It is a little strange, therefore, that it has generally been regarded as a work of profound pessimism.

It was probably the hero-narrator himself, Braz Cubas,

who put ideas of pessimism into the critics' heads in the first place, with his prefatory note, "To the Reader."

> If I have adopted the free form of a Sterne or of a Xavier de Maistre, I am not sure but what I have also inserted a certain cantankerous pessimism of my own.

And, finally, there is his remark on the last page of the novel, the remark that no critic neglects to quote, the remark from which William Grossman coined the title for his translation, *Epitaph of a Small Winner*. When he balanced his life's accounts, says Braz, the good against the evil, he discovered he had a small amount on the credit side: he had never had a child, had transmitted to no living being the legacy of our human wretchedness. True, there seems to be a bitter taste here, but if we have followed the narration closely, this remark will invite an amusing as well as a pessimistic interpretation.

From the title of the book, *Posthumous Memoirs of Braz Cubas*, one assumes, correctly, that the hero of the tale, Braz Cubas, narrates his own story. But, as he informs us straightaway, posthumous memoirs does not mean merely memoirs published after their author's death. No, the words mean that the author of the memoirs did not begin to compose them until after he was dead. He wrote them, he says, from the life beyond, to while away the tedium of eternity. The dedicatory inscription on the first page brings home to us his physical state at the time of writing.

To the Worm

Who

First Sank His Teeth Into The Cold Flesh

Of My Cadaver

I Offer

In Fond Remembrance

These

P O S T H U M O U S   M E M O I R S[2]

The first half of the title, "posthumous memoirs," surely rings a bell with us whose native tongue is English, calling to mind Charles Dickens's *Posthumous Papers of the Pickwick Club*,[3] a kind of Victorian picaresque novel in which the eminently respectable, rich and portly Mr. Pickwick made a journey in the interest of science—that is, to prove by actual observation his theory of the tittlebat. On that scholarly junket he fell in with various shady characters, with consequent misadventures—was sued for breach of promise, put in the Fleet, caught hiding behind the door in a young ladies' seminary, and otherwise placed in a number of degrading and undignified postures.

Before we have got through Braz Cubas's title and preface then, we have been reminded of two English authors often mentioned in connection with the picaresque type story: Charles Dickens and Laurence Sterne. Further allusions to both are to come up in the course of the *Memoirs*. The relation to Sterne is the closer. When Braz states that he has adopted "the free form of a Sterne," he is, I believe, referring not so much to Shandy's superficial mannerisms as to basic matters of general structure, character portrayal, and narrative method.

As Sterne in *Tristram Shandy* borrowed from, and at the same time burlesqued and parodied, the epics, romances, comic epics, and picaresque tales of his predecessors, Machado de Assis in this novel did the same for Sterne. Sterne, in order to satirize the long romance that begins with the birth or childhood of the hero and gradually takes him up to maturity, or beyond into middle age, began his *Life and Opinions of Tristram Shandy* before his hero's birth, with his begetting. It took the first three of the novel's nine volumes to get him born, almost another volume to get him through the first day of his life, another half-volume or so to get him into breeches, and, so far as the narrative goes, it is difficult to determine whether he ever did come of age.

Machado de Assis, in his turn, parodied the older romances, and *Tristram Shandy* into the bargain. Only, he went about it from the opposite direction. *His* hero-author, Braz Cubas, begins his story with his own death notice, which runs somewhat as follows: I passed away at two o'clock on a Friday afternoon, in the month of August, 1869, at my fine estate on the outskirts of Rio de Janeiro. I was sixty-four, of a rugged constitution, rich, and a bachelor.

He goes on to describe his funeral, to explain why it was so poorly attended—rain, lack of publicity, and so forth. He then continues, still in reverse, to relate the cause of his death—pneumonia brought on by an idea for an invention, an idea for a medicinal plaster to cure men's melancholy. When the idea came to him he got overheated by inspiration and the prospect of fame, got in a draft, caught cold, neglected the cold, pneumonia set in, then agony and death.

Next, we have his last illness, and here we see that Braz's narrative method, like Shandy's, is not so rambling and crazy as we had been led to believe. Tristram Shandy remarked of his method, "My work is digressive, and it is progressive too,—and at the same time."[4] Braz Cubas's method is a refinement on Shandy's. It too progresses through digressions, and even through retrogressions, that are economical and dramatic. Here is the way we are introduced to Virgilia, his "great sin," as he calls her.

> I saw her loom in the doorway to the bedroom—pale, moved, dressed in black. She stood there a whole minute, without the courage to enter. . . . I gazed at her . . . forgetting to greet her by word or gesture. I had not seen her for two years, and I saw her now, not as she *was*, but as she *had been*—both of us as we had been, because a mysterious Hezekiah made the sun turn backward to the days of our youth. The sun turned back, I shook off all life's wretchedness, and this handful of earth that death was about to

scatter to eternal nothingness suddenly had more power than time—time, which is death's minister. No water from the Fountain of Youth could have accomplished what was done by nothing more than *longing*.[5]

The comparison to Hezekiah is apropos. He too was on his death bed. The turning back of the sun was a sign that the Lord would heal him and add fifteen years to his life, because he had walked before the Lord in truth and with a perfect heart and had done what was good in the Lord's eyes. Braz, of course, received much less time—some two or three days. In this chapter, however, the sight of Virgilia rolled back time to the days of his youth. In the chapter that follows, "The Delirium," time is rolled back to the beginning, "past Eden." That chapter (vii) sheds considerable light on the novel's theme, as we shall discover later. From his final "delirium," Braz quickly arrived at his birth with another of his methodically mad transitions. But before we let him tell any more of his history let us take another look at his title, *Posthumous Memoirs of Braz Cubas*.

As its first half brought to mind the Victorian pseudo-picaro Pickwick, the title's second half perhaps bears a trace of that picaresque novel par excellence, *Gil Blas de Santillane* by Le Sage. The name Braz is the Portuguese form of the Spanish *Blas*, and Assis, who frequently mentions Le Sage's hero in his writings, always refers to him as Gil Braz.[6] Conversely, the Spanish translations of *Posthumous Memoirs* have been titled *Memorias Póstumas de Blas Cubas*.

The more or less usual recipe for the picaresque hero as exemplified in Le Sage, in some of his Spanish forerunners, and in English imitations such as *Tom Jones* and *David Copperfield* (the latter a well-watered-down picaro, to be sure), is somewhat as follows. A young boy of rather well-to-do but otherwise obscure family is introduced by chance into the criminal set or outer fringes of respectable society, and after many escapades with thieves, women, and the law, in ups and downs of fortune in both high and low life, as he feels middle age coming on, marries a sweet, innocent girl who proves a model wife (she is likely to have a wealthy middle-class father and the hero settles down comfortably on his in-laws' cash), has a minimum of two children—a boy and a girl—is elected to the city council, made the director of the local bank, or something of the sort—in short becomes a thoroughly respectable middle-class paterfamilias.

Braz Cubas attempted to follow a pattern of that sort, but somehow failed on all counts. Partly, perhaps, because he was a nineteenth-century Brazilian, born and bred in Rio de Janeiro, the cultured court-city of the Braganças. The name *Braz* certainly suggests the word Brazil. It had been borne by a famous Brazilian patriot, founder of the city São Vicente, and inventor of the mill commonly used in Brazil for refining sugar. Braz's father had so named him in an attempt to connect his own rather obscure family with the proud descendants of the sixteenth-century patriot.[7]

Braz had the right kind of genealogy for a picaresque hero. The Portuguese word *cuba* means vat or barrel, and, as we learn in chapter iii, a not too remote ancestor had originally made his living mending and fabricating those plebeian articles, then turned planter, became rich, sent his son to the University of Coimbra . . . and thus the Cubas family became *old-family* in less than no time. Braz's father, Bento, made up a fanciful story to explain away the hogs-heady smell of the name. One is reminded of Gil Blas's forged letters of nobility and the consolation offered him by his servant Scipio on his want of true nobility: "You have Letters of Nobility. That's enough for your posterity. When time has covered these letters with the impenetrable veil with which it conceals the origin of all great houses, after four or five generations, the race of Santillanes will be among the most illustrious."[8]

Braz was born in 1805, the only son of doting parents,

both of wealthy family. He was a spoiled child, tyrannizing over family, slaves, and visitors without pity. His two uncles did not add much to his upbringing. One, João, a rough soldier, was, in Braz's words, "a man of unbridled tongue, loose life, and picaresque vocabulary."[9] The other, Ildefonso, a priest and canon of the Church, offered constant criticism but his influence was negligible. Though of blameless life himself, Ildefonso was so much concerned with the outward shows of religion as to have little time for inculcating virtue in others: a slip in a paternoster, an ill-timed genuflection, was worse than breaking any number of commandments. Braz's father met Ildefonso's criticisms by maintaining that he was following an educational system vastly superior to the usual one. And, says Braz, "in this way, without answering his brother's arguments, he succeeded in deluding himself." (Bento Cubas's educational system is decidedly reminiscent of Walter Shandy's Tristrapaedia[10] as well as his theories of childbirth and of the influence of names.) In spite of faults of upbringing Braz turned out to be not such a bad fellow, although he did cause his father disappointment.

Like a good picaro, he got his introduction to low life and the wrong kind of women at a tender age. When he was seventeen his uncle the captain took him to a supper party "with women." The party was held at the house of Marcella, a high-priced Spanish girl whom he had already admired in the street. It took him thirty days to reach Marcella's heart, and then, he tells us, the world was his, but not for a trifling consideration. "Marcella loved me for fifteen months and eleven thousand milreis," he recalled. At the end of that time, his father, concerned for the diminishing Cubas coffers, shanghaied his son (with Marcella's help): Braz was put on a ship for Portugal and the University of Coimbra. Although he had every intention of throwing himself overboard, he did not; and long before the ship touched port,

Marcella had been expunged from his mind and heart. His vanity was intent on the glory of a university career.

He received a degree, but the "career" had been a little less than glorious. Then, after traveling through Europe for several years, he returned to Rio de Janeiro in time to see his mother die. There follows a pathetic interlude of some five pages, in the course of which he spent a few solitary days in the civilized wilds of Mt. Tijuca, where, he informs us, he acquired the melancholy from which he was never again to be free. The pathetic interlude ends on a comic note. His seclusion, with which he was already getting bored, was interrupted by two things. His father suddenly appeared, bringing a combination proposal of marriage and political career, that is, of a bride with a father influential in political circles. Secondly, Braz learned that the family acquaintance who had prepared his mother's body for burial was in the neighborhood and wished to see him. He felt an obligation to see her for another reason: she had been the unfortunate victim of one of his many acts of childish cruelty. This woman had a daughter, Eugenia, illegitimate but young, innocent, pretty, ardent. Again there was promise of a love affair, but it came to nothing. Braz discovered she was lame: his vanity retreated before the idea of marriage with a lame girl; his more generous feelings shied away from the brutality of seducing her. Besides, his father had another marriage in view for him: he told himself it was right to obey his father, proper that he "embrace a political career . . . the constitution . . . his bride . . . his horse. . . ."

He had no difficulty in accepting "the bride," Virgilia, a beautiful girl of sixteen, nor the seat in the Chamber of Deputies which was to be furnished by her father. Virgilia and her father accepted Braz. But another young man happened along—a more ambitious young man, Lobo Neves—and promised Virgilia he would make her a marchioness.

At the same time, Marcella appeared out of Braz's past and gave him a nasty psychological turn that interfered with the smooth course of his courtship. Lobo Neves got the girl and the political career that were to have been Braz's.

This double loss was a great disappointment to Bento Cubas. Many children fail to live up to the expectation of their parents, and the parents manage to adjust to the situation. Braz's father did not make the adjustment. He died four months later of shock at this blow to the "illustrious" house of Cubas. Braz himself felt only some short-lived pain in his personal vanity. As for the rest, he remembered that his not very distant forebears had mended barrels for a living, and bore any affront to the illustrious Cubas name with great calm. Even his personal feelings were soon soothed in the company of N, Z, and U; and to otherwise pass the time he wrote poetry and fiery political articles, achieving some reputation in both fields.

About eleven years after Virgilia's marriage, Lobo Neves returned with his family from São Paulo and took up residence in Rio. Braz waltzed with Virgilia at a ball; they fell in love. To quote Braz's words:

> Some plants bud and sprout quickly, others are slow and never reach full development. Our love was of the former type; it sprouted with such impetus and so much sap that in a short time it was the largest, the leafiest, and the most exuberant creature of the woods. I cannot tell you exactly how long it continued to grow. I remember, however, the night it first blossomed into flower with a kiss, if you can call it that, a kiss that she gave me, trembling—poor thing—trembling with fear because we were standing at the gate to the grounds of her husband's estate. This single kiss united us, this kiss, ardent and brief, prologue to a life of delight, of remorse, of pleasures ending in grief, of troubles blossoming into joy, of patient, systematic hypocrisy, the only restraint upon an otherwise unbridled love—a life of nervousness, of anger, of despair, of jealousy,

all of them paid for in full by one hour; but another hour would come and would swallow up the first and everything that went with it, leaving only the nervousness and the dregs, and the dregs of the dregs, which are satiety and disgust: such was to be the book of which this kiss was the prologue.[11]

There you have it—an illicit affair such as you might find in *Gil Blas, Guzmán de Alfarache,* or *Tom Jones,* only it follows a most unpicaresque line of development. Braz Cubas's bedroom adventures are nothing if not disappointing. He lacked the rough and tumble stuff of a true picaresque hero. As he says of himself, he had too much of the refinement of his country and age.

The story of his first love, Marcella, was pure farce. The Coimbra loves were only a passing reference. Eugenia, the lame girl, was a brief, humorous-sentimental incident; the nameless N, Z, and U left behind them a faint scent of their perfume, nothing more—even their names were forgotten; and now Virgilia, a Cleopatra cut down to 1842 Rio de Janeiro comic proportions, but still a charmer.

For some years the affair with Virgilia went on, right under her husband's nose, practically without incident. When Rio society began to notice the frequent regularity of Braz's visits to the Neves house, the lovers did not flee the country as Braz proposed; Virgilia refused. She wanted to go on with the love affair and keep her reputation too. Braz found a gem of a cottage on the city's edge where their rendezvouses would draw less attention, and persuaded a respectable but poor woman, Dona Placida, much against her more respectable feelings, to live there and act as a screen for their clandestine meetings. (Indeed, in order to put Dona Placida's scruples to sleep, Braz told her a pitiful tale of how he and Virgilia had been separated by their parents, and she forced to marry Neves, and a lot of other baseless lies.) Occasionally there is promise of something piquant, but our hopes are always dashed. Virgilia conceived a child that Braz presumed to be his, but there was a miscarriage and no child of his ever saw the light of this world. On another occasion, when Lobo Neves was offered the governorship of a province, he invited Braz to go along as his secretary . . . and Braz accepted. They were—Neves, Virgilia, and Braz—to go off into the idyllic wilds, far from the malicious tongues of the capital—a cozy ménage à trois. As Braz put it, "A governor, a governor's lady, and the governor's secretary: that's what you call solving matters in truly administrative style." The appointment, however, was made on the thirteenth day of the month; Neves was superstitious; he declined the position. Thus this situation with its explosive possibilities was deactivated by Fortune, and Braz and Virgilia went their way of humdrum adultery.

At last another offer of a governorship came to Neves. The appointment this time had the digits of the date reversed: instead of "13," it was dated "31." Neves accepted. He and his family sailed out of the harbor. Virgilia passed out of Braz's life without a drop of blood being shed. Neves, it is plain, knew the truth, had known it for some time, but held his peace from a fear of society's ridicule.

And now Braz made his final bid as a picaresque hero. He was in his forties. It was time for him to marry the innocent young girl. She came along on schedule—pretty, nineteen years old, rather poor, her father on the low and vulgar side. She was a relative of Braz's brother-in-law Cotrim. All seemed propitious. And then, after a brief preparatory paragraph discussing the closeness of life and death, Braz transcribes her epitaph for us: "Here lies Dona Eulalia Damascena de Brito, dead at nineteen years of age. Pray for her!"[12] She died in the first epidemic of yellow fever to strike Rio de Janeiro, December, 1849;[13] and this gives her death an ironic, fatalistic twist. Braz's conniving, avaricious brother-in-law Cotrim was in the slave-smuggling line.

(Importation of slaves had been banned by law in 1831.) It was Cotrim who was pushing the marriage with Eulalia in order to bring his low relations into the pseudoaristocratic Cubas family. Since it was commonly believed that this epidemic of yellow fever had been introduced into Brazil by a boatload of contraband African slaves, the superstitious regarded it as divine retribution for the godless traffic. The mosquito theory was not advanced until 1881, a year after *Memórias Posthumas de Braz Cubas* first appeared in print.

With his betrothed dead, Braz could say at the end of his memoirs that as a hero of romance and even as a picaresque hero he was something of a failure. He listed his defeats: no page with blood on it; he suffered no remorse; with Don Quixote he did not win fame, although, like him, he had tried to win it—through his medicinal plaster to cure melancholy, the disease of which Don Quixote was thought to have died. He never became "caliph" or "minister," never knew marriage, had no children—not even the two-child minimum, the boy and girl of a Gil Blas or Tom Jones. Finally he adds in a tone between regret and perhaps genuine relief the phrase that has been taken ever so seriously and applied to Machado de Assis as well as, or even more than, to his creature Braz Cubas—the remark about leaving no legacy of our human misery to a child of his.[14]

In spirit, however, Braz was a Gil Blas, though an unsuccessful one. Wide-awake, witty, handsome, reckless, light-minded, of an easy virtue and adaptable morals, accepting all situations and turning most of them to his own advantage, tolerant of vice in himself and in others, yet not completely vicious—he gradually learned something as he made his "circuit of life"; but, unlike the more conventional, the true picaro, he never got around to reforming or having any regrets. Yet his story contains traces of pessimism, he says: he warns of it in his prefatory note, "To the Reader," and frequently reminds us in the course of the narrative that his is a lugubrious tale, that it reeks of death; and he will drive home a point by saying, "I assure you of this from the depths of my tomb." Athough he thus insists on his pessimism, his manner is far from pessimistic. He is about as carefree a corpse as one is likely to come across. Even the worm of his dedication, that is, death (perhaps his critics also), is patted on the back, so to speak, with a certain camaraderie, and one suspects that Braz's tomb was a snug affair with hot and cold running water and a good library.

Life, as well as death, is given the comic treatment. The butt of the comedy is in all cases the same—human vanity. All the characters suffer from it, some more than others, none more than Braz, except, perhaps, his father. The elder Cubas is the incarnation of vanity—a simple, unaffected, undisguised, harmless, and inoffensive vanity—Bento, who died of shock at the blow administered to the nonexistent nobility of the Cubases by Braz's politicosocial failure but whose last moments were brightened by the visit of one of the emperor's ministers to his sick bed.

Practically all the characters are vain, comically so. There is no villain among them, no consistently vicious person. The one personage who comes closest to being a villain is Braz's brother-in-law Cotrim. Opposed to and overshadowing his vanity are his sadism, avarice, hypocritical scheming, and cowardice. We are not much inclined to laugh at Cotrim's treatment of his slaves, but in his struggle between avarice and vanity he too is funny.

Marcella at the beginning was a comic character. There was the contrast between her eagerness to parade through the Rio streets, her magnificences and gaudy style of life, and, on the other hand, her careless attitude toward the city's vice code. But early in the book there is indication of a change occurring in Marcella. The insecurity of her harmless but silly vanity is indicated by her interest in something more solid than men's admiration, to wit, money. When she briefly reentered Braz's life after an interval of some seven or eight years, her beauty was gone, the old arrogance and flashiness were gone. Her soul, Braz informs us, was dead, killed by love of gain, "which," he says, "was the worm that gnawed away her soul's life."[15]

Eugenia, the lame girl, is not really comic. We dare not laugh at her. She was not vain, though pretty, because of her lameness; she was sad, bitter, proud, and stoical. She was not cruel, except to herself.

Some probably do not find Dona Placida particularly funny but only pathetic. Yet, with her artless ambition to rise above her birth as the illegitimate child of two most repulsive parents; her lifelong ambition to be an "honest woman"; the numerous setbacks this vain little ambition suffered at the hands of her mother, her daughter, and the men in her life; her embarrassment at being cajoled by Virgilia and Braz, and forced by her poverty, into playing the bawd to a couple of irresponsible adulterers—poor old Dona Placida is funny, even when she is most pathetic. But the others, Braz and Virgilia with all their friends and relations —one can laugh at their vanities without restraint.

Vanity is the backbone, the very viscera, not only of silly and of vicious acts on the part of the characters, but of their good and generous actions as well. Take charity for example: nothing could have induced Cotrim to make donations to charity except to get his generosity written up in the newspaper or to have his portrait painted in oils and hung on the wall of a benevolent society.

Vanity begets ambition, which in Braz's world is what stokes the engine of human progress. Ambition, he shows us, promotes science (exemplified in his invention), politics and letters (to cite himself, Neves, and Luiz Dutra), and snobbery, or social distinction if you prefer, like Bento Cubas's.

Vanity is the very essence of sexual love and fidelity: it

was in great measure responsible not only for Braz's love of Virgilia but also for his faithfulness to her over so many years. Curiously enough Braz more or less exempts women from this last vanity. Woman, he says, gives herself for love's sake ... whether it be romantic love, "or the purely physical love known to certain ladies of ancient Rome, to women among the Polynesians, Laplanders and Kaffirs, and perhaps among some other civilized races; but man—and I speak only of men in a cultured and elegant society—man joins vanity to the sentiment of love."[16]

Vanity is responsible for honesty; and it is honesty, we are told, that gives rise to dishonesty. When Braz found a gold piece in the street and took it to the police station, this honest act not only gave his ego a warm inner glow of superiority, but he was showered with praise at the station, he received a letter of commendation from the captain of the precinct, and his friends learned of it. Word reached the chief of police, who personally congratulated him on his honesty, and finally Virgilia herself learned of it. With his vanity thus surfeited on probity, when he found five thousand milreis wrapped in an old newspaper on the beach, he took them to the Bank of Brazil and deposited them in the name of Braz Cubas, and to the devil with pats on the back.

When vanity is stifled, it is replaced by some less amusing form of self-love, as we have seen in Marcella and Cotrim. The same happened to Braz: when he recognized that Luiz Dutra was a better writer than he, he elaborately withheld the approbation so eagerly sought by the sensitive Luiz. "My purpose," he confides, "was to make him lose confidence, discourage him, eliminate him."[17]

It is not often that Braz's vanity fails him. He is such a thoroughgoing egoist, so sure in his superior wisdom, so indulgent toward his own imperfections, that it is no wonder he can view with Olympian calm the slips and errors of the less than perfect mortals that bask in the sun of his presence.

The villain of the piece is not any of the personages. It is human nature, life itself.

When Braz closes the Virgilia episode, he states that this is not the end of his history, that the best is yet to come. With this brief warning he more or less turns the book over, lock, stock, and barrel, to *Humanitism*. Humanitism is the philosophy developed by Braz's former schoolmate Quincas Borba, a man of attractive personality who had gone crazy. The only son of a tremendously wealthy mother, Quincas, as a boy, had been a nabob among the other boys of the school. Years after, when Braz ran into him on the street, the nabob, who had dispersed his fortune, was a dirty, penniless beggar, a philosopher, and a thief. On that occasion he picked Braz's pocket before they parted. Later he inherited more money and turned up again with new ethics and a new philosophy to fit his new economic status.[18] The basis of this philosophy is *humanitas*. Quincas uses the Latin term, not in its accepted sense of "culture," but with a quite contrary meaning, which he foists upon it.

In the beginning of his memoirs, as mentioned above, Braz related the substance of a delirious hallucination he had experienced in his last illness. In his delirium he seemed to be first a Chinese barber shaving a mandarin, then a de luxe, illustrated edition of St. Thomas Aquinas's *Summa Theologica*, and, finally returning to his own person, he was carried off on the back of a talking hippopotamus that traveled swiftly backward through the ages—past Eden to the beginnings of time, a region of eternal ice and snow—where a great female creature who called herself Pandora hulked at him. She defined herself as Imperishable Nature with all things in her box, death as well as life, and her law as egoism. She showed Braz the centuries passing in review—the hopes, labor, love, hate, greed, and joys of men working with and against one another, pushing forward and holding back the march of civilization. Each age brought its share of light and of darkness, its parade of systems, of new ideas, of new illusions; in each the verdure of spring burst forth, grew yellow with age, and then, young once more, burst forth again.

Humanitism, the philosophy invented by the mad Quincas Borba, is a kind of exuberant development of Pandora— a thoroughgoing egoism.[19] According to Quincas Borba's explanation, humanitas, the principle of all things, is Man shared by and summed up in every man. Each man is not merely humanitas's vehicle; he is at one and the same time vehicle, driver, and passenger.

Quincas Borba's Humanitism has been interpreted variously by various critics—as a satire on Leibnitz, Nietzsche, evolution, and so on.[20] Probably there are shafts at these and some other philosophies in it; but there is little doubt that superficially Assis was poking fun at Auguste Comte and Positivism with its professed aim of securing the victory of altruism over egoism. We have already had a glimpse of what Assis thought of Naturalism, the literary aspect of Positivism.[21] Naturalism was not the only form of Comte's philosophy popular in Brazil. Positivism in all its phases— philosophical, political, and theological—had a tremendous vogue there, and for many years. We still see the Positivist motto on the national flag: *Ordem e Progresso*—Order and Progress. Brazil was one of the few countries where the Positivist religion took root and where its ritual was observed in temples.[22] Machado de Assis delivered many a body blow to Positivism in the columns of his journalism, and in other writings also.[23]

The superficial resemblances between Borba's philosophy and Comte's are numerous. For example, there is a similarity of terminology: *humanitas* and *humanité*. Corresponding to Positivism's four stages, the theologic, metaphysical, abstract, and positive, there are four phases of Humanitism. They are not the same as Comte's but a kind of pseudoscientific parody of them: the *static*, prior to all creation, the *expansive*, which is the beginning of things, the *dispersive*, which is the appearance of men; and finally the *contractive*, which is the reabsorption of men and things into humanitas.[24]

Comte had little use for his predecessors. Borba considered Pascal's formula inferior to his own,[25] and asserted that the Stoicism of Zeno and Seneca was child's play compared to Humanitism.[26] Indeed, he, like Comte, sneered at all the Greeks except Aristotle,[27] and said that Humanitism was a system of philosophy destined to put all the other systems out of business.[28] (Of course, the tendency to disparage other systems is perhaps common to most philosophers.)

Humanitism has the all-embracing quality of Positivism: it covers metaphysics, ethics, science, literature, economics, and has a religious dogma with liturgies. Quincas spent a great deal of thought and perspiration over his liturgies for the Church of Humanitism. Humanitism, he explained to Braz, was to be the church of the future, the only true religion; Christianity was all right for women and beggars, and other religions in his opinion were no better.[29]

There are many small echoes of Positivism in Humanitism. Comte elevated the dog, "the noble dog," to a place beside man. Quincas did the same in the novel *Quincas Borba*, which is a sequel to *Posthumous Memoirs of Braz Cubas*. Another example is Quincas's insanity; Comte spent two or three years in a mental hospital.

All these resemblances, however, are more apparent than real. Assis is poking fun not only at Positivism but at all other illusory *isms*, and particularly at materialistic ones. In addition, I believe, he is poking fun at himself, as though to say, "The opinions Braz Cubas spouts and this Pandora I inserted into his delirium are the same as Quincas Borba's philosophy; they are as crazy as Positivism. I am as crazy as Quincas Borba, that is, I am as crazy as Auguste Comte."

Perhaps it is worth noting that Quincas is the nickname for Joaquim, which was Assis's first name as well as Borba's.

Egoism then is the basis of humanitas, as it is of Pandora-Nature, as it is of Braz Cubas, who is only a piece of Pandora—as he reminds her in his delirium: "Why will you harm yourself by killing me?"[30] Indeed, egoism is the motive power of all the other characters.

Quincas Borba's philosophical arguments and Braz Cubas's rationalizations about himself and about the other personages have a certain crazy resemblance. Braz explains Cotrim's avarice by showing that avarice is only an exaggeration of a virtue, that is, thrift; "and," adds Braz, "naturally one cannot have too much of a good thing."[31] Hence avarice is really a virtue. In the same manner, Quincas brilliantly demonstrates that envy is one of the noblest, if not *the* noblest of all human virtues. Envy, he explains, is only admiration in action, struggling aggressively; and, since struggle is the proper function of the human organism, it is envy's hostile actions that most contribute to the advancement of science, letters, and the arts, and to human progress in general. Hence, it turns out envy is a virtue.[32]

Finally, the determinism to be found both in Positivism and in Quincas's Humanitism is also a part of the Cubas philosophy, and as such is turned to artistic purpose: it becomes a dramatic device in the novel. Quincas Borba constantly maintains that since humanitas is in all men, and vice versa all men are a part of humanitas, every man has a stake in every other man's life, thought, and actions. As he gnaws a chicken wing, he gives the following explanation.

> The sublimity of my system really requires no better documentation than this very chicken. It was fed on corn that was planted, let us say, by an African imported from Angola. This African was born, grew up, was sold; a ship brought him here, a ship built of wood cut in the forest by ten or twelve men and driven by sails that eight or ten

men wove, not to mention the rope and the rest of the nautical apparatus. Thus, this chicken, on which I have just lunched, is the result of a multitude of efforts and struggles carried on for the sole ultimate purpose of satisfying my appetite."[33]

Braz's determinism is much less complex than Quincas's. He calls it his "theory of rolling balls,"[34] and illustrates with Marcella. When Braz was engaged to Virgilia, Marcella, through a chance circumstance, reinserted herself into Braz's life. The emotional reactions, memories, and thoughts thus aroused by Marcella and the past, interfered with his feeling toward Virgilia and his relation toward her; in short they were partially responsible at least for the breaking off of their engagement and consequently of Virgilia's marriage to Lobo Neves. Braz likens himself and others to rolling balls: the ball Marcella rolled against the ball Braz; it, set in motion, rolled against Virgilia. Thus one may say Marcella changed the course of Virgilia's life, and even of Lobo Neves's without coming into contact with either of them. Another example of this theory is the implication that the slaves brought illegally to Rio de Janeiro by Cotrim changed the course of Braz's life through the death of Eulalia. (Here the nexus is more like Quincas Borba's with Africa, slaves, a ship, and yellow fever completing the connection.) In the same way, the purpose of Dona Placida's birth and existence, and of the unlovely coupling of her parents, was to foster an illicit love affair between Braz and Virgilia.[35] The witty Braz remarks that the principle of the rolling balls is responsible for the "solidarity of human boredom."[36]

Although Braz laughs and blames everything on Nature, the projection of his rolling-balls theory into the novel's action does inject a moral tone—a suggestion of human responsibility. Thus a combination, or interlocking, of human will and chance seems to close round the characters with the vicelike grip of inescapable Fate, and is perhaps one more reason for critics calling this novel "pessimistic." The individual cannot escape his own past and that of his parents and ancestors, nor even from acts—present and past —of strangers.

CHAPTER ELEVEN

MELANCHOLY AND
AN EPIC HERO

Braz mentions his pessimism and his melancholy in his prefatory note, "To the Reader." The first two chapters tell of his idea for an invention, a patent medicine in the form of a plaster, to cure the melancholy of the world. His own melancholy, to which he recurs again and again, appears to have some connection with Quincas Borba's dictum on "struggle."[1] Braz acquired this pale, morbid flower, as he calls it, during his self-imposed solitude on Mt. Tijuca after his mother's death. He was sitting under a tamarind tree reading *As You Like It*. When he came to the line, " 'Tis good to be sad and say nothing!," he felt a "delightful echo" within him and hugged the tedium of lonely sorrow to his breast with a sensation of voluptuous pleasure.[2] This is Jaques's melancholy, "a sentimental self-indulgent humor," as Dowden called it, or to quote another Shakespearean critic, "[Jaques] sips the cup of woe with the gust of an epicure."[3] The Pandora of his delirium called Braz a "grande lascivo" (great lecher); the duke says to Jaques,

> For thou thyself hast been a libertine
> As sensual as the brutish sting itself.[4]

When the first installment of *Posthumous Memoirs of Braz Cubas* appeared in the *Revista Brasileira*, March 15, 1880, it had as a posy the English sentence, "I will chide no breather in the world but myself, against whom I know most faults."[5] This quotation is also from *As You Like It*; but it is Orlando speaking, Orlando the lover, Orlando after he met Rosalind. Before, one recalls, he chided his elder brother Oliver for a matter of some sixty lines.[6] In the first book-edition of the *Memoirs*, 1881, Assis removed the posy. It would seem that he wished to leave Orlando out of it and associate Braz only with the melancholy Jaques. Jaques's melancholy, as explained by himself, arose out of "the sundry contemplation of my travels, in which my often rumination wraps me in a most humourous sadness."[7] Rosalind further defines his melancholy for him in her parting speech, "Farewell, Monsieur Traveller: look you lisp, and wear strange suits; disable all the benefits of your own country: be out of love with your nativity, and almost chide God for making you that countenance you are; or I will scarce think you have swam in a gondola."[8]

Although Assis removed, in the 1881 edition, the posy from *As You Like It*, he substituted in the so-called fourth edition, 1899, a foreword that has appeared in all subsequent editions.[9] In it, he remarks that Braz's literary forebears—Laurence Sterne, Sterne's French imitator Xavier de Maistre, and the Portuguese imitator of both, Almeida Garrett

> were all travelers. Xavier de Maistre traveled around his bedroom, Garrett in his own land, Sterne in the land of others. Of Braz Cubas it may be said perhaps that he traveled all the way around life.[10]

In other words, Braz Cubas's melancholy, like Jaques's, was a traveler's melancholy: as Rosalind had said of Jaques, Braz had full eyes and empty hands,[11] and thus could count himself a failure as a bourgeois-picaresque ideal. Like Jaques he was an onlooker, a critic of life. He did not struggle, although Quincas Borba warned, "Life without struggle is a dead sea in the universal organism."[12] Quincas's admonition to him not to lie and weep at the river's edge is apparently another allusion to Jaques's melancholy—to his weeping stag swelling the already swollen river with its tears; Quincas's river was time, and Braz was cautioned not to try to stop its ceaseless flow but to take advantage of it, to live, to struggle.[13] Quincas believed in struggle; so too did Machado de Assis.[14] We never hear of Braz's struggles: we hear his opinions. And this is the part of Sterne's method that Machado de Assis imitated most closely; or should one say that Braz Cubas imitated the Shandy method?

Like Tristram Shandy, Braz gives minute analyses not only of his own thoughts, but smells out the secret opinions, feelings, and ambitions of all the other characters as well. It is through these opinions and sentiments, rather than through their actions, that Assis's personages, like Sterne's, come alive, grow on our affections, and move our pity or laughter. More often than not it is our laughter, for that, after all, is Braz's purpose. That was the purpose of both Jaques and Shandy. Jaques asked the duke to let him turn jester, to give him a suit of motley and leave to speak his mind. "And [he says] I will through and through / Cleanse the foul body of th' infected world, / If they will patiently receive my medicine."[15] Tristram Shandy's purpose was also medicinal. After disclaiming that his work was a satire against various prominent figures and evils, he concludes,

> My book . . . is wrote against the spleen [a synonym for melancholy in Sterne's day] in order, by a more frequent and a more convulsive elevation and depression of the diaphragm, and the succussations of the intercostal and abdominal muscles in laughter, to drive the gall and other bitter juices from the gall-bladder, liver and sweet bread, of his majesty's subjects, with all the inimicitious passions which belong to them, down into their duodenums.[16]

At the time of his death, Braz Cubas was on the eve of inventing a medicinal plaster to cure men's melancholy. Is it possible that these *Memoirs* are the postmortem perfected version of that plaster?

If such was the symbolism intended by Assis it might explain a bibliographical mystery. In a contract dated September 30, 1869, he agreed to deliver to his publisher B. L. Garnier by mid-March, 1870, a work entitled *The Manuscript of Licentiate Gaspar* (*O Manuscripto do Licenciado Gaspar*); but there is nowhere any further reference, by Assis or by his contemporaries, to this projected book, although Brazilian scholars have endeavored to discover traces of it.[17] The name Gaspar was used by Assis for two different characters in two short stories—"O Rei dos Caiporas" ("The King of Jonahs") (1870)[18] and "D. Monica" (1876); but he did not even include these stories in any of his collections, and, on the surface at least, they do not appear to have any connection with the title, *O Manuscripto do Licenciado Gaspar*.

A relationship between *Posthumous Memoirs of Braz Cubas* and *Gil Blas* was suggested above (p. 77). I now offer a further suggestion for strengthening that relationship—a suggestion which, at the same time, makes one wonder if the "lost" *Manuscript of Licentiate Gaspar* did not actually become *Posthumous Memoirs of Braz Cubas*.

Gil Blas, like *Posthumous Memoirs of Braz Cubas*, opens in an atmosphere of death, with an epitaph. Like Braz Cubas, Gil Blas prefaced his story with a note entitled, "To the Reader," in which he, again like Braz, laid claim to a seriousness of purpose. In this note he relates a parable, in which two students traveling together to Salamanca stopped by the way to refresh themselves at a spring.

> They noticed nearby a stone, level with the earth, on which there were traces of writing, partly effaced by time and the hooves of herds that had come to drink at the spring. They threw some water on the stone to clean it

and read these words of Spanish, *Aqui está encerrada el alma del Licenciado Pedro Garcias—Here lies buried the soul of Licenciate Pedro Garcias.*

The younger of the two students, who was quick and thoughtless, immediately said with a hearty laugh, "What could be more absurd? Here is buried the soul! . . . A buried soul! . . . I would like to know what eccentric composed such a ridiculous epitaph!" With these words, he stood up and prepared to go on his way.

His companion, a youth of greater discernment, said to himself, "There is some mystery here. I will stay behind and clear it up." He let his companion depart; and, without losing any time, began to loosen the stone with his knife. He found beneath it a leather purse containing a hundred ducats and a sheaf of paper bearing these words in Latin, "Be my heir, you who had the wit to unravel the meaning of the inscription; make better use, than I, of my money." The student, overjoyed by the discovery, replaced the stone and continued on his way, taking with him the licentiate's soul.

Whoever you may be, dear reader, you will resemble one or the other of those two students. If you read my adventures without heeding the moral instructions that lie buried in them you will derive no profit from this work; but, if you read attentively, you will find herein, as Horace teaches, the useful mingled with the pleasant.[19]

Blas's and Braz's heritage is the same, namely, the essence of their story. Blas makes it plain that his heir is his "reader." Braz's heir is a worm, as we read in his dedication. Who, or what, is this worm? Elsewhere in Assis's writing, "worm" is used to symbolize some form of death—as envy, time, greed, and so on. In this novel, for example, greed was the worm that killed Marcella's soul. The bookworms mentioned in chapter xvii of *Dom Casmurro*, besides their more profound implication, undoubtedly refer to critics. Here, too, in the dedication to the *Memoirs*, I believe "worm" means critic, that is, reader. Hence the two heirs, of Braz Cubas and of Gil Blas, are the same. To reduce the whole metaphor to its lowest terms: as Gil Blas's (metaphorical) soul was a purse full of ducats, so Braz Cubas's was a medicinal plaster, that is, both novels contain moral instruction —one "salutary," the other (being French) "valuable" in a more substantial sense. This places Braz in the British camp alongside Jaques and Tristram Shandy, whose respective purposes were medicinal.

There are other allusions to *As You Like It,* beyond the ones noted above; but echoes of *Tristram Shandy* are countless.[20] Even Braz's famous "pessimistic" final sentence may stem from the remark by Toby Shandy's valet, Corporal Trim: "I have neither wife or child—I can have no sorrows in this world."[21] As often noted, Braz apes the superficial quirks of the Shandy style. The peculiarity of a dedication to a coffin worm vies with the Shandy dedication placed at the end of Book I, chapter 8, where it is offered for sale to the highest bidder. Tristram Shandy expected "millions" of readers; Braz boils his expectations from one hundred down to one. There are his chapters consisting wholly of asterisks and exclamation points, appeals to the Laplanders as exponents of the highest culture, pseudosentimental digressions involving not only human persons, but also donkeys, flies, and other nonhuman souls, in such a way as to amuse, and to illuminate the main characters. But Assis turns Shandean mannerisms to a new use of his own. Compare the story of Uncle Toby and the fly with that of Braz's fly and ant.

The gentle Toby had "scarce a heart to retaliate upon a fly."

> —Go—says he, one day at dinner, to an overgrown one which had buzzed about his nose, and tormented him cruelly all dinner-time,—and which after infinite attempts, he had caught at last, as it flew by him;—I'll not hurt thee,

says my uncle Toby, rising from his chair, and going across the room, with the fly in his hand,—I'll not hurt a hair of thy head:—Go, says he, lifting up the sash, and opening his hand as he spoke, to let it escape: go, poor devil, get thee gone, why should I hurt thee?—This world surely is wide enough to hold both thee and me.[22]

During a quarrel with Virgilia, as Braz sat looking down at the floor, he noticed a fly dragging along an ant, which was chewing on his (the fly's) foot as they traveled. "Poor fly; poor ant!" writes Braz. A few minutes later, when the human lovers had patched up their quarrel, Braz leaned over to pick up Virgilia's earring, which had fallen off during the rigors of reconciliation, but the fly, still carrying the ant, which was still chewing on his foot, had climbed up on the earring.

Then [writes Braz] I, with the inborn delicacy of a man of our century, placed that tormented couple in the palm of my hand, calculated the distance from my hand to the planet Saturn, and asked myself what universal interest there could be in such a wretched little episode. If you conclude from this that I was an uncivilized brute, you are mistaken because I then asked Virgilia for a hairpin in order to separate the two insects; but the fly got wind of my intention, opened his wings, and flew off. Poor fly! poor ant! And God saw that this was good, as they say in the Scriptures.[23]

While Sterne forced the philosophies of his day to serve comedy and help build his characters, with a view to propagating a philosophy of his own perhaps,[24] Machado de Assis purloined Shandean comedy for a purpose that was essentially narrative. Braz's fly-and-ant not only illumines the humane ways of a Brazilian gentleman, it also epitomizes the relationship existing between him and Virgilia, and serves as a poetic transition to their separation, which occurs in the next and following chapters—a separation initiated by higher powers, as with the fly and ant, but taken advantage of by both insects; Braz flies off; and Virgilia, with only a faint show of resistance, gladly goes her separate way. Assis's metaphor goes to the narrative heart of things, the basic theme of his novels—love at war with self-love, life with death. Braz Cubas is not only a romantic, picaresque hero gone wrong, there is about him a suggestion of epic proportions and a certain mordant trace of tragedy.

The name Braz surely suggests the country Brazil; and Braz Cubas was perhaps intended to bear somewhat the same relation to Assis's Brazil as Aeneas bore to Virgil's Rome. When Bento Cubas came to Tijuca, where his son was grieving over his mother's death, Braz exhibited the same filial obedience as *pius Aeneas*, but in calmer, more Brazilian style. When Mercury brought Jove's order to leave Carthage, Aeneas was stunned; his hair stood on end, and his voice stuck in his throat. Braz, on the contrary, received his father without either "perturbation or protest."

> "My son, you must bow to the will of Heaven."
> "I already have," was my reply, and I kissed his hand.[25]

When his father told of the marriage he had arranged for him with the beautiful daughter of an influential politician, and the resulting political career in store for the young man, Braz reflected, and his subconscious desires were expressed on paper: he wrote, over and over, "as if in a trance," the first three words of the *Aeneid*: *Arma virumque cano*, "I sing the warlike exploits and the hero," but each time ending on the word *virumque*, "and the hero." He was identifying himself with Aeneas, hero-founder of the Roman state. In his next novel, *Quincas Borba*, Assis employed the same mechanism for the same purpose: the protagonist, Rubião, wrote, over and over, the words, "Marquis of Barbacena"—it was a title the crazed Rubião was taking to himself.[26]

Braz obeyed his father. He left Tijuca, abandoned his

Dido (Eugenia), to go marry a powerful king's daughter (Virgilia). He left in the name of *pietas*, that is, to comply with a father's wish, for family preferment, for the good of the Empire. At the same time, Braz savors strongly of the Cervantic Aeneas—a version already alluded to in *Resurrection*—Aeneas the faithless philanderer and cad, true scion of the perjured race of Laomedon.[27] For Braz, you will recall, concludes his account of his descent down the mountain: "I kept telling myself it was right to obey my father, that it was fitting and proper to embrace a political career, that the constitution, that my bride, that my horse . . ."[28]

In somewhat the same spirit, Braz adapted Virgil's "ants" to his own nefarious purpose. After killing the ill-omened black butterfly with a towel, when he finally picked it up and threw it out the window, he remarked that it was time because "the provident ants were already arriving" to carry off the butterfly's corpse.[29] The "provident ants"[30] are Camoens's: the sea nymphs that pushed Vasco de Gama's ships off the sandbars are compared to "provident ants." But Camoens had borrowed these insects from Virgil. When Dido looked down from her watchtower, the Trojans carrying supplies for their ships looked like a line of ants laying in supplies for winter.[31] For all the comic adaptation by Camoens and by Assis, there lingers in the Eugenia episode something of the Phoenician queen's black magic and evil omens. And certainly Eugenia on horseback has the queenly bearing of equestrian Dido.

As the living Aeneas journeyed to Hades, where the Sibyl disclosed secrets of life and death and showed him souls of men dead and of men yet to be born,[32] so Braz, while still alive, traveled to a kind of Hades, a region of snow and ice where time began; and Pandora, a great Sibyl-like creature, showed him the march of centuries—ages past and ages still to be.[33] But this brings us to another epic, one much nearer Assis's heart than the *Aeneid*.

The *arma virumque cano* continued under Braz's pencil into another concept. He wrote:

$$\text{arma virumque cano}$$

A
Arma virumque cano
       arma virumque cano
     arma virumque
         arma virumque cano
       virumque
Vir   Virgilio
   Virgilio   Virgilio
     Virgilio
                     Virgilio[34]

That is, the *vir*, the hero Aeneas, has become Virgil: Braz has become Virgil. And Virgil was Dante's guide through Hell and Purgatory, then he vanished and Beatrice became his guide to Paradise.[35] Braz Cubas partakes of the nature of Virgil, Dante's guide, who is thought to represent human reason: Braz is nothing if not rational. As the mental specialist sent by Quincas Borba to examine his sanity said, few men had his soundness of mind and judgment.[36] It is passion, love, that Braz lacks. And as Virgil disappeared as Dante's guide on Mt. Purgatory because human reason could take him no further, and Beatrice, "love," became the guide, so Braz's life is not only a failure in the picaresque cadre, it is incomplete in another sense.

At the beginning of his delirium he thought he was a de luxe edition of Thomas Aquinas's *Summa Theologica*, a book that purports to be an exposition of theology on rational principles; it is also an *unfinished* book. A man's life, Braz wrote, is a series of editions, each one corrected by the succeeding one, with the final edition presented by the publisher to the worms.[37] Braz never had a "final" edition. He was himself a kind of march of civilization in miniature; and, just as there was no visible end to the marching centuries Pandora showed him, there is no end to Braz. Like the *Summa Theologica,* he is an unfinished book, an incomplete book: he possessed reason; he never fully attained love; he examined human folly, his own included, with detachment, without much emotion. In Dante's *Inferno,* the lowest depth of Hell is a region of cold, of ice and snow, and of souls immersed in frozen rivers to their lips: that is, the maximum penalty, the worst torture man can suffer is insensibility.[38] And some of the tortured souls in Dante's frozen landscape still have warm bodies on earth: it is only their souls, their hearts, that are dead. When Braz, in his delirium, was carried to a region of snow and bitter cold, he thought he was dead, but Pandora told him, "You are alive. . . . Yes, worm, you live." Long before (chap. xcvi), Virgilia recoiled from his kiss as if it were a dead man's— "beijo de defuncto." In Assis's sixth novel, *Quincas Borba,* the heroine, Sophia, "put her soul in a cedar box and the cedar box in the day's leaden coffin, and abandoned herself to being dead in earnest."[39] As in Dante, the soul, or heart, can die before the body, and in that respect Braz's heart bears some resemblance to Felix's heart in the novel, *Resurrection.* But *Resurrection* aimed at tragedy; and there are faint echoes of tragedy in Braz's *Memoirs.*

When the idea for an invention to cure melancholy poised itself in Braz's brain, it took the form of an X and addressed him: "Decipher me or I devour you." These are the words of the Theban Sphinx, which posed the riddle of man's life.[40] Like Sophocles' Oedipus, Braz tried to solve the riddle of existence with his intelligence and failed. It was not till Oedipus had learned the true meaning of love through his blind life with Antigone and Ismene that he enjoyed a hero's death and joined the gods. Braz did not learn. In his delirium, he said to Pandora, "Open your maw and devour me." Her only answer was to constrain him to look at the marching centuries, where among the rest he saw "hundred-gated Thebes." He expected to find in the last one of the future the "decipherment of eternity," but his eyesight failed him.

Like Macbeth, he heard the call of the witches, "Why should you *not* be Minister, Cubas?"[41] When Macbeth's ambitions were unrealized, life became a "tale told by an idiot, full of sound and fury signifying nothing." Braz's life became meaningless. But these echoes of *Oedipus* and *Macbeth* are only the appurtenances of tragedy. The *Memoirs* is not a serious epic because the hero is comic. The book could have been tragic if Braz had had a different constitution. In his essays on the actress Adelaide Ristori (1869), Assis laid down as the basis of tragedy "human emotion."[42] Braz's emotions do not run high: he is reasonable.

Braz is not heroic in the tragic sense: he did not fight with his destiny, he accommodated himself to it, with a maximum of comfort. He went along easily with the prevailing customs of society. He saw how cruel and ridiculous they were but did not try for serious reform: his single political reform as Deputy, one recalls, provided for cutting down the size of the soldier's cap.[43] He offered nothing, for example, to ameliorate the lot of the Eugenias and Placidas of the world. If he gave a fillip now and then to society, it was because he was a comedian (and a picaro, one of whose traits is to satirize the society on which he is a parasite). Thus his epic accomplishments leave something to be desired: he did not found a kingdom; he did not even reach port. Braz's epic is a comic epic, with roots in Cervantes.

In discussing the romance, that is, the novel, as a literary form, Don Quixote's Canon from Toledo declared that an epic may be written in prose as well as in verse and that the author can combine in a single hero the virtues and vices of all the epic heroes—Ulysses' cleverness, Aeneas's "piety," Achilles' valor, and so on; and he can weave into *his* work adornments from other literary genres, as the lyric, the tragic, and the comic—because the "loose form" of the "romance" permits such mixtures.[44]

These Cervantic ideas were also accepted by Machado de Assis. In a literary criticism of 1866, he defined as his ideal for the Brazilian novel "the literary novel, a novel that combines the study of the human passions with poetry's delicate and original touches."[45]

Braz Cubas, in his note to the reader, claimed to have adopted a "free form" apparently for the better effecting of the Canon of Toledo's mixtures.

Just three years before the publication of *Posthumous Memoirs of Braz Cubas,* in a light-hearted column announcing the "resurrection of the grand bore Rocambole on the stage," Assis wrote that the heroes Achilles, Aeneas, Don Quixote, and Rocambole were natural links in a chain.

> Each age has its *Iliad*; the various *Iliads* go to form the epopeia of the human mind. In the mind's infancy, the hero was Achilles—the childlike warrior, haughty, quick to anger, but simple, unaffected, boldly carved in granite, his profile standing out against the sky of golden Hellas. . . .
>
> Aeneas is the second hero—valiant, travel-weary as a Roman centurion, poetic, melancholy, civilized, a mixture of the Greek and Latin mind. This Aeneas lived on into the Middle Ages, became a Christian soldier with the name Tancred, and ended up in chivalrous exploits of high and low degree.
>
> But chivalry, after battering men's bodies, went on to battering people's ears and patience. Hence arose Don Quixote, the third hero—a generous and noble soul but ridiculous in his actions, although sublime in his intentions. Even in this third hero there still glowed a little of Achilles' brightness along with modern colors—a glow that has faded away in the glare of today's practical gaslight.
>
> It was Rocambole's turn. This hero, seeing Priam's palace level with the ground, and La Mancha's windmills down, laid hold of what remained, became a police hero,

and set himself to wrestling with the Code and common sense.[46]

It is doubtful that Rocambole, "the cursed bore of modern times," entered into the composition of Assis's heroes, especially since Assis said he had never read any of the books of his exploits. But certainly Braz Cubas took to himself several of Don Quixote's attributes. Although Braz tells us it was Shakespeare who first awaked his melancholy, still his disease bears some resemblance to Don Quixote's. Don Quixote died of melancholy because he failed in his ambition to perform chivalrous exploits that would spread his name abroad and down time. But his melancholy must have been latent for a long while, because, in the beginning of their adventures, Sancho dubbed him Knight of the Sad Countenance (*de la triste figura*). Braz, when all his other ambitions had failed, tried to win immortality by inventing a plaster to cure men's melancholy. Even this medicinal plaster, which was to have been patented "Emplasto Braz Cubas," finds a kind of progenitor in *Don Quixote*—although Assis himself had long been addicted to the invention of patent medicines to cure various ills, as: hunger, pregnancy, political revolutions, bad governors, nonpayment of debts, homicide, robbery, and so on. Such cures were a way of satirizing, in one package, medical science and commerce, politics, or other social evils. Nevertheless, the Emplasto Braz Cubas does call to mind Quixote's prescription for a medicine that not only cured any wound but even the fear of death itself. Its name, as Don Quixote gave it, was Balsam of Fierabrás (Balsamo de Fierabrás); but, later, Sancho (whose ear for Castilian was none of the best), when he had been badly beaten up in one of their adventures, asked Don Quixote if he could not give him a sip of "aquella bebida del feo Blás," that is, "of ugly Braz's tonic." There is something in all this so redolent of Assis's congenital exuberance in the matter of word play that one is tempted to suspect that what seem to be Cervantic echoes in the name of Braz's invention are not accidental. The end results of Quixote's "balsam"—vomiting and diarrhea—only add to the temptation.[47]

Assis also borrowed from the Spanish knight various conceits for his hero, as, for example, Braz's psychological formula entitled "the equivalence of windows," which seems to stem from the axiom Don Quixote applies to fortune, "When one door shuts, another opens."[48] Braz uses expressions such as "these eyes that the earth will consume," finds himself in rather strained attitudes and gestures, and is very minute and explicit about the content of chapters coming up—all in the Cervantic manner.[49] And Assis conferred some of Don Quixote's minor attributes upon the Brazilian hero: Braz is a sportsman, a hunter (unlike Jaques, who criticized the duke for killing deer), and he is a gentleman, although he seldom displays Don Quixote's lofty indifference to money. Braz is not above using money to get what he wants; he quietly keeps found money, with no attempt to restore it to its rightful owner; and he quarrels with his sister over their inheritance. In these sordid details he is pure picaro.

There are other, major, differences between the two heroes. Both have a ladylove. Don Quixote explains that his love for Dulcinea "has always been platonic."[50] None of Assis's heroes seem ever to have heard that word—platonic. Braz Cubas was not mad; indeed he was certified to be of sound mind by one of the best medical authorities in the field. It was on Braz's old schoolmate Quincas Borba that Assis bestowed Quixote's madness:[51] Borba was in fact a kind of Brazilian Quixote with a wildly Cervantic nag—his philosophy, Humanitism. Braz, on the contrary, had his feet firmly on the ground: he took no wild flights of fancy, no rides on Rosinante. It was Sancho's "ass of patience," he tells us, that conveyed him to Marcella's heart, in a matter of thirty days.[52] (This Spanish girl, by the way, had a progenitress, whom she strongly resembled, Marcella the heartless shepherdess of *Don Quixote*, Part I, chap. 12 and following.) Braz was shrewd and practical. Like Sancho he salted away found money, and like him, believed in the enobling effect of wealth;[53] and he gives us to understand that he rarely, if ever, missed a meal out of sentimental reasons.[54] Even Braz's father had a bit of Panza blood in him. As Sancho came to believe in Dulcinea's enchantment, although he had made up the story himself, so Bento Cubas came to regard as genuine the "noble" origin of the Cubas line although it was he who had fabricated the improbable tale.[55] In short, the great Spanish ferment that worked in Le Sage, Sterne, Fielding, and Dickens pervades this book, and was to continue with equal force in Assis's sixth novel, *Quincas Borba*.

For all his resemblances to Sancho Panza, Braz still has a certain epic grandeur. Compounded after the recipe suggested by the Canon of Toledo, he is a mixture of epic heroes. Besides Aeneas's piety; Quixote's melancholy, detachment, and thirst for fame; and the intellect and reason of Dante's Virgil; he has the wiliness of the Portuguese Ulysses, Vasco da Gama; and he has a bit of Achilles in his nature—not Achilles' valor, but Achilles' joy in revenge. Rather Achilles' revenge than Lady Macbeth's remorseful bloody hand! he exclaims as he exults over his cuckolding of Lobo Neves and the failure of Neves's political ambitions.[56] His da Gama wiliness is exerted, not on a powerful eastern prince but on the poor, witless old lady Dona Placida. And, besides mirroring the glorious Brazilian Empire of the Braganças as Aeneas did Augustus's Rome, Braz Cubas shared the Trojan hero's reputation for philandering. In short, Braz's epic is a comic epic. He is by nature more a hero out of comedy than out of romance. As with Don Quixote, as with all truly comic heroes, there is a certain India rubber resilience in his soul. But Braz Cubas lacked Don Quixote's enthusiasm. Don Quixote battled for his ideal with serious fervor. If he sometimes dealt an uppercut to the status quo—as when he freed the criminals condemned to galley service or manhandled monks and squires and government men—it is we, the readers, who enjoy an unholy satisfaction at the routing of respectable society; it was the picaro Panza who pocketed the food and other good things left behind by the fleeing victims. Don Quixote was oblivious of the nature of his triumphs. Braz Cubas was not so ingenuous. He was more Aristophanic, developing techniques, scrupulous and unscrupulous, ridiculous or canny, for advancing his own interests—often at the expense of others' happiness; but he did not *fight* society. He had no consuming passion—no madness.

A frequently repeated word in *Posthumous Memoirs of Braz Cubas* is *espectáculo*—spectacle, show—as a synonym for life or for a man's life. The *spectacle* is always a struggle against death in some form: it may be the death agony itself; it may be against hunger or greed. Sometimes this life spectacle is symbolized by a dogfight or a cockfight or a storm at sea.[57] Whatever form the spectacle, Braz merely looked on. He was not a part of life but a traveler round it, as Assis wrote in his preface. Like the melancholy Jaques he was an onlooker. Jaques said, "All the world's a stage, and all the men and women merely players. . . ." They both viewed the show from the cold plain of the spiritually dead. As the scene with Pandora suggests, Braz was spiritually dead before his physical death. The same thing happened to Jaques. When Duke Frederick was converted to a religious life and so became dead to the world of men, Jaques decided to follow him and thus also became dead. In proof of it, he made a series of "bequests" to the other personages who were to remain behind in the world.[58]

The "plaster" to free his fellowmen from melancholy

symbolizes Braz's attempt to love and thus to win immortal life; it was, in his words, "divine" and "an inspiration from heaven." The wish took form too late and never resulted in action. We are left with his comico-pessimistic summation of his life, in which he would have us believe there had been no genuine pleasures of the spirit but only brief physical sensations and fleeting satisfactions of vanity—that is, of self-love, of hugging himself—the rest, surfeit, lack of pain but a weakness of spirit. During the delirium of the illness brought on by his enthusiasm for the plaster, he set out on a quest to discover what life (and death) was, to solve the "mystery." But it was a mad idea of Folly's, he tells us. At the end of the delirium Folly pleaded for only ten more minutes and she could solve the mystery. Reason laughed and turned Folly out of the "house."[59] Earlier, after his mother's cruel, lingering death, Braz had taken up this same quest for a day or two; on that occasion also, Reason prevailed: "I put in my trunk the problem of life and death, the Poet's [Shakespeare's] hypochondriacal characters, my shirts, meditations, and neckties. . . .[60]

For all the comedy, we are left in no doubt as to the nature of Braz's melancholy: like Jaques's it is a self-indulgent humor. And there is no reason to believe that Assis wholeheartedly concurred in Braz's satisfaction that he had never had to work for a living, had not died in poverty nor suffered a semimadness like Quincas Borba and, best of all, had had no children. What Assis's thoughts were concerning the advantages of wealth over poverty and of a detached sanity over a lovable insanity are perhaps open to question. It is certain, however, that he was no enemy to work;[61] and he and Carolina are reported to have often lamented their lack of children—something he himself seems to confirm in his last novel. It is also certain that he objected to being called pessimist as a term of opprobrium. He insisted that *pessimism* did not connote impenetrable gloom and despair, and that Schopenhauer was a jolly old man.[62] Perhaps his definition of a pessimist differed from that of his contemporaries. An optimist, in his opinion, was an idiot; a pessimist, an idealist:[63] one almost seems to be a degree of the other. Certainly, he did not take his pessimism seriously. In any event, he took care to dissociate himself from his created character in the preface he wrote for the third edition[64] of the *Posthumous Memoirs* by making Braz Cubas answer the book's critics, and by speaking of Braz as of a real person distinct from himself. In the novel itself he leaves Braz to shift for himself and make what impression he will with his memoirs. This is a far cry from *Resurrection*, into which the author frequently entered without ceremony to explain the faults, virtues, and doubts of his characters. The participation of a character in a novel's narration was something Assis was to experiment with, with increasing boldness, right up to his last book. In *Posthumous Memoirs*, by using Sterne's technique, that is, by permitting the narrator Braz Cubas to analyze the actions and ideas of the other personages, he made those personages come alive to an extent far surpassing that of his preceding novels. Although the least personages of Braz's *Memoirs* vibrate with a life of their own, still we must never forget that we see them in the mirrors of Braz's mind.

Another point of difference between Braz and his creator is this matter of Humanitism. Although Braz seems to subscribe to Quincas Borba's mad philosophy, there is no reason to believe that Assis did. There is some reason to believe he did not. As mentioned, Humanitism has some of the outward trappings of Positivism—even to a literary theory. And Braz Cubas puns on the word *positive* in at least two places in his *Memoirs*.[65] It is in the same spirit of fun that Assis referred to Positivism in his journalistic columns. Apparently he could not bring himself to speak seriously of a system that excluded psychology in favor of phrenology as a method for studying the intellectual processes.[66] Positivism's literary outgrowth, Naturalism, on the whole, he loathed. He particularly condemned a writer's use of shocking physical details with little or no motivation, and implied that Zola sometimes followed such practices with a view to increasing his income.[67]

Two years before *Posthumous Memoirs of Braz Cubas* began to appear in the *Revista Brasileira*, Assis wrote what has often been considered a harsh review of Eça de Queiroz's *Cousin Bazilio* (*O Primo Bazílio*). By way of criticizing faults of the Naturalist novel, he summed up the heroine's unmotivated fall from virtue in the following words:

> Such was the beginning of a fall that no moral reason explains, no passion—sublime or second-rate—no grudge, no perversion even. Luiza slips into the mire without desire, without repugnance, without compunction. Bazilio does no more than give her a shove, like the inert matter she is. Once fallen, since no spiritual flame animates her, she does not find in sin the satisfaction that the great criminal passions give: she simply wallows.[68]

Posthumous Memoirs of Braz Cubas, however, is remarkable among Assis's novels for the amount of ugly physical deformity and disease it portrays: smallpox, cancer, pneumonia, tuberculosis, asthma, heart lesion, yellow fever; and Viegas, the disgusting old man from whom Virgilia hoped to inherit a fortune, was, in Braz's words, a whole hospital in himself.[69] Such sordid details seem to bring the novel within the confines of the Naturalist formula. And this has puzzled some readers. The truth of the matter is, Braz Cubas was a member of the hated School. He showed an interest in it at an early stage. In chapter xxii he refused to say anything about romanticism, although he had been present at its birth in Europe. In chapter xiv he had already remarked that romanticism wore out Pegasus and left him by the roadside, where the Naturalists found him starved and diseased, and out of pity put him in their books. One aspect of his friend Quincas Borba that Braz particularly admired was "his talent for observation, the way he described the gestation and growth of vice within his own body and soul, his inner struggles, easy capitulations, and habituation to wallowing in the mire."[70] In other words, what Braz admired was Quincas's Zola-esque style of "narration."

Braz himself was adept at the "realist" style, as attested by his long description of the loathsome invalid Viegas (which ended in comedy of course—no legacy for Virgilia). And there are a number of the book's passages reminiscent of *Cousin Bazilio*. Marcella with her leg hanging out of the hammock (chap. xvii) recalls Luiza's ways in Bazilio's "paradise." The Marcella affair, it is true, was animated from beginning to end by none too subtle comedy. Besides, Marcella was not a wife: one would expect her gestures to be those of a professional. But the erring Virgilia's fluttery arrival at the love nest, "the toy," bears a singular resemblance to Luiza's arrival at the "paradise."[71] The refections or love feasts in the two places are almost identical. Braz, like Bazilio, was motivated in the affair mostly by vanity. Finally, when Luiza was packing her bag to run away with her lover, she put in a photograph of her husband. Assis, in his criticism, remarked that he could find no "physiological or psychological reason for this testimonial of conjugal tenderness." His own Virgilia, however, over the years of her affair with Braz, maintained a conjugal tenderness for *her* husband. Virgilia, it is plain, was endowed with the very flaws that Assis censured in Luiza: she slipped into vice without the motivation of a strong emotion—and suffered no remorse. But the Brazilian "love" episode terminated in comedy, the Portuguese in unhappy melodrama. Braz had applied "the only moral" Assis found in *Cousin Bazilio*, namely, that "a proper choice of servants is the requisite of a peaceful adultery." The episode turned out to be, in Virgilia's life, what Assis said it should have been in Luiza's, to wit, "a simple parenthesis in the conjugal sentence."

Virgilia showed little more sensibility than Luiza but she is a comic character and has the same India rubber resilience as Braz. She does not have the pride, nor the dignity, of Assis's serious heroines; Eugenia comes closer to the Machadean feminine ideal. What appears to be Naturalism in *Posthumous Memoirs of Braz Cubas* has a way of turning into travesty of the School—or into symbolism. When Quincas Borba steals Braz's watch, it is a realistic, picaresque detail; but it soon appears that the watch represents *time*. Braz has been relieved of the past and goes to Virgilia, "the soft, warm, fragrant pillow" of the present.[72] Symbolism lifts the *Memoirs* to universal heights, where tragedy and comedy rub shoulders, and where life and death and time, good and evil, love and self-love, carry on their eternal wars.

CHAPTER TWELVE

PUBLIC OPINION—
THE WORMS

Machado de Assis did not have the last laugh on the Naturalists.

In 1952, when *Memórias Posthumas de Braz Cubas* first appeared in English translation in the United States under the title *Epitaph of a Small Winner*,[1] it was greeted with exclamations of wonder and admiration by reviewer after reviewer our country over, although more than seventy years had passed since its initial publication in Portuguese. Unbelievable as it may seem, this novel—with its astounding originality of conception, wit, and irony—caused scarcely a ripple in the Brazilian public opinion of 1881.[2] The answer is partially to be found in the then prevailing popularity of the Naturalist novel.[3]

Although Machado de Assis had denounced the Naturalist school of fiction in critical articles,[4] had pilloried it in journalistic columns, and even had parodied its manner in passages of *Posthumous Memoirs of Braz Cubas*, the school flourished throughout Brazil. When he began to write, the romantic novel had not yet passed its heyday: its reigning monarch in Brazil was José de Alencar, whose most popular works, such as *O Guarani* and *Iracema*, portrayed the Herculean feats and gentlemanly sentiments of the noble savage. Machado de Assis deliberately turned away from romanticism, which he called "that great moribund Muse that gave birth to our generation";[5] but he was also opposed to the Positivist ideal that a literary work should be "a compendium of philosophy or of social propaganda."[6] In fiction, he favored the representation of what he termed "reality," that is, of "aesthetic truth" as opposed to the "realism of nature."[7] The latter, he perceived, had a way of degenerating into the extreme form that came to be known as Naturalism. While the vogue of the new method infected his contemporaries, it had little effect on Assis. He was a privateer in the service of art. He laid bold hands on the literary wealth of the Western world: epics, tragedies, comedies, histories, philosophies, satires, and works of fiction—none of them were safe from him. With the stolen metal, he attempted to forge new and strange works that would body forth man's passion in its essential forms. His first four novels represent his struggle with the newfound medium; in the fifth, *Posthumous Memoirs of Braz Cubas*, he mastered it; in the remaining four, he perfected, adapted, experimented—with increasing skill.

His criticism of the Naturalist novel was that it aimed at representing superficial appearance—content to be an "inventory of events and fortuitous" actions unmotivated by human passion and, in its most extreme form, a photographic and slavish reproduction of the low and ignoble—sordid details related for the purpose of politico-social propaganda or with nothing more than a view to arousing momentary physical sensation in the reader, and with no meaning beyond.[8]

Machado de Assis was battling against the current of popular taste, as he himself well knew. *Posthumous Memoirs of Braz Cubas* came out in book form, January, 1881. The same year saw the publication of *The Mulatto* (*O Mulato*), a novel of the Naturalist genre, by the Brazilian Aluísio Azevedo. During that whole year, only three reviews of *Posthumous Memoirs of Braz Cubas* appeared;

within a comparable period, over one hundred articles are reported to have been published on *The Mulatto*.[9]

The most important of the three reviews of *Posthumous Memoirs of Braz Cubas* was written by Capistrano de Abreu, to whom Assis had given a puff only a year before, calling him "one of our fine talents."[10] The "fine talent," as may be surmised from the "Foreword to the Third Edition" of the *Memoirs*, proved inadequate to an appreciation of that book's literary merit.[11] After saying some clever things to the effect that *Posthumous Memoirs of Braz Cubas* is not really a novel but a description of manners and the social philosophy implicit therein, a philosophy that combines "La Rochefoucauld and Sancho Panza"—"skepticism" and "satisfaction with this best of all possible worlds"—"a gloomy philosophy," whose "formula" is Quincas Borba's Humanitism, and after giving a lengthy summary of the plot by way of illustrating the above remarks, the reviewer concludes that a consideration of the book as a literary work would be an enormous task because it is a collection of unrelated stories that have to be studied separately. He says he will not undertake such a study because there are many things he does not understand. His final advice to his reader is: *"Tolle et lege,"* "take the book and read it yourself."

> Perhaps you might wish for more animation and variety in the style, that certain antitheses be employed less often, that transitions be less abrupt, and the contrasts less crude. Never mind. *Tolle et lege.* If you understand it, you have several unique hours in store—a mixture of gall, madness, rictus. If you do not understand it, so much the better. It is proof that you are an untainted soul: conscientious, steadfast, ingenuous, that is, a little foolish.[12]

In this review, the resumé of the story, for all its length, omits one rather essential detail: namely, that Quincas Borba was mad—that the "philosophy which consoled" Braz was the outpouring of a deranged mind. Yet the omitted detail makes pointless much of Abreu's cleverness. And it was for reviews like this that Machado de Assis was to be grateful.

The canny Braz had foreseen what would happen to his *Memoirs* at the hands of public and critics. He perhaps saw it more clearly after the initial publication in serial form, for he added to the first edition of the *book*, the prefatory note, "To the Reader," in which he expressed doubts of his *Memoirs'* attaining popularity:

> Because the frivolous will be disappointed at not finding their customary romantic novel and the serious-minded will find the book frivolous because of its threads of romance, and these are the two main pillars of public opinion.

Braz added to this edition his dedication "To the worm that first sank its teeth into the cold flesh of my cadaver." That there existed some kind of relationship in Braz's mind between worms (death) on the one hand and critics on the other is shown by his remark in chapter xxvii of the *Memoirs*, to the effect that life is a series of editions, each one corrected by the succeeding one, with the final edition presented by the publishers to the worms. Twenty years later Assis's fictional narrator, Dom Casmurro, produced his chapter entitled, "The Worms"—which implied that critics (and scholars) grow fat on the books they gnaw but "know absolutely nothing of the texts they gnaw." And Cubas ended his "To the reader" on a defiant note: "If you like it, I am repaid for my labor; if you don't like it, you will be repaid with a fillip, and a good day to you!" The novel *Quincas Borba*, sequel to the *Memoirs*, and written by Machado de Assis in his own person, ends on the same note, but sounded *fortissimo*: Weep! if you have tears; if you don't want to weep, laugh. It's all the same to the Southern Cross.

But, Machado de Assis was no "Southern Cross." He was

by no means indifferent to neglect or to unfavorable criticism. A letter from his brother-in-law Miguel de Novaes, written to him from Lisbon, July 21, 1882, indicates that Machado had been depressed by the public's response to *Posthumous Memoirs of Braz Cubas*. The last paragraph of Miguel's letter reads:

> It seems to me you are wrong to be discouraged, and you should go on writing, always. What does it matter that the majority of the public did not understand your latest book? Some books are for everyone; others are for only the few. Your last book is in the second category, and I know that it was greatly appreciated by all who understood it. It is not—as you, my dear friend, well know—the books with the greatest vogue that have the greatest worth. Do not think about nor concern yourself with public opinion when you write. Justice will be given you sooner or later, you may be sure of that. And, as the sermon has ended with the paper, I'll finish also, begging you to give our love to Carolina, and for you my friend a hug from your sincere friend, Miguel de Novaes.[13]

It is perhaps otiose to mention that Machado de Assis did not give up writing and probably never had any intention of doing so. As we have seen in his letter to a younger contemporary on the matter of choosing a career that would leave time and energy for writing, he wrote that every career had its drawbacks, which one learned to endure. "The main thing [he continued] is not to neglect letters. Do not take this as advice. A true call to letters does not need such admonitions, it goes of itself whichever way it must go and finds in actual practice its own best exhortations."[14] Machado de Assis's was a "true call." As his brother-in-law advised, he "went on writing always." It was ten years, however, before he completed another novel.

He recognized that a writer needs encouragement. Not

only did he bestow praise liberally on others—especially on younger writers,[15] but he sought it for himself.

"You will not weary me with kind words," he wrote in a column of the *Gazeta de Notícias*, "rather, you will give me new heart for other undertakings. Who knows if I shan't go even much, much further? A man cannot tell what he will do in this world before he does something; even so, he does not become aware of his power immediately."[16]

He sometimes nudged his friends to give him encouragement. To Salvador de Mendonça he wrote: "They say it [*Helena*] is the least bad of my books. I don't know; you shall judge."[17] After Carolina's death these hints have a certain insistency: "I gather you did not receive *Esaú e Jacob*. I will send you another copy in the same post with this letter. I do not know whether this book is more bitter than its predecessors, as you anticipate. Write me what you think."[18] Or again: "Read the *Memorial* and write me."[19] "My *Memorial de Ayres* is on its way to you. You must tell me what you think of it."[20]

As we have seen, Machado de Assis had cause to repine at critics' neglect of *Posthumous Memoirs of Braz Cubas* in the 1880's. The reception accorded *Quincas Borba* in the early nineties was scarcely more hearty.[21] In the autumn of 1897, however, he received attention of a thundering sort that "took care" of both those novels and everything else he had written to date. A book entitled *Machado de Assis* was published in Rio de Janeiro—the first of many books to be written about him.[22] The author, Sylvio Romero, had introduced the so-called scientific method of criticism in Brazil in 1870.[23] As its chief exponent he had already written some rather unfavorable reviews of Assis in 1870, in 1880, and in 1885.[24] He states in this book that his former antipathies have weakened and that Machado de Assis, Brazil's most highly praised, most complete man of letters, is a

figure worthy of serious study.[25] In spite of such protesta-
tions, the book is, on the whole, an attack on Assis's writing
from every point of view. His approval of Assis's fiction is
limited to Braz Cubas's "delirium," which he praises for its
language and style.[26] As for the rest of the *Posthumous
Memoirs*, his opinion is that it is without meaning or depth,
its imagination puerile, its originality of an inferior order,
its wit seldom funny, its only virtue a few realistic scenes
from Braz's childhood.[27] In all Assis's fiction, Romero fails
to find a single complete, true, vitalized character. His
prose style is termed colorless and feeble, his humor forced
and impoverished, his philosophy superficial.[28] In spite of
his distaste for the author's work, the number of pages Romero quotes from Assis's fiction would lay him open to
legal action under present-day copyright restrictions.

Friends sprang to Assis's defense with articles answering
Romero's emphatic inconsistencies, notably Lafayette Rodrigues Pereira, a well-known jurist and politician, ex-
senator of the Empire and governor under the Republic,
who wrote a long rebuttal in the form of four articles that
appeared over the pseudonym "Labieno";[29] and there were
younger men to defend him, such as Magalhães de Azeredo
and Araripe Júnior.[30] In his correspondence Assis expresses
gratitude to the distinguished Pereira, and delight at being
championed by the younger writers.[31] For his own part, he
did not seem to be greatly perturbed by Romero's book,
probably because, knowing the man's temperament and
blind prejudices, he did not think highly of his judgment.
As he wrote to Azeredo, "[Romero] does not possess a calm
mind, he is aggressive by nature. One cannot write criticism
under those circumstances, but, then, I am suspect."[32] The
only public reference Assis made to the matter was a brief
mention in the foreword to the third edition of *Quincas
Borba* (1899), where he thanked the "brave and generous
voices" that had defended him.

Even these friends who had spoken out for him were not in complete sympathy with his artistic aims. The critic José Veríssimo, close friend and public admirer of Assis's genius, later admitted to a feeling of antagonism toward his fiction. He even went so far as to state that after pondering the matter for thirty-five years he still could not say for sure whether the impression left on him by Assis's first novel, *Resurrection,* was "agreeable or disagreeable."[33] Veríssimo, noting this same resistance and lack of comprehension among other contemporaries, gave an explanation that had been suggested earlier by the critic Clovis Beviláqua: namely, that these writers had come from outside the capital—most of them from the north, Maranhão, Ceará, and Bahia—where there existed an antipathy to the capital, its views, and way of life.[34]

A historic event had set Rio de Janeiro apart from the rest of Brazil and given it a life and atmosphere unique in the New World. In November, 1807, when Napoleon's troops were nearing Lisbon, the Prince Regent of Portugal, later King João VI, fled to Brazil to save the monarchy. He and his court were conveyed thither by the British navy. After a stormy crossing, on March 7, 1808, João, his family, furniture, jewels, riches, and a library—along with his court, comprising generals, counselors, justices, musicians, clergy, lords and ladies, some ten thousand persons in all, with *their* furniture, jewels, and wealth—disembarked at Rio de Janeiro, where the colonials had prepared a gala reception, many giving up their own residences to house their noble Portuguese guests. Brazil derived important benefits from João's stay. He raised the country from colonial status to that of kingdom and conferred new rights and privileges that fostered its development. It was the capital itself, however, that most benefited. With the influx of scholars, diplomats, artists, nobles, and with João's establishment of a press, library, school of fine arts, and other cultural institutions in the city, Rio de Janeiro quickly acquired the refinement, elegance, luxury, and ceremony of a European court city. Indeed it came to be known as The Court; many of Assis's letters have simply that heading, *A corte.* For Dom João lived on in Rio even after he became king. When he did return to Portugal in 1821, he left his son Pedro on Brazil's throne; and Rio de Janeiro remained a court city until 1889, when Pedro II, João's grandson and Brazil's second emperor, gave way before the Republic—of which, of course, Rio de Janeiro continued to be the capital.[35]

Machado de Assis, a "Carioca *enragé*," as he called himself,[36] was, according to his contemporary, Clovis Beviláqua, much read in the capital but did not enjoy the same popularity among the provincials of the north.[37] Beviláqua himself, José Veríssimo, Sylvio Romero, Araripe Júnior, Capistrano de Abreu, Pedro de Couto, among other critics of Machado de Assis, were from the north. And it was in the north that Naturalism first took root in Brazil;[38] it was in the north that the "scientific" school of literary criticism sprang up, with its narrow Positivist point of view that an author must contribute to the good of his fellowmen by writing social propaganda. In Romero's words, "I do not write for the pleasure of writing but with the idea of being useful to my country. . . . *Art for art's* sake in literature is an antiquated romantic sin, a leprosy that must be banished from this progressive age."[39]

These provincials, evidently, regarded themselves as the true, the real Brazil in contradistinction to the effete capital, and their literary productions as the uncontaminated national expression. Assis had opposed the Naturalist school of fiction. His regard for the Positivist critical standard was no greater. For him art was all.[40] Science and its inventions he could view with a certain dispassionate calm, as he speculated whether, for example, the dispatches soon to race over the Atlantic cable would be more remarkable for sense and originality than the letters that had been coming by slow boat.[41] But, in science's growing ascendancy over men's minds, he saw a terrible threat to intellectual freedom. Art, on the other hand, offered consolation and strength for living and improving.

> Long live the Muses! Those beautiful, ancient maids that do not grow old or ugly. They are the most solid thing there is beneath the sun.[42]

Assis thought the writer could offer nothing greater to his country or to his fellowmen than a work of *art*.[43] But, as we have seen, he was forced to recognize that few, if any, of his colleagues were in sympathy with his artistic efforts. Braz Cubas, in the prefatory note to his *Memoirs*, despaired of achieving popularity but still hoped to arrest the passing sympathy of the public. In this he succeeded; but the appreciation of his art which Assis desired was not forthcoming in his own time. As early as the *Posthumous Memoirs* he had come to suspect that he would have to wait for vindication at the hands of future generations and began, perhaps, to write more and more for posterity. Braz Cubas imagined his reader of 1939.[44] This date, it must be noted, would be the centennial year of Machado de Assis's birth. As time went on, the day of justice mentioned by Miguel de Novaes seems to have receded farther into the future. In a column dated August 19, 1894, Assis addresses a scholar of the twentieth century, as follows:

> When you leaf through the *Gazeta de Notícias'* collection for the year of our grace 1894, and come upon these lines, do not go on without understanding this observation of mine. Not that you will find a gold mine buried in it, nor even great merit. But it will be agreeable to my *manes* to know that a man of 1944 pays some attention to a fusty chronicle a half-century old. And if you carry your piety to the point of writing in some book or review, *A writer of the nineteenth century cites a case of local color*

which seems to us not devoid of interest. . . . If you do
this, you might add, like the soldier of the French ballad:

Du haut du ciel—ta demeure dernière.
Mon colonel, tu dois être content.

Yes, my young captain, I shall be content.[45]

In spite of such hints that he looked to posterity for recognition, he continued to write for his contemporaries, and
apparently continued to hope that a small audience among
them would understand and feel the power of his books.[46]
In the years from his first novel (1872) to *Quincas Borba*
(1891), he published, in addition to the 6 novels, some 138
short stories, 4 comedies, 324 columns and articles, and
nearly 4,000 lines of verse—not to mention translations and
technical compilations. In much of the prose, and even in
his lighter verse, he continued to belabor the Naturalist
school of fiction and Positivism in its various forms.

QUINCAS BORBA
AND DOM CASMURRO

CHAPTER THIRTEEN

QUINCAS BORBA

Some have thought Assis took a step backward, artistically speaking, with *Quincas Borba*.[1] It is true he reverted to the third-person omniscient narrator of his first four novels, and, as in those novels, society here plays a considerable role in the drama, which does not all take place within a protagonist's psyche as happened with the hero of the *Memoirs*. This sixth novel, however, is indissolubly linked to *Posthumous Memoirs of Braz Cubas* by the presence of Braz's mentor, the mad philosopher Quincas Borba. His spirit dominates its action in much the same way that the dead Caesar's spirit dominates Shakespeare's tragedy *Julius Caesar*. This novel's protagonist became Quincas Borba's sole heir. Borba bequeathed not only all his wealth but also his philosophy and his dog to his fellow townsman Rubião, a simple provincial schoolmaster who had closed his school to nurse Quincas through a fever. In the course of the convalescence Rubião became an eager listener to the mad philosopher's discourses, which he only imperfectly understood. Toward the end of the *Memoirs*, Braz mentioned a trip Quincas took to his birthplace, Barbacena, in the province of Minas Gerais, his subsequent return to the capital, and his death shortly thereafter. As the new novel reveals, it was during the stay in Barbacena that Quincas acquired his new disciple.

In spite of the all-embracing character of Humanitism as expounded to Braz in the *Memoirs*, we find it expanded and improved upon in *Quincas Borba*. There have been added, touches of Darwin and Malthus: for example, the treatment of war, epidemics, and the like. In the *Memoirs* Quincas Borba explained that these scourges (blessings in disguise) served to break the universal monotony and offered a man the pleasure of sacrificing himself to humanitas; epidemics though disastrous for a few gave joy to the others in the thought of having escaped a like fate.[2] In one of his lectures to Rubião, however, Quincas Borba illustrated this thesis of war as a benefit to mankind with a story of a field of potatoes and two starving tribes. If the tribes peacefully divided the potatoes there would not be enough to properly nourish anybody and all would die of inanition. But if one tribe exterminated the other by war the victorious tribe would get all the potatoes, and so live. "To the victor the potatoes!"[3] This illustration seems to contain a reference to Malthus's principle of population. (Quincas, it might be noted in passing, disposed of the exterminated's humiliation by handily applying the Democritean law of the indestructibility of matter.)[4]

His application of the Darwinian theory of natural selection is perhaps still less subtle, because Machado de Assis evidently regarded the very expression "survival of the fittest" as a clear example of British brutality.[5] Quincas Borba illustrated the Darwinian theory by relating to Rubião the story of his grandmother's death: As she started across a church square to go to her sedan chair waiting on the corner, she was run down and crushed to death under the wheels of a heavy chaise. But, explained Quincas, it was neither an accident nor regrettable. The owner of the chaise was hungry; the coachman whipped up his mules to fetch his master to dinner and so conserve humanitas. There was an obstacle in the way of this act of conservation, namely,

Quincas's grandmother. The obstacle had to be overcome. It would have made no difference if it had been a cat or a mouse—except that the grandmother would not have died —the principle would have remained—or if it had been a poet, Gonçalves Dias or Byron. The only difference in that case would be the increased number of obituaries and *in memoriams*. The world would not stand still for lack of a few poems that happened to perish prematurely in the head of some poet or other.[6]

Besides bolstering his philosophy with such Malthusian and Darwinian refinements, Quincas Borba added one more definitely Positivist principle to his new course of lectures. Comte had elevated man's friend the dog, "the noble dog," to the human level. Borba had a fine hound, dark gray with black spots, to which he had given his own name, Quincas Borba. Since the life-principle humanitas was in everything, as he explained to Rubião, it was also in the dog, which could thus receive a person's name "be it Christian or Muslim." His book, *The Philosophy of Humanitism* "in ninety-one parts" would make him immortal among the literate; the dog (for Borba felt his own death near) would give him a brief immortality among *il*literates, who would recall the philosopher when they heard the dog called by his name.[7] The only condition attached to Rubião's legacy was that he always keep the dog with him and tenderly care for it as if it were the human being Quincas Borba himself.[8]

When Rubião came into possession of the legacy, suddenly he seemed to understand the philosopher's words, "To the victor the potatoes!" They had been obscure and incomprehensible before—right up to the time the will was read. He, Rubião, had been one of the "exterminated"; now he was a victor. It was his role to be "hard and implacable because he was powerful and strong." "To the victor the potatoes!" This was to be his battle cry henceforth. He had been of the starveling tribe, Borba a victor; Borba died, Rubião became the victor. The thought was perhaps a little hard to follow but that often happened in philosophies. As the author remarks, it was all a matter of geography, point of view. "The best way of appreciating the whip is to have hold of its handle."[9] Rubião debated whether to assert his new superiority in Barbacena, his native city, where he had many friends but also where he had been a laughingstock because of his loyal friendship for a crazy man; or whether to enjoy life among strangers and the sophisticated pleasures of the "court city." He decided for the latter. *He could always return to Barbacena.*[10]

This simple provincial Brazilian went forth to take up residence in the metropolis, his sole companion the dog Quincas Borba. What does this dog signify in relation to its master? Rubião and Quincas Borba each identified the dog with himself; the dog identified Rubião with Quincas Borba—which would lead one to believe that the animal symbolized some quality of soul shared by the two men.[11] Rubião compared his own loyalty and friendship for Quincas Borba to the dog's,[12] and later saw in the dog's loving, faithful glance the "soul" of the dead philosopher.[13] Comte's reason for elevating the dog was this same loving, faithful quality of companionship to man.[14] The author, Assis, identified Rubião's sense of honor and loyalty with the dog; he gave Rubião and his dog the same look of flying when they ran so that their limbs appeared to be wings; and, at the end of the book, dog and man are merged into one being.[15]

In the capital, the dog Quincas Borba found only one kindred spirit—the lady Fernanda.[16] His companion, Rubião, a walking bit of humanitas from Barbacena, did not find life there the chain of neat causal successions that Borba's Positivistic philosophy required. On the surface at least Rubião was abandoned by his author to the tender mercies of a society in which Darwin's law of survival, generally speaking, held sway; but *this* fight for survival was not the clear-cut struggle of a scientist's dream. It was a far cry too from Comte's third, or scientific, state, although Comtean elements were present. Rio de Janeiro society was an anarchy. Assis has in other writings compared life to a game of chess. In one such instance he justifies the comparison on the grounds that chess is an image of anarchy "in which the queen devours the pawn; the pawn devours the bishop; the bishop, the knight; the knight, the queen; and everybody devours everybody. Darling anarchy—all this without wheels that turn or ballot boxes that speak!"[17]

The innocent capitalist from Barbacena was not equal to this game. He was taken advantage of, slighted, or abused in some way by almost every person he met: sharp businessmen, politicians, society snobs, street rabble, the beautiful, vain social climber Sophia (who served as a silent partner to her husband's financial schemes), parasites of various sorts, fancy foreign white servants. . . . He poured out all his wealth in business ventures, charities, luxury, dinners, and regal presents. Finally he went insane. Was he driven to it by the cruel treatment of a ruthless society? Assis's answer is "no." Rubião was a morsel of Borba's humanitas. He is also a piece of Machado de Assis's humanity: the combatants of an inner psychological struggle each joined forces with those on the outside. Though buffeted about in a cruel society, he was not run down by the chaise of another's hunger but by his own. The "fault," as with Brutus, was in himself; the prime confusion was in his own soul.

This theme of confusion is sounded in the first paragraph of the novel. In the second paragraph it is stated as a formula: there is an unfathomed abyss between mind and heart. His "heart" rejoiced in his possessions and in the thought that his sister had died before she could marry Quincas Borba—perhaps she would have had a child, and he, Ru-

bião, would have been cut out of the will; now he was sole
heir. His "mind" shocked at his "heart's" thoughts, quickly
changed the subject and gazed fixedly out to sea, at a row-
boat going along in the bay; "but his heart continued to
pound joyfully." Assis seems to be saying that there is an
abyss between the conscious mind and its wayward sister
the subconscious; the thoughts and desires generated by the
subconscious are inadmissable to the conscious mind's probity. More simply, there is an abyss between regard for
others and love of oneself.

The same chasm yawned between the two aspects of
Quincas Borba's spirit: between the dog Quincas Borba and
the glorious capitalist-philosopher, possessor of the potatoes. The dog is the real humanitas, the true human principle; it is he who has the qualities of the humane man:
gentleness; sensitivity to the feelings of others; a capacity
for companionship, loyalty, and devotion; simple, unsuspecting friendliness toward everyone, holding no resent-
ment even toward those who rebuff him with kicks or
shrinking aversion. Rubião had these qualities, in superla-
tive degree. But even before the inheritance, his "heart"
had felt tremors of greed and sensuality.[18]

Barbacena was the proper home of this dog and his master. In Barbacena the dog had accompanied his master
everywhere; in Rio de Janeiro he passed much of his life
chained up, for Rubião was often from home or entertain-
ing guests, and, as mentioned above, only one of his new
found acquaintances was to prove sympathetic to the dog.
Even there at the beginning of the story, as Rubião's "heart"
gloated over his material possessions and longed to possess
his friend Palha's wife, Quincas Borba whimpered to be
unchained and admitted to his presence. Rubião said, "I
will go untie him," but he did not, he went on thinking of
his possessions and of Sophia.[19] The same symbolism appears
in later scenes of the book: for example, when Rubião's

hunger to possess Sophia had become a torture, he untied Quincas Borba and was himself temporarily released from his guilt-ridden desires.[20]

It was the inheritance that separated Rubião from the dog. It was the inheritance that widened the abyss between "mind" and "heart." Rubião himself recognized the fact: he pondered marriage as a cure. "It might be a way [he reflected] of restoring to my life the unity that it lost with the change of milieu and of fortune."[21] The dog Quincas Borba counseled marriage; and Rubião's "mind hovered above the abyss"—the abyss of madness into which he was to plunge again and again.[22]

One of the books in Assis's library (and in Braz Cubas's also, for he cribbed as well as quoted from it) was Erasmus's *Praise of Folly*.[23] Folly, according to Erasmus, is the daughter of Plutus (the Greek word for "wealth"), the most powerful of all the gods, at whose single beck all things sacred and profane are turned topsy-turvy—by whom war, peace, empire, assemblies, marriages, law, the arts . . . in short, all public and private businesses, are governed. Folly was born in the Fortunate Isles, where all things grew without plowing or sowing, among lovely flowers. She did not cry as other children do, but smiled. Her mother was the nymph Youth. She was suckled by two other lovely nymphs—Drunkenness and Ignorance. Self-love became her constant companion along with Flattery, Pleasure, Indolence, Revelry, Sensuality, Madness, Oblivion, and Deep Sleep. With these as servants and counselors, Folly has subjected all things to her dominion.

Rubião was Plutus's child, his male-child and in his own fancy his birth was as blessed as the female Folly's.[24] The attendants in Rubião's train were the same as hers—self-love, flattery, and the rest. It is perhaps not for nothing that the woman he sought in adultery was named Sophia—the Greek word for "wisdom." She was in almost all respects the opposite of Rubião. Still, the name is ironic: she was wise, but with a small, crafty, cautious wisdom, the wisdom of self-interest.

Rubião's name also fits his character, and his story. The Portuguese common noun *rubião* is a word sometimes applied to a red ear of grain, in particular to a red ear of Indian corn—a symbol of good luck among Portuguese and Brazilians. At husking bees its finder is named "King Milho" (maize) becomes master of the feast, and among other privileges is entitled to kiss any or all of the women present.[25] Our Rubião was a solid ear in relation to Palha ("straw" or "chaff"), the entrepreneur who used Rubião's simplicity and generosity for his own selfish ends. Rubião entered Rio de Janeiro a kind of natural king in his moral superiority—as shown in his devotion to Borba through illness,[26] in his friendly simplicity and good nature, in his liberality in regard to emancipation of slaves,[27] in his honor in the matter of the found letter,[28] in his love of his native state,[29] and in his active conscience.[30] He was king of the feast, so to speak, by the luck of his newfound wealth; and, in his own eyes, as victor over the potato patch he was emperor with the right to kiss the woman Sophia and make her his empress. By the counsel of the companions that attend on Plutus's children, the Rubião of Barbacena, the good, conscientious man of small pretensions, was changed into a grotesque, though not unsympathetic, monster. For Rubião's life in the city was not in all respects the life of a corrupt "heart." He engaged in acts of loyalty, generosity, and physical courage. Both in his madness and without it he displayed a certain magnanimity, a Quixotic greatness of soul and, like Cervantes's hero, an Olympian indifference to the small impedimenta of reality. His intemperance, as Plutus's child and Folly's own brother, has a Spanish grandeur in its very outrageousness. There are, for example, the ideas, acts, and emotions that go to form the vast project of adultery with his friend's wife: the princely gifts, the wild scenes of jealousy over Sophia's suspected betrayal with *another* (although he, Rubião, was neither her husband nor her lover), the bringing of the whole world to her feet, the imperial luxury of dress, equipage, ceremony—all products of an unbridled imagination. But running through this waking dream there is a sensuality not to be found in Don Quixote's dreams. Don Quixote's love for Dulcinea, as he explained to Sancho, was on a purely "platonic" level; whatever sexual urges he had were repressed—his interests that way being symbolized by Rosinante's gambols with the Galician mares.[31] "Platonic love," as I have mentioned before, was a little known expression among Assis's heroes.

Before Quincas Borba died Rubião had played Sancho Panza to Borba's Don Quixote—eagerly imbibing the mad wisdom of Humanitism, the knight errantry of a scientific age. Unamuno has explained how Don Quixote loved humanity in Sancho. One should love one's neighbor and not mankind, says Unamuno, because mankind is an abstraction that each of us makes concrete in himself. "To preach love of mankind is therefore to preach self-love, of which by original sin Quixote was full, his whole career being but a refinement thereof. He learned to love all of his kind by loving Sancho."[32] Just as in Sancho, humanity ceased to be an egoistic abstraction for Don Quixote, so Quincas's humanitas was realized in Rubião—in whom he loved all humankind as Quixote had loved it in Sancho Panza. Quincas identified himself with Don Quixote and implied that his spirit would live on in Rubião. "Do you see this book [he asked Rubião]? It is *Don Quixote*. If I destroy my copy, the work will live on in the remaining copies and in later editions."[33]

After Quincas's death, Rubião, it would appear, assumed the dead philosopher's ideas and manners but retained his own simplicity and Panza-like pleasure in possession and

other forms of sensuality, becoming an amalgamation of
Quixote and Panza in one man. For all his Panza-like traits,
Borba's heir carried on the Quixotic tradition. Clothed in
a thin armor of self-confident illusion, he issued forth from
Barbacena to do deeds of knight-errantry—perhaps more by
Sancho's definition than by Don Quixote's. "A knight er-
rant [said Sancho] is beaten up one day and made emperor
the next."[34] Rubião was no more wise to the wiles of Rio de
Janeiro than Don Quixote had been to those of Spain. He
became a slave to a scheming, heartless beauty who fell off
a horse—[35]who was no more a Dulcinea than the garlic-
breathing peasant girl who fell off a donkey and repulsed
Don Quixote's gallant attempts to right her. Our Brazilian
knight tried to serve his country by backing a rascally political publisher; he succored and consoled the unfortunate
with the noblesse oblige of a true gentleman; with a true
knight's reckless and athletic courage he saved a child from
a horrible death beneath horses' hooves and a cart's wheels;
he nourished his illusions as emperor and lover by reading,
not romances of chivalry but French novels by Dumas and
O. Feuillet.[36] He had, in short, a large strain of Don Quixote
in him. And his Rio de Janeiro had elements of Quixote's
Spain, though it was not so cruel. It was corrupted by luxury
and false foreign ways perhaps;[37] it was cunning and cow-
ardly; but, infused with a certain Brazilian mildness, it did
not have the robust brutality nor brazen chicanery of Cervantic Spain.

Rubião's Rio was an anarchy created by a society of
dreamers. In chapter lxxxii Machado de Assis placed Prospero and his whole island of dreams in our Rubião's head.
Rubião was the great dreamer; but everyone in that Rio de
Janeiro, except one, was enclosed in a dream world of his
own, everyone a Prospero dreaming dreams that others entered only as servants of the dreamer—a Prospero creating
spells with an enslaved Ariel. Rubião was the great dreamer,

carried off into madness by the subconscious horses of desire: he was Emperor of France with his Empress Sophia
beside him in the carriage, and the dog Quincas Borba at
her feet.[38] Sophia dreamed on social eminence, on adulation
of her beauty, and on adultery with Carlos Maria. Carlos
Maria dreamed of his own apotheosis. Maria Benedicta, at
the left hand of the god Carlos Maria, dreamed of herself as
Virgin Mary with the Christ child leaping in her womb.[39]
Palha dreamed on possession and more possession, and display of possessions.[40] Dr. Falcão dreamed little foxy dreams
in which he appeared as a great detective of sin in private
lives. Camacho dreamed of fame and power as political
journalist and publisher. The spinster Toninha dreamed
of domestic joy; and her father, Major Siqueira, sought to
revive the romantic past by reading and rereading *St. Clair
des Isles,* which (says Machado de Assis) constituted his
whole library.[41] Theophilo dreamed of saving his country
from political disaster. It was only Fernanda, Theophilo's wife, who touched reality. It was only Fernanda who
reached out of her own dream to embrace the lives of
others. She could penetrate even into the heart and mind of
a dog—the dog Quincas Borba.[42]

In short, *Quincas Borba*'s theme is the same one as in
Assis's other novels—the old duel between love and self-
love. Prospero's dreams (like all dreams, according to
Freud) were selfish dreams, his magic served egotistical desires for justice and revenge; but finally he broke his wand,
freed the enslaved Ariel, and set sail for reality. It was a sea,
not an abyss, that stretched between Prospero's lonely isle
and the mainland—a sea over which Ariel was to conduct
Prospero and his company in safety. Just so, Rubião, with
only his dog to accompany him, returned to Barbacena, the
little city that was for him the symbol of his "life's whole-
ness"—the proper marriage of "mind" and "heart."[43]

As they began to go up its street named for Brazil's great

liberator Tiradentes, Rubião cried out, "To the victor the potatoes." He had forgotten the original meaning, which he had taken as the first rule of life, but "suddenly, as if the syllables had remained fixed in the air, intact, waiting for someone to understand them, he united them, recomposed the formula, and gave it utterance. . . . He did not quite remember the allegory, but the words gave him a vague feeling of struggle and victory."[44] His natal city was beginning to reassert itself in his memory, when a sudden storm burst over Barbacena. In the reverberations of its thunder Rubião's madness again came upon him.

There is a kind of paradox in this scene. It is not for nothing that it reminds one of *King Lear*. The formula, "To the victor the potatoes," says Assis, was *re*composed and gave a *vague* idea of struggle and victory. The formula is not really ironic on Rubião's lips, for it has a new meaning. Lear became a true king only at the end, and through madness. Rubião also became king. He did not crown himself with Quixote's golden helmet (the barber's basin),[45] that is, with illusion. He crowned himself with "nothing": it was a spiritual crown. Although he was mad and an emperor, his palace was the arch of heaven, the stars its candles. When he ordered its lights put out, there is an allusion, I believe, to Othello's lines, "Put out the light; and put out the light," and "Out brief candle." It is Assis's poetic way of saying that Rubião's madness was soon to end but with it his life. He had come home to Barbacena, the dog became part of him as they slept on the church steps.[46] Though he still thought himself Emperor of France and victor over the potatoes,[47] it was a bigger conquest—a bigger victory—but he received the crown too late. His "abdication" followed immediately on the coronation. Like Lear, it was only in death that Rubião received the crown of life.

In the author's final injunction (Weep if you have tears, laugh if you have only laughter, it will be all the same to the stars in the Southern Cross, for they are too high to dis-

tinguish men's tears from their laughter), some readers find
a bitter outcry against an external nature or universal law.
This assumption, it seems to me, is unwarranted. A perusal
of Assis's writings discloses that he was not interested in an
external nature (or external god of any sort) except as it
furnished valuable symbols with which to express inner
psychological states, or manifestations of them. He commonly used "star" and "stars" to express a certain loftiness
in human character, especially toward the emotion of pity
and even of self-pity—as, for example, in the character of
Yayá Garcia's stepmother, who was named "star," Estella.
Sometimes the plural, "stars," "Pleiades," "Southern Cross"
(the last a peculiarly Brazilian constellation for Machado
de Assis, and, as Rubião notes, a Brazilian honorary order as
well) are only metaphors for high society.[48] Even in this
novel *Quincas Borba*, "the moon," "the individual,"[49] is
distinguished from "the stars," "a group of laughing, heartless virgins." And here, at the end of the novel, with these
last three sentences, the author advises that reader who is as
far above human pity as a distant star to laugh like those
giddy girlstars he had described in chapter xl. With these
same final words, he modestly and justly assessed his novel,
as if to say, "I thought to write a tragedy but I am not sure
that I have."

For all the modesty of Assis's final remark, no reader,
probably, has remained unmoved by this book. In one respect, certainly, it represents an advance over *Posthumous
Memoirs of Braz Cubas*, as that novel represented an advance over the one before it, and so on back to Assis's first
novel, *Resurrection*. The characters of *Quincas Borba* are
all individual, human, complicated and contradictory,
moving. And the spell they have over us, as I have tried to
suggest, is created not by realistic detail but by a subtle web
of allusion and symbol. With *Quincas Borba*, Assis crossed
over into the borders of tragedy.[50] In his next novel, he
seized the citadel.

CHAPTER FOURTEEN

DOM CASMURRO[1]

Assis's seventh novel, *Dom Casmurro*,[2] is the culmination of the six that preceded it. Not only does it surpass the others as an artistic work, but elements of the first six novels appear here in more perfect form: composition of characters, narrative structures, theme developments—the whole novelist's art. In particular, Assis's ever-increasing strands of symbolism send subtle threads all through these other elements and weave a wonderful thing.

Rubião, as we saw, although a kind of tragic hero, was a combination of two comic ones—Don Quixote's noble ideals warring against Sancho Panza's more fleshly yearnings. And it was with the vast credulity of both Cervantic heroes that Rubião faced the wiles of a corrupt society—a society that in itself reflected his inner struggle. Rubião's credulity—his vain belief that he was fortune's darling and that no one would do him harm, his flouting of the demands of human nature in others—this utter trustfulness, constituted a kind of tragic flaw that set vicious elements in motion against him: Sophia's meretricious arts, Palha's greed and dishonesty, Camacho's brutal treachery . . . If this had been Rubião's only flaw, however, the story would certainly have ended differently—perhaps in comedy, like that of Fielding's Parson Adams. But Rubião shared the human nature he denied to Palha, Camacho, and the others. His struggle assumed two fronts when "the devil" prompted

him to lust after his friend Palha's wife.³ Attacked front and
rear, Rubião lost his reason.

Still, Rubião's drama is not of truly tragic proportions.
We are moved to pity by his conflict ending in madness and
death, but we do not have the sense of shock, as though
there had been some "essential change in the face of the
universe," which comes with tragedy.⁴ Besides, his *actions*
like Don Quixote's were often ridiculous no matter how
grand his intentions.

Dom Casmurro's hero, Bento Santiago, also has two men
within him, but his is a more sinister combination: Othello
and Iago. In addition to superior passion, Santiago was possessed of attributes essential to a tragic hero—attributes in
which Rubião was sadly deficient—namely, those of high
degree. Rubião was a humble peasant of an odd countri-
fied appearance,⁵ of limited education and mental capac-
ity.⁶ Santiago was born to wealth and position; he was
handsome, well educated, and by no means stupid. Since
he narrates his own story, he not only manages to convey
the impression that he is the aristocratic descendant of a
long line of great plantation owners with countless slaves,
he also contrives to envelop himself in an aura of super-
stitiously religious, almost divine, eminence. This he does
by dwelling on a special relationship between his mother
and God and by insinuating that his very birth was a miracle, and so regarded by the family priest. He informs us
that his story was Othello's—except that his Desdemona
was guilty. But soon, however, we discover the hidden Iago.
With a criminal's urge to talk, he discloses, in carefully
guarded metaphor, that his jealousy was rooted in aborigi-
nal evil, that it antedated its object, groped until it found
an object, then pursued and clung to it with obdurate
blindness.

Since Machado de Assis allowed Santiago to tell his own
story without interference, the surface is all bland, indul-

gent irony and humor, only now and again spiced with traces of brutal wit and skepticism—recollections in old age, of his childhood, of his adolescent lovemaking, and of his "betrayal." There are recollections of his widowed mother, gracious lady of latifundia and close to God, with her circle of third-rate intellects, dependents of her house, easy-living descendants of the great navigators: Dr. Costa, medically speaking somewhat of a nonentity (his habitual therapeutics being leeches and emetics) but indispensable at the card table; the kindly priest Cabral, condemned by his profession to an austere cuisine little suited to his gourmet's taste; the busybody José Dias, whom Santiago termed an Iago; the poor relatives—his obese lawyer uncle, who had been a political hothead in his youth and a devil with the women but had "lost all ardor both political and sexual"; the sharp, suspicious Cousin Justina who always "said frankly to Peter, the evil she thought of Paul, and to Paul what she thought of Peter . . ."

It is gentle wit that plays over Capitu, the playmate turned woman: her lovely arms; her eyes a treacherous tide that drew one into its dark depths; her dark, luxuriant hair, combed by the youthful hero's eager, fumbling hands—to his undoing; her maidenly reticence punctuated with sudden almost masculine aggressiveness; her sly wit over their new relationship; her bursts of jealous anger; and her womanly pride. Mild wit still plays over the youthful years of waiting, and over the wedding, but suspicion and hate were already growing in the dark recesses of his heart. Beneath the civilized surface, there was (in his own words) "the subterranean man"; and *he*, as Santiago knew but refused to acknowledge, was a monster—a man who denied his love to any other human being, living or dead, and refused the love offered him.

The titles of Assis's novels are in every instance an important element of the whole. Each is what he called in his preface to *Esau and Jacob* a resumé of the *matter*. For his first two novels, *Resurrection* and *Hand and Glove*, he made the meaning of the title explicitly clear in the body of the work. For the remaining seven, he left this task of explaining the title to the reader. In *Dom Casmurro* he went so far as to permit his hero-narrator to deliberately mislead us.

Santiago tells how the nickname Dom Casmurro had been given him by an irate neighbor, and explains that *casmurro*, as applied to him means a morose, tight-lipped man withdrawn within himself, a definition not to be found in dictionaries. Since those days, however, Portuguese dictionaries have expanded their definition to include the meaning Santiago gives. In Assis's day, they defined casmurro as "obstinate, stubborn, wrong-headed." And this, perhaps is the more important definition for the understanding of the novel. Santiago did become casmurro by *his* definition, but he also had in his nature that "resistance to persuasion" found in Sophocles' tragic heroes.

The dom, Santiago informs us, was intended to make fun of his aristocratic airs, for this word is a titular prefix to the name of a member of the higher nobility. In Brazil this use of dom was confined to the monarch and his legitimate sons. In Portugal also this is the rule, but, there, dom is sometimes informally applied to a few heads of old houses. The title dom is used, too, for members of the higher clergy.[7]

Both the noble and the priestly significance are appropriate to Santiago. Not only does he display his family's aristocratic lineage; the youthful Bento had a daydream in which the Emperor Dom Pedro II (who was, perhaps, a father image to many Brazilians) drove up to the front door in his royal coach, entered the Santiago house, and solved the boy's problems by telling his mother to send him to medical school instead of to the seminary. As for the word's religious connotation, Santiago's priestly talents and his mother's piety are dwelt upon at some length. But there is a further suggestion of sanctity about the word—which is derived from Latin *dominus*, "master," a term applied in the Vulgate and in the Roman ritual to God or to the Christ. In *Quincas Borba*, Carlos Maria's belief that he is a kind of god, and his young wife's worship of him, and of her child as a Christ-child, find a parallel—a more psychologically plausible parallel—in Santiago's feeling about the relationship existing between God and his mother. Santiago is a witty man. He holds up to frequent ridicule both his mother's and his own casuistic "deals" and bargains with their "Multimillionaire Creditor," whom they pay, when they pay, in prayers and ill-kept promises. But, though he laughs, one feels that deep within he has a superstitious belief in this special relationship to God, and that *dom*, for him, is only short for *dominus*.

True to Machado de Assis's formula, the title epitomizes the matter of the novel. The old man's nickname, Dom Casmurro, indicates the change wrought in the hero Bento Santiago by time and by life's events as he himself narrates them, and by the evil in his nature that killed the good— the Iago that dominated and destroyed the loving Othello, the Christ-child that became the Prince of Evil.

The superficial story Santiago would tell us is of his betrayal by Capitu with his friend, Escobar. Through the language of metaphor, however, he tells a different story. Machado de Assis, in his dramatic criticism, stated that the basis of tragedy is human emotion and that (in modern times) the law that regulates tragic acts is moral or spiritual freedom.[8] His definition of the most proper structure for a novel was: the action resulting from the interplay of contrasting natures.[9] *Dom Casmurro*'s tragedy takes place within Santiago's own psyche, the war of passions, the exercise of moral freedom. It is he who makes the choice between good and evil, and, although time hardens his cold heart, he cannot rid himself of twinges of guilt. That is why he tells his story. The interplay of natures is within him—his generous, loving nature fighting against and finally overcome by the strong powers of evil. Although these latter are within himself, he projects them upon others—especially upon Capitu; but, as he himself tells us, he carried "death on his own retina." Good in this novel is equated with love, and love with life; evil with self-love and death. Santiago's struggle with his destiny resembles that of Felix, the hero of *Resurrection,* who tried to revive his dead heart. "I appear to be alive but am not," Santiago tells us. I am a corpse painted and made up to look like life, but the "inner structure will not take dye." He repeats this theme louder and more clearly: "I tried to connect the two ends of my life—restore adolescence (love) in old age (lack-love), but the middle, myself (the essential part, love, life), is missing." He tore down the old house (his heart) and had the original duplicated in another part of town. He tried to bring ghosts to life. He could not fill in the sonnet "battle of life," between the first and last line, because love failed him. Rubião, like Lear, won the battle: victory was late and of the Pyrrhic sort; it was, as the maddened Rubião termed it, a "Battle of Solferino." Santiago won life but lost the battle, as he himself intimates. All these symbols tell the same story: living death, death in life. Although he lived on, his soul, like Dante's traitorous Alberigo's, was in the icy depths of hell.

The cause of death in the case of Felix's heart was vague, barely suggested. There was a hint of submerged evil in Rubião's nature which came to the surface in a recollection of an old memory of going to a hanging;[10] and there was Rubião's dream of killing Palha,[11] and his transfiguration in the garden as he wooed Sophia, when he folded up his archangel's wings and put them in his pocket and suddenly showed a fiend's two horns sunk in his forehead.[12] But these hints were vague. Evil assumes a more terrifying aspect in *Dom Casmurro*. The death of Santiago's heart is enveloped in an atmosphere of mystery and ominous suggestion: ghosts, revenge, guilt, torture, broken vows, Faust and Macbeth—both of whom were in league with the powers of darkness; the libretto of his life's "opera" was written by God, music by Satan—and Santiago danced to that music. These innuendos give one a feeling that unholy murder has been done. Santiago insinuates that it was his wife Capitu and his friend Escobar who murdered his heart with their cruel betrayal. But his own words give him the lie: his metaphors tell the more forthright tale. He himself murdered the loving Bento and projected that murder upon Capitu and Escobar. Many readers, convinced by Santiago's cunning, believe implicitly the plain Portuguese of his clever insinuations. But even if Capitu were guilty of adultery with Escobar, the tragedy of Dom Casmurro would remain: it is *in him*. Santiago's "heart" had been killed long before the supposed betrayal—his jealous cruelty manifested itself before Capitu ever saw Escobar. If Capitu deceived him, it was not the loving Bento she deceived: it was Dom Casmurro. The title of the book is *Dom Casmurro*, not *Capitu*; the tragedy is his—the terror of a life without love, and Santiago was formed for love. Yet his life, like Macbeth's, became "a tale told by an idiot." When we finally recognize the fate that has closed in upon him we are struck with awe and horror; and, as in great tragedies, we have a feeling that there has been a "change in the face of the universe." Our sadness over the sacrifice of Capitu's love and beauty is not unmixed with a kind of joy. She won life's battle: her self-love, her original vanities and jealousies, were driven out; only love remained in her life. This victory of hers was mirrored in the soul's battles of the other characters—José Dias, Dona Gloria, Cousin Justina, and the rest.

But all these personages, and even the portraits on the wall, who seem to speak with their mute eyes and gesture, are melded into the life of the principal character, Santiago, into his very brain, so to speak. It is he who tells us of them; they are, or become in the telling, aspects of his personality. It is he who dominates the story, dominates the mystery-charged atmosphere, dominates our emotions—on which he leaves a mark that never completely fades away. He stands at the center of the whole structure; everything—plot, symbolism, characters, theme—all converge in him, making this Assis's most emotionally powerful work.

LAST TWO NOVELS:
ESAU AND JACOB
AND AYRES'S MEMORIAL

CHAPTER FIFTEEN

AYRES NARRATOR

When *Dom Casmurro* was published, José Veríssimo wrote a review in which he expressed disappointment that this novel did not continue the artistic "evolution" promised by *Quincas Borba*'s advance over *Posthumous Memoirs of Braz Cubas*.[1] At our distant remove, it seems impossible that anyone could express disappointment over *Dom Casmurro*; but we have already noted Veríssimo's confessed antipathy to his friend's writing. He was quite evidently sincere in his opinion that *Dom Casmurro* was inferior to *Quincas Borba*. He believed the author had "retrogressed" to the "detached intellectual attitude" of the *Posthumous Memoirs of Braz Cubas*, and that in Santiago, Machado de Assis had repeated the character Braz Cubas, that these two personages—allowing for minor differences of manner resulting from the different social periods in which they had been born—were "twins."

Santiago and Cubas may fairly be called twins, perhaps; but they are by no means identical, as Veríssimo would have it. They are rather the two halves of drama's mask—comedy and tragedy. As Veríssimo remarks, these two heroes were of a similar social background—Braz Cubas frankly summed up his father's household as a collection of vulgar, ostentatious, weak-willed, capricious natures.[2] The same description might be used for Dona Gloria's establishment with two important modifications: Santiago had only one parent

—a strong-willed mother; and Christian piety had become the fashion in his time. Both Braz and Santiago, given a free hand by Machado de Assis, explored their own psyches and those of their friends and relations for the benefit of their readers. The purpose of the two authors, however, was quite different. Braz Cubas's aim was to amuse and instruct, both himself and his reader, by recounting his travels around life and his tilts with society and with his own nature. The result is comedy. Santiago on the other hand had a more specific aim, a deadly serious one—to do away with his own guilt feelings, to convince himself, by convincing the reader, that he had not committed a crime.[3] We are not amused for long by his narrative. He arouses our pity, and our horror at the enormity of the change in a human being who once had the love of all about him and the reader's affection as well. It is difficult for us today to understand how Veríssimo could state that the emotion aroused in the reader by *Dom Casmurro* is purely intellectual.

Machado de Assis created a third author, the old diplomat Ayres, to write his last two novels for him: *Esau and Jacob* (1904) and *Ayres's Memorial* (1908).[4] The first of these was reviewed by Veríssimo;[5] and again, as with *Dom Casmurro*, he found in it a certain "monotony and repetition" of style and character: that is, he regarded Cubas, Santiago, and Ayres as all pretty much of a piece. True, they were all old men at the time they composed their works, they were Cariocas, and they lived in the nineteenth century; but if one wishes to convince himself of their different temperaments, it is only necessary to examine their way with comedy (the major element present in all Assis's prose). Ayres's comic Muse bears no relation to Braz's exuberant, impudent glee, nor to Santiago's by-turns sentimental humor and brutal wit. Ayres's laughter is often gentle, lighthearted, and fanciful, always restrained, indulgent but never sentimental, never rude.

All this is not to say that there were no resemblances between the three authors—Cubas, Santiago, and Ayres—nor
even that they did not share certain narrative techniques
with their maker, Machado de Assis. Although Cubas and
Santiago were given a free hand by Assis, they were not omniscient; but only related their own story as they saw it, or
would have others see it, and in the first person. The narrator of *Esau and Jacob*, however, is an omniscient author,
telling all in the third person, although he also enters the
story as a character. This dual role—of author and character—gives him added narrative power. Because we know
Ayres to be the author, all his thoughts, speeches, and actions as a character in the narrative, along with quotations
from character Ayres's diary, throw light on the author's
ways of thinking and thus on the meaning of the story itself. And, since the author does not speak in the first person, we are all the more willing to believe what he tells us,
for, I suppose, we forget momentarily or paradoxically that
the two men are one and the same. Perhaps Ayres took a leaf
from Julius Caesar in this matter, or more likely from
Xenophon, who employed the same method in his *Anabasis*.
We know Ayres read Xenophon; he tells us so in *Esau and
Jacob*, chapter lxi, "Reading Xenophon," and quotes a passage from the *Cyropaedia*. Ayres resembled that Greek in
certain other respects: both were interested in politics, both
were diplomatic—knew how to advise, persuade, and lead
men; both retired from public life to lead the life of gentlemen, and passed their leisure in writing; both observed
men's words and actions (their own included) with a certain
indulgent detachment. Although Xenophon had mentioned himself a couple of times previously in his *Anabasis*,
it was not until the beginning of that work's fourth book
that he made the formal introduction, and in this way:
"There was, you see, a certain fellow in the army, Xenophon by name . . ." Author Ayres introduced character

Ayres in much the same casual manner at the beginning of his twelfth chapter: "This fellow Ayres, who appears here . . ."

Although the reticence Ayres displays in his own regard does not extend to the other characters, he does, for all his omniscience, maintain a respectful distance, so to speak. In this particular, as in several others, he resembles his creator Assis, who does not, as an author, boldly enter the innermost recesses of his hero's, or heroine's, heart, but stops with a certain native politeness on the threshold. This is noticeably true of *Quincas Borba*, the only one of the last five novels that is narrated by Machado de Assis in propria persona. We never learn, for example, enough of Rubião's past to be sure of the actual nature and origin of the insanity that had lain dormant in his psyche for so many years. The only information[6] given us about his life before he met Quincas Borba, when he was some forty years of age, is that he was a native of Barbacena, had been a schoolmaster, had tried his hand at several other occupations without success, and that when he was young and very poor he had passed some time in Rio de Janeiro. Aside from slight abnormalities such as his preoccupation with gold, the only indication of the madness to come dated from that visit to the capital of so many years before. One day he had yielded to a strange desire to go to a hanging: "Inner forces each offered him their horse, one to take him back or on to his own affairs, another to see the black man hanged."[7] In the first four novels, all directly narrated by Assis, the author is more explicit about his characters' thoughts and feelings; still, the reticence mentioned above is present. For example, somewhat the same vagueness that surrounds Rubião's psychic past envelops that of Felix, the hero of *Resurrection*.[8]

Both Assis and Ayres, it would seem, disclaim perfect omniscience. Ayres, in particular, often admits bafflement and lack of penetration in regard to his personages—even of character Ayres, the one person whose thoughts we might reasonably expect him to be a party to. In *Esau and Jacob*, chapter lx, he wrote, "I do not swear this was so, because the day was long ago, and the people were strangers to me. Ayres himself, if he suspected such a thing, did not mention it to anyone, nor did he strain his ears to catch the rest."

In the face of all this circumspection and lack of information on the part of their author (whether he be real or fictional), it is not surprising that Assis's characters early exhibited a tendency to assert themselves. This was mentioned above in the discussion of *Resurrection*.[9] In the second novel, *Hand and Glove*, we are told that the effect of the heroine's beauty on the author was quite different from its effect on the character Estevam.[10] With succeeding novels author and personage grew farther apart. In his fifth novel, Assis deliberately dissociated himself from his protagonist Braz Cubas by means of a preface, leaving him to tell his story as he would and answer the critics.[11] Santiago, the protagonist-narrator of *Dom Casmurro*, was given the same letters patent; and, in my opinion, he made use of the privilege to look down his nose at his creator—that is to belittle Assis's literary pretensions.[12] Nine years before Santiago's arrogant gesture, however, *Quincas Borba*'s personages already had an air of autonomy. Ayres, who followed the same system as his master in this regard, explains it to us:

> Well, there is the epigraph of the book, if I should wish to give it one, and no other occurred to me. It is not only a way of rounding out the characters and their ideas, but it is also a pair of spectacles with which the reader may penetrate whatever seems not quite clear or wholly obscure.
>
> Furthermore, there is an advantage in having the characters of my story collaborate in it, aiding the author in accordance with a law of solidarity, a kind of exchange of services between the chess-player and his men.

If you accept the comparison, you will recognize the
king and the queen, the bishop and the knight, and that
the knight cannot become a castle, nor the castle a pawn.
There is of course the difference of color, white and black,
but this does not affect the power of each piece to move,
and finally one side or the other wins the game, and so
goes the world. Perhaps it would have been a good idea
to insert, from time to time (as in chess books), the favorable positions or the difficult ones. With no chessboard,
that procedure is a great aid for following the moves, but
then it may be that you have enough vision to reproduce
the various situations from memory. Yes, I think so. Away
with diagrams! Everything will go along as if you were
actually witnessing a game between two players or, to be
more precise, between God and the devil.[13]

That is, the good and the evil in their natures make the
action; the characters write the story.

Consonant with this attitude toward his characters' free
will and freedom of action, Ayres had little use for the determinism of the Naturalist novel, or its methods. Long,
superficial descriptions, especially those including sensa-
tional physical details—what Assis termed "the exact inventory of the disreputable and obscene"[14]—are not only
shunned but are ridiculed. As the Assis of *Quincas Borba*
parodied *Cousin Bazilio*'s pornographic "paradise," with
Rubião's hallucinatory dream of Sophia coming to an am-
orous tryst with him—which ended with the mad lover's
rather Machadean remark to his Sophia, "And yet, my blos-
som, those hours were long as the devil!"—[15] so Ayres related
the ex-thief-nabob Nobrega's vision of putting silk stock-
ings on Flora[16] in order to parody, I believe, the overabun-
dance of *un*dressing of Bazilio's Luiza. Ayres also laments
the difficulty of his artistic method as compared to that of
the Naturalistic type description when he tries to convey
Flora's emotional crisis over the twins.

There is nothing worse than talking about sensations that

do not have a name. Believe me, my dear sir, and you, madam, who are no less dear to me, believe me, I would rather tell over the lace ruffles on the young lady's dressing gown, the hairs that were caught up at the back of her head, the threads in the carpet, the boards in the ceiling, and when it comes to that, the sputterings of the night lamp, whose flame was dying. . . . It would be boring, but readers would understand.[17]

Here we find Ayres politely echoing Assis's sarcastic remark in the famous criticism of *Cousin Bazilio*: "The new poetics will not reach perfection until that day when it tells us the exact number of threads in a fine linen handkerchief or in a dish clout."

Although the patriotic aim in *Esau and Jacob* comes closer to the Positivist ideal that a work of art should directly serve the state than any other of Assis's novels, its narrative method is the furthest removed from the Naturalistic. Ayres, as we have seen, relies on his characters to create the action, instead of being created by it in the Naturalistic manner. And, instead of leaving nothing to the imagination, he calls on his reader to fill in many of the details by himself, and to fathom the meaning if he can.

Henry Fielding, who claimed to be "the founder of a new province of writing" and hence could make what laws he chose, gave notice to his reader that he would leave great vacant spaces of time for him to fill in with his own conjectures since he (the reader) had been thoroughly and properly trained for these exercises by the author's lectures on the new art—which we know as that of the novel.[18] Machado de Assis, old friend of Fielding's works, tried to draw his reader into his effort from his very first novel, and with his second novel, *Hand and Glove*, he began to leave "vacant spaces" for the reader to fill in, but fearfully and gingerly and not without stooping to rhetorical praetermissions as in the following passage:

A perspicacious reader, as I suppose this book's reader

must be, will dispense with my recounting the many diverse and contradictory plans he wove, as are reasonable
in such situations. I will only mention that he thought
three times of suicide, twice of leaving the city, four times
of drowning his earthly woes in that still more earthly
slough of corruption in which youth's flower so frequently
rots and dies.[19]

Four novels later, in *Quincas Borba,* Assis scolds the
reader for letting himself be taken in by the characters'
thoughts and conversations, and for not drawing the proper
conclusions.

> [The trouble is] the reader lost his way and could not fit
> together Sophia's hurt anger with the cab-driver's tale;
> and so asks in bewilderment, "Then the rendez-vous of
> Rua da Harmonia, Sophia, Carlos Maria—this tinkling
> flim-flam of sweet, guilty-sounding rhymes—is all calum-
> ny?"
> All calumny—the reader's and Rubião's, not the poor
> cabby's, for he mentioned no names, was not even report-
> ing an actual case. You would have seen this for yourself
> if you had read slowly and reflectively. Yes, benighted
> reader, only consider: it would be highly improbable for
> a man going on an *adventure* of the sort to have the cab
> wait in front of the hideaway. It would establish a witness
> to the crime. There are more streets in heaven and earth
> than are dreamt of in your philosophy—cross-streets where
> the cab could have waited very nicely.[20]

The fictional narrators Braz Cubas and Santiago also left
spaces to be filled in by the reader. Braz called his "leaps"
or "jumps"[21] and defended the practice: for example, in the
passage in which he compressed Nhan-loló's illness, death,
and funeral—as well as his own disappointed hopes of prog-
eny and domestic bliss—into a transcription of the epitaph
on her headstone: "Here lies Dona Eulalia Damascena de
Brito, dead at nineteen years of age. Pray for her!"[22] Santi-

ago explained the purpose of *his* blanks, much as Fielding had:

> There is no way of emending a confused book, but everything may be supplied in the case of books with omissions. For my part, when I read one of the latter type I am not bothered a bit. What I do, on arriving at the end, is to shut my eyes and evoke all the things which I did not find in it. How many fine ideas come to me then! What profound reflections! The rivers, mountains, churches, which I did not find on the written page, all now appear to me with their waters, their trees, their altars; and the generals draw swords that never left their scabbards, and the clarion releases notes that slept in the metal, and everything marches with sudden soul.
>
> The fact is, everything is to be found outside a book that has gaps, gentle reader. This is the way I fill in other men's lacunae; in the same way you may fill in mine.[23]

He also required his reader to act as judge and jury and hand down a decision on his guilt or innocence.

The principle of the "blank space" is still more important to Ayres's artistic procedure. Like Assis in *Quincas Borba*, he frequently warns his reader to pay strict attention and to reread, as in the following passages:

> This was Ayres's conclusion, as one may read it in the *Memorial*. This will be the reader's, if he cares to conclude. Note that I have spared him Ayres's work; this time I did not oblige him to find out everything for himself as he has been obliged to do on other occasions. For, the attentive, truly ruminative reader has four stomachs in his brain, and through these he passes and repasses the actions and events, until he deduces the truth which was, or seemed to be, hidden.[24]

> Explanations eat up time and paper, delay the action, and end by boring. The best thing is for you to read attentively.[25]

> Let my lady reader figure it out if she can: I give her
> twenty chapters to do it in.[26]

This cavalier attitude is a far cry from the conciliatory ad-
dress by the author of *Hand and Glove*—unless, of course,
that was irony. The reason for Ayres's insistent manner is
that in *Esau and Jacob* the empty space has become the
center of the picture as in some old Chinese painting. Our
imagination must enter and fill the void. The artist, however, has painted faintly into the edge of the vacancy those
"delicate touches of poetry" that Assis demanded for the
ideal Brazilian novel.[27] These sprays of fancy will direct and
inspire our thoughts—or, as Ayres words it, give us "a pair
of spectacles with which the reader may penetrate whatever
seems not quite clear or wholly obscure."[28] Through an
elaborate nexus of such "poetic touches"—that is, literary
allusions and symbols—Assis contrived another of his novel-
istic experiments. The experiment does not reside in the
interplay amongst real author, fictional narrator, autonomous characters, and reader, mentioned above, although
this lively system of intercourse surely helps it along. No,
the innovation attempted in the novel *Esau and Jacob* has
to do with the nature of the protagonist, who presents many
faces, masculine and feminine, yet remains himself and
true to his destiny, or perhaps one should say *herself* and
her destiny. The society that played a secondary role in
Quincas Borba, in *Esau and Jacob* has become the principal
actor playing out a comic struggle with its destiny in a kind
of shadowboxing, for the antagonist is invisible—"invisible
Time."[29]

In the novel *Quincas Borba* it was not only Rubião who
had within him the seeds of madness. Incipient madness
was present in the whole society. Palha's financial success
was pushing him that way. Sophia already struggled in a
strait jacket of repressions. The wealthy Carlos Maria and

his simple bride had retreated into the cult of themselves as
a Holy Family. And the less well-off dwelt in lesser states of
alienation from reality—with Fernanda the only truly sane
member of all that mad group. *Esau and Jacob* carries Rio
de Janeiro society twenty-five years further down the same
road, through the years from 1869 to 1894.

As had become usual with Assis, the keynote is sounded
on the first page with these words, "Not everyone can say
he knows a whole city." For "city," read "society," because
Rio de Janeiro was Brazil's capital—political, financial, cultural—and in this novel it is to be taken as the whole people.
Brazil, in all its history, resides in the personages of this
"city"—in the flesh and blood individuals and in what Ayres
called their "souls," that is, in what each represents in essence or metaphorically.

Immediately, upon the above pronouncement, author
Ayres proceeds to show us "the whole city," that is, its "soul"
as well as its outer physical aspect. He shows it to us in a multitude of brief scenes and tableaux that fuse, superimpose,
and change almost imperceptibly. To start us off spiritually
on the right foot, he placed a posy at the very beginning, a
verse from Dante's *Inferno* (v, 7): *Dico, che quando l'anima
mal nata* . . . ("I say that when the ignobly born soul . . .").
In chapters xii and xiii, he partially explains this epigraph
by applying the verse to a company of guests at Santos's
house—"insipid bores" who spent the evening discussing a
fortuneteller. He also quotes an old Portuguese proverb
over these persons: "What the cradle holds only the grave
will take away." The Dantean context is much more refined: *Anima mal nata* designates an individual born with a
nature capable of accomplishing a great destiny but predestined by God not to fulfill the destiny promised by his
nature. Minos, the judge of Hell, assigns such *mal nate* souls
to their proper circle of Hell by the number of times he

lashes his tail. Later in our novel, Santos himself "lashed his
tongue seven times," thus landing himself in the seventh
circle with the bankers and usurers—where, in fact, he belonged.[30] From this and other allusions of the sort, and from
the verse being placed at the head of the book, it is apparent
that its application extends beyond Santos's guests of a
single evening, to the whole generation, all of whose souls
are *mal nate*.

In chapters xxxii and xxxiii we are told Ayres's experience on his return to his native city and retirement from the
foreign service. Again the narrator uses the "pair of spectacles" method. He alludes to the psalm in which David returned after fighting the Philistines and "saw the City all
full of wickedness and contention," and "in the marketplace nothing but usury and fraud."[31] Ayres took for his
device the psalmist's words, "I fled afar off and dwelt in
solitude,"[32] for he too fled to escape the Philistines who were
in all the land: he roamed the streets of his boyhood and
dwelt alone with old letters and memories. Assis, however,
like Dante, believed in man's capacity for evolving and
improving and, also like Dante, that man could achieve the
end destined for him only by remaining in society. Ayres
returned to the marketplace, to the drawing rooms, to the
whole *City* and dwelt with those Carioca Philistines.[33] He
himself was not yet quite aware of his motive in so doing:
he said he did it to "kill time, deathless time."

Dantean and biblical allusions such as these are comple-
mented by the novel's titles. In his foreword, Assis informs
us that the name Ayres gave his narrative was *Último*,
"Last," and he pretends to be puzzled by its meaning. Yet
he himself sold the novel to his publisher Garnier under
that title, and it is still on the manuscript of the work, which
is in the Brazilian Academy of Letters in Rio de Janeiro.
Indeed, the title *Último* was not changed to *Esau and Jacob*

until after galley proofs.[34] Assis also mentions in his preface still another title that "would epitomize the matter" of the book—*Ab Ovo*, from the egg. The titles *Esau and Jacob* and *Ab Ovo*—like the *anima mal nata* of the epigraph—point directly to predestination. *Último*, "Last," I believe, emphasizes the *nature* of the society that is the substance of the narrative. Although the title *Esau and Jacob* contains an allusion to the biblical story and its Old Testament interpretation of two nations warring in Rebekah's womb,[35] Dante's symbolic use of the story has greater significance for our novel. Dante, following St. Paul and other Church fathers, used Esau and Jacob as a symbol of God's grace, which He bestows or withholds in an embarrassingly capricious manner, often condemning a good soul before birth to the fate of not fulfilling its natural capabilities—as happened to the souls that appeared before Minos. In particular, Dante used Esau's red hair to symbolize God's practice of conferring diverse natures on men, even on sons of the same father and mother—twins—so that not only do brothers not necessarily resemble one another, children often do not resemble their parents.[36] Flora, the lovely heroine of Ayres's narrative, is in this last category. As Ayres jocosely said of her, "Children do not always reproduce their parents"; and Flora, like Esau, had red hair.[37] *Último*, perhaps contains an allusion to Matthew 12:45 where we find, in the version owned by Machado de Assis:[38] ". . . e o ultimo estado de aquelle homem fica sendo peor do que o primeiro. Assim tambem acontecerá a esta geração pessima." (. . . and the last state of that man is worse than the first. Even so shall it be also for this most wicked generation.) That is, *Último* names the "last" generation of the Brazilian Empire—which is the setting and the subject of this novel. It is not difficult to connect this "most wicked generation" with the wicked men David saw throughout the "whole City," es-

specially when one finds (still in Assis's Bible) on the page
facing the psalm quoted by Ayres (54) Psalm 57, which also
treats of the wicked in the City. Its verse 4 reads:

> Os peccadores se alienárão des da nascença: elles se
> extraviárão des de que sahírão do ventre de sua mãi: fal-
> lárão falsidades.

> (The sinners are doomed to turn against each other from
> birth; to go astray from the moment they leave their moth-
> er's womb; to speak falsehoods.)

Again predestination: a society predestined to strife, cheat-
ing, and lying.

This theme of predestination, which had been announced
by the book's title, preface, and epigraph, is at once taken
up by Ayres's narrative in his first chapter, for it is an important element of "the whole city" that is about to be
revealed to us.

Natividade, the wife of a prominent banker, and her sister
Perpetua climb the steep mountainlike hill Morro do Castello to consult a fortuneteller about Natividade's baby
sons, the identical twins, Paulo and Pedro. The fortuneteller, Barbara, is a *cabocla*, a girl of mixed blood from the
backlands. She prophesies that the babies will be great men;
she also discloses that they fought in their mother's womb
and are destined to fight in life. This prediction is the beginning of the plot: the parents' efforts to further the boys'
greatness, and the still greater efforts to prevent their fighting—for both the mother and father believed in the cabocla.
The reader, however, who is already immersed in the implications of the book's title, preface, and epigraph, is bound
to feel a little dubious about this prophecy. Add Ayres's
description of the seeress—all gentle wit and satire, plus an
"old dandy's" delight in a pretty face and figure. As for
Assis, we know from other writings that he had little faith
in fortunetellers.[39] Even the name of the *morro* on which

the cabocla lived points to unfulfilled dreams: *castello,*
castle, in Machadean symbolism means air castles.[40] There
is a destiny doomed not to be fulfilled, either in its bright
hopes or in its strife. The climbing of the morro tells the
same story. First a playful allusion to Dante's mountain of
repentance (which, appropriately, was located in the Southern Hemisphere):[41] the ladies climbed up the steep, stony
path "as if it were penance." Contrary to Dante's mountain,
however, where the ascent became easier the higher one
went, here it was "better coming down than going up"—
perhaps a glance at Dante's guide Virgil as well, for the
Sibyl's warning to Aeneas was, "The downward path to hell
is easy . . . but to retrace your steps and regain the upper air,
this is the task, this, the toil."[42] It was this task, this struggle,
that the último generation rejected.

The *Morro do Castello* is here a monument of Brazil's
past, a symbol of the history of Brazil's capital. There was
no real city until the first Portuguese settlement removed to
this rock. It was from there that the Portuguese drove the
French from the bay in 1581. It was on this hill that Father
Manuel de Nóbrega founded the great Jesuit college in the
sixteenth century. Anchieta taught there and preached in
the Jesuit church that bore the date 1567 on its lintel.[43] In
1871, when Natividade and her sister visited the morro, all
this early civilization was long since gone, church and college had been abandoned by the Jesuits. The Morro do
Castello was now nothing but an old neighborhood with
banana peels underfoot and washing hung up to dry in the
windows.[44] It was no longer the home of cultivated Jesuits:
a fortuneteller reigned there in 1871, Ayres tells us.

At the foot of the hill was a man who bore the same name
as the founder of the abandoned church and college, Nóbrega, a lay-brother begging alms for souls in purgatory. He
stole the banknote Natividade put in his alms bowl. The
faiths of all the members of the society Ayres describes rep-

resent a falling off from the vigorous faith of the Jesuit
fathers who gave early Brazil its character. They all do lip
service to Catholicism, and with the customary rites, but
their real devotion is reserved for other gods. We have wit-
nessed Natividade's faith in fortunetellers. Her sons, Paulo
and Pedro, came to worship political saints: Robespierre
and Louis XVI respectively, until they replaced these with
their own parents, a banker and his wife. The three Bap-
tistas each had a different superstition. Ayres recited odes of
Horace's in place of prayers. Santos, the banker, was a de-
votee of spiritualism—a practice particularly abhorrent to
the Church because of its keeping souls earthbound so that
they cannot finish their proper business in purgatory and
continue on their way to heaven. At one point he was willing to believe he was the father of two reincarnated apostles
—Peter and Paul.[45] His spiritualism, however, gave way to
another, more powerful cult—Mammon. He could not
spare even a few minutes to summon the spirit of his dead
teacher, Placido, because he was extremely busy with some
"lucrative liquidations."[46] But Santos's religious fervor did
not stop there. As his name perhaps indicates, he was a man
of many "saints," and his holy-of-holies was symbolized by
the statue in his garden—a statue of Narcissus, which he
particularly admired.

The moral fiber of this society was on a par with its religious practices—not conspicuously vicious but frivolous,
foolish, contemptuous of its heritage, and not averse to the
practice of dishonesty. Nóbrega, as we have seen, was a
thief; he became a millionaire. Santos had a distinct talent,
we are told, for making money and making other people
lose theirs.[47] Baptista's ethical standards in the matter of
political patronage also appear to have been questionable.
The times were propitious to crooked dealings; but, as
Ayres tells us, the occasion makes the theft, it does not make
the thief.[48] The thief (he says) is born not made—and we

are back with the *anima mal nata* and a city filled with
sinners "doomed to go astray from the moment they leave
their mother's womb." Ayres was not dishonest: he was discreet and diplomatic. He shared some of the other weak-
nesses of the age, however.

The women of this society are less offensive than the men,
at least to our narrator Ayres, but he was not blind to their
faults. Although he was charmed by Natividade in particular, he does not conceal from us that she was vain, passionate, selfish, snobbish, unreasonable, and somewhat mean to
start with. Motherhood and time gradually changed her. As
Ayres phrased it, she rounded the Cape of Storms with only
a torn sail or two, quickly mended them, and calmly pursued the route to India.[49]

Flora, the heroine, is an exception among the women of
this novel, as her third suitor, the young bureaucrat-poet
Gouvêa is an exception among the men. Love is what distinguishes these two. But, Flora is more than a lover; she is
more than a human being. As our narrator presents her, she
appears a charming Portuguese-Brazilian-Catholic girl of
the time: innocent, modest, sweet, gentle, artistic, poetically
romantic, superstitious, and subject to vapors like a true
Victorian lady.[50] The character Ayres, however, found something strange about her: a will, an ambition, and a more
than human desire for perfection. She loved the identical
twins Pedro and Paulo equally; because for her their
"souls" were also identical, except that each had "something indefinable" that the other lacked. Paulo's dreams for
the future stirred her; she found peace and contentment in
Pedro's satisfaction with the way things were.[51] Dante saw
the double nature of incarnate love in Beatrice's eyes, now
as wholly divine, now as wholly human, but could not see
the two as one thing and one person until the beatific vision
at the end of the *Paradiso*. So Flora, just before her death,
saw the twins as one. The others, our narrator informs us,

thought it was "the beginning of the delirium"; Ayres "rejected the delirium."[52]

This is more than a real girl—sane and lovely in spite of her hallucinations and her strange desire. Our narrator gives a key to her identity, especially with his metaphors. Her name was Flora—goddess of flowers. She was "Orpheus the sweet singer," a will-o-the wisp,[53] a "fragile vase,"[54] "flower of a single morning,"[55] fit subject "for a tender elegy,"[56] a "rose growing beside a crumbling wall,"[57] ruins of a partly-built house that was never finished,[58] a spring that never had a summer.[59] She did not resemble her parents —the unenlightened Imperial politicians Baptista and Dona Claudia; she was the spiritual child of the literary, career diplomat Ayres. Ayres—the intellectual, the free-thinking man of European culture—read in the classics, suave, kindly, moderate, urbane, and eternally youthful.[60] She was born in the year 1871, which marked the struggle over the law of *free birth* in the Chamber of Deputies—the law that declared every child born, free.[61] Her intellectual progress in speaking, reading, writing, was dated by ministries.[62] All these symbols, facts, and images connect her with the establishment of the Brazilian Republic—the ideal republic. *It* was born of the emancipation movement, the ideal of the brotherhood of man, the spiritual child of poets and intellectuals. Quintino Bocayuva, Assis's old literary colleague, was known as the father of the Republic and led in the formation of the new government. But Bocayuva and the other intellectual idealists abandoned the new government within a matter of months.[63] During the first troubled days of Floriano Peixoto's regime Flora died; "her funeral passed through a city in a state of siege."[64] The ideal republic was dead. Her pallbearers, listed for us by Ayres, were Baptista, Santos, Ayres, Pedro, Paulo, and Nóbrega[65] (government, finance, diplomacy, the conservative and liberal parties of the new era, and the new wealth). There was a wreath on her grave from "her loving friend Natividade" (the old Portuguese Brazil). And then this company withdrew to Petropolis,[66] "the city of peace, luxury, and gallantry," the "international city," founded by the internationally-minded Emperor Pedro II, and named for him. The emperor had been deposed but his city remained. As Natividade remarked, not even the name had been changed, "Pedro's City"[67]—the plutocracy itself, as Ayres implies when he tells us that after the capital again became quiet, "Petropolis abandoned Petropolis," and came down to the city.[68] That is, after the demise of the *republic*, the old crowd returned to power. Everything went back to its status quo.

The conservative party-man Baptista became convinced he was a liberal;[69] Santos, banker and baron of Imperial Brazil, did not show respect for the old emperor's fall by abstaining from cards for a single evening.[70] Custódio's signboard would be changed from Imperial Pastryshop (*Confeitaria do Império*) to Custódio's Pastryshop (*Confeitaria do Custódio*);[71] that is, there would be no change, because Custódio *was* the Empire. Natividade confused the old terms with the new: province with state, court with capital, emperor with president, but her sons both addressed her as "Baroness."[72] The portraits of Robespierre and Louis XVI which hung over their beds would be replaced with the portraits of their own parents.[73] Pedro, the monarchist, accepted the new government; Paulo, the republican, was opposed to it: it was not the republic of his dreams; but his dream republic too was of the past—the Venetian Republic.[74] The age was destined by its own vacillating nature not to achieve its destiny. Ayres, the incarnate spirit of compromise, appears as the Genius or tutelary deity that presides over this irresolute company of souls.

The past had taken over. Flora, the present, the beautiful moment in Brazil's history, the republic, ideal of brotherly love, was dead *forever*. Our narrator weeps over it.[75]

> There is no novelty in funerals. That one happened to pass through streets that were in a state of siege. Come to think of it, death is nothing more than the suspension of the liberty to live, perpetual suspension, whereas the decree of that day lasted only seventy-two hours. At the end of seventy-two hours, all the liberties were restored, except that of returning to life. Whoever died, was dead. That was the case with Flora. But what crime could that girl have committed, except the crime of living, and perchance of loving, it is not known whom, but of loving? Forgive these obscure questions, which are not appropriate, but rather strike a discordant note. The reason for them is that I do not record this death without pain, and I still see the funeral . . .[76]

Brazil it would seem, was destined never to realize her dreams, never to enjoy a present, but only a future that would be identical with her past. That is what all the personages of the book secretly wanted. Time is a specter that stalks this novel's pages just as it did *Dom Casmurro*'s; but here the bouts with the invincible antagonist are for the most part comic, and the old fellow is often knocked out and put in chains—though not for long. His opponents tried to escape his grasp by clinging to the past: a letter written by the Marquis de Pombal, an antique inkwell,[77] an old signboard.[78] Or they fortified themselves with other weapons and stratagems. Baptista would have turned back the clock if he could.[79] Nóbrega rubbed imported toilet waters on a face already badly battered and bruised by time.[80] Ayres drank deep at European springs of wisdom.[81] Santos changed the cut of his beard and the brand of his cigars.[82] When his old signboard gave way, Custódio had a new one made—with the old message in new paint. Natividade sought help from her dressmaker but she had two other more powerful allies: nature and, finally, love.[83] The two men who dyed their beards, called sexual love to their aid— to little purpose. They held "Time captive" a while; but then, as Ayres wrote, God granted Time a writ of habeas corpus. One man's beard turned white, the other man died.[84]

Flora's concern with time was of another sort. She tried to escape the present through her music. "For her, music had the advantage of not being past, present, or future: it was a thing outside time and space, pure idea." Nevertheless, there was in her music "a kind of harmony with the present hour."[85] That is, there is only one way of holding "Time captive"—through love. Love for Assis is the present moment,[86] and its major symbol a flower. Flora was the present, she was the Republic, which was also a symbol of love—born out of the emancipation movement, with its ideal of brotherhood. In contemporary prints, the Republic was regularly represented as a beautiful young woman, or girl, with roses and rose petals all about her.[87] Flora too was a "rose growing beside a crumbling wall," and the "red rose of dawn";[88] her mother gathered flowers for her to wear at the republican ball.[89] In other of Assis's writings roses are "God's thoughts";[90] these flowers, it is plain, are political ideals or ideas that "keep growing." As republic, Flora died; as love, as present, she disappeared; but her brief presence and strangely beautiful death drew the other main characters of the novel together: what she had stirred in their hearts lingered on as a sainted memory symbolized by "immortelles" and "forget-me-nots."

But there are no consistent allegories for Machado de Assis—no *Pilgrims' Progresses*. Flora is as paradoxical as the other characters, and she too was tainted with the weakness of the age. The only person truly flesh of her flesh and spirit of her spirit was the young, obscure, poetic government employee Gouvêa, from whose worshipful glances she steadily averted her eyes. We are told she put her faith in Ayres (Brazil's traditional diplomacy?), in Natividade (Imperial Brazil?), in Santos (finance), in the army's widow Perpetua, in the five stars of the Southern Cross (Brazil's glory?), in the nine Muses (the poets), in the angels, archangels, virgins, and martyrs (the Church?), in an old ivory crucifix given her by her grandmother (old Portuguese faith and superstition?).[91] Except for the nine Muses perhaps these were all adjuncts of the status quo. She too preferred the past's illusions. She chose candles rather than gaslight, so that she could not see clearly when Pedro and Paulo appeared to her (past and future).[92]

Machadean allegory does not embalm the characters into fixed attitudes, nor slow their action: it infuses life and vigor. This novel's real plot scarcely moves, even on place: where will the mediocre talents and halfhearted bickering of a couple of rich boys lead? and the answer, nowhere. Not much there to raise the blood pressure. But, an age, a great country, human progress itself, missing a rendezvous with its destiny? The thematic action is poignant, suspenseful, and witty. The wit is not made leaden by allegory: it is given wings. Santos's fads in religion, financial speculation, beards, and governments are funny in an individual banker or banker type; they are still more ridiculous in the Bank of Brazil. Our mild amusement over the childish hopes and superstitions of the banker's wife deepens when these are seen to be the illusory dreams of Imperial Brazil, whose womb teemed, not with "royal kings," but with republican political parties—conservative and liberal—which were indistinguishable twins. Flora's parents, eccentric individuals, funny as they are, are also a caricature of the imperial political baggage carried over into the new republican government. The more stature thrust upon these figures the more laughable become their failures, and demifailures, to at-

tain the height of their dreams. The lovely Flora defined
governing as retiring into a corner and taking her fill of
contemplation and piano-playing[93]—and we smile; but,
when we perceive that this lovely girl is the Brazilian Republic, our laughter takes on a special inner delight. Ayres's
wit carries us far beyond Brazil's borders. His talkative
cabby is another individual who appears to be native to
the place. On the morning of November 15, 1889, after
hearing some disturbing news on the Rua do Ouvidor,
Ayres stepped into a tilbury and told the driver to take him
to his house on the Rua do Cattete.

> He did not ask the driver anything: *he*, however, told him
> the whole thing and a lot more. He told of a revolution,
> of two Ministers killed, one gone into hiding, the rest
> thrown in jail. The Emperor had been seized in Petropolis
> and was being brought down the mountainside.

It seems the cabdriver had heard the whole story from a man
he had picked up on the Rua dos Inválidos and driven across
the city to the Largo da Glória. He suspected the man had
blood on his hands (though it might have been clay), any-
way he was in a great hurry and his hat was mashed in, and
he paid double the legal fare, rightly so, too, for it was pretty
risky business driving people about in such dangerous times.
The old diplomat did not take the hint; and, part way
through this rambling discourse,

> Ayres glanced at the driver, whose words came forth sweet
> with news. He was not unknown to him, this person. He
> had seen him before, without his tilbury, in the street or
> in the drawing room, at church, or on board ship; he was
> not always a man, sometimes he was a woman, dressed in
> silk, or in calico.[94]

Thus, we see, this man is not the local Genius of the Rua
do Ouvidor: he is the great goddess Rumor herself.
The cabdriver's elevation to universal eminence is not

an isolated instance. Every person in the book has a universal essence. Narrator Ayres early advises us that the epigraph from the *Inferno*, "*Dico, che quando l'anima mal nata*" will help round out the characters. As Dante's *Divina Comedia* is filled with "souls," so *soul* is the keyword repeated on every page of the novel. Not only human beings but also animals (donkeys, horses),[95] inanimate objects (a signboard, an inkwell, the stones of the street, the walls of houses; the sea, winds, and sky), and even activities like the soothsayer's rites, all have a "soul," an impelling spirit, an essence, a metaphorical life. Although at times it may seem that a person is possessed of more than one "soul," this is actually not so: they are only aspects of the same essential quality. Santos's soul, for example, was his Bank, his cigars, his house, his carriage, his wife, his sons, his statue of Narcissus, et cetera—that is, his possessions. His "spiritualism," that is, his immortal soul, or essence, symbolizes the incarnation and reincarnation of his self-love in those other many souls that are indicated by his plural name, Santos, "saints." Most of the personages have more than one aspect but their names point to their soul's essence. We have considered the lovely changeling Flora—daughter of ignorance, foster child of intellect, "flower of a single morning," a fragile poem, ephemeral joys and dashed hopes, vacillation, music, youth, a spring that promised a summer never to come, a thing of unsubstantial air, of life and death, the present's moment, love, the ideal republic that passed away.

The Santos twins were named for the saints, Paul and Peter, whom Assis had often used as symbols of the future and of the past: St. Paul, the spirit of progress; St. Peter, the conservative, the rock, the strength of the past.[96]

The soul of the supreme guardian or "custodian" of the past, Custódio, was singular in number and named for the Guardian Angel. His Imperial Pastry Shop was the old order, stocked with its traditional cakes and pasties made

from old Portuguese recipes.[97] Perpetua, another stout
worshiper of Brazil's past, was also properly named.[98] Many
if not all the names, have a somewhat ironic flavor—none
more so than the one borne by that prophet of spiritism,
Placido. Not only did Placido lend "placid" assent to
others' beliefs—Ayres's agnosticism, the fortuneteller's art
("Teste David cum Sibylla")[99] but like most Brazilians he
was named for a saint, Placid, the abbot who founded a
monastery sacred to the chief of all the spirits, *Sanctus
Spiritus*, that is, the Holy Ghost.

Barbara, the cabocla fortuneteller, is an example of the
lengths to which old word-lover Assis would go in the fash-
ioning of a name's allegory. Not only does the name Barbara suggest the uncivilized, the wilds from which she came,
so too does her descriptive title *cabocla*, which in addition
marks her as indigenous—the true Brazilian, though of
mixed blood. She probably represents the three racial
strains of Brazil's ethnic substructure. In her are combined
gentleness, innocent beauty, rhythmic grace, and the mystic
ignorance of Indian, Negro, and Portuguese folklore and
superstition. As a fortuneteller she was a mixture of universal mumbo-jumbo. Ayres mockingly compared her to
the ancient oracle at Delphi—in her numerous clientele, in
her vague, double-tongued prophecies, and in the sacrificial
fires represented by the smoke from her cigarette. The fifty-
milreis note given her by Natividade was "the equivalent,
or more than the equivalent of Croesus's rich offerings to
the Pythia." She was "the Pythia of the north." Yet the
Dogma of the Immaculate Conception hung on her wall.
Her headdress of crumpled ribbon with a tassle of rue is
likened to a Catholic priest's zuccheto.[100] And the *Saints'
Legend* figures in her name, her dress, and her situation.
Barbara, a most popular saint among the Portuguese, was
shut up in a tower by her pagan father, who finally killed
her. St. Barbara's attributes are a tower and the palm of

martyrdom; and she is regularly portrayed in a white tunic —sent her by the angels, according to the *Golden Legend*. Our fortuneteller Barbara lived in a stone house on a steep stone cliff—much like a tower, and was, so to speak, under the management of her father, an old caboclo who acted as her receptionist, brought her on stage with the cue, "Enter Barbara," and supplied the ritual music—a sambalike ballad that told of a *palm* tree and a girl dressed in a *white* skirt. Plainly, Afro-Brazilian elements had been introduced into the Christian proceedings. Rue was a homely, but powerful, charm against bad luck and sorcery throughout Brazil, especially among the Negresses.[101] The old caboclo's song is a type of work-song used by slaves on northern plantations; but its sexual overtones also suggest primitive religious rites. Its music must have suited this mood, for Barbara shook off her divine ecstasy by moving her hips to the song's familiar rhythms.

Natividade felt an affinity for this girl. She "understood" her prophecy; she believed it. Natividade believed her sons would be "great and glorious." As for their "fighting," this would cease, because Natividade "believed in time,"[102] in time's power to accomplish miracles. Time would cure her son's quarreling, change it to amity; time would make her sons great and famous. Natividade was allied to time by her name. She was named for a holiday—the holy day commemorating the Virgin Mary's birthday (Natividade da Virgem).[103] And she was not one to forget anniversaries— "whosesoever they were, friends' or relatives', she knew them all by heart."[104] In an apologue, written by Assis in 1890, "How Almanacs Were Invented," we seem to find a forerunner of Natividade. The apologue tells how old Father Time fell in love with a girl of fifteen—Hope, and asked her to marry him. She told him he was too old. Time invented the almanac and showered copies of it over the earth, in order to let Hope see that the years would pass and she too would grow old. But his scheme did not have the desired effect. Hope seized upon the almanac because it showed her when to celebrate her friends' birthdays, holidays, et cetera. Each year Time showered down his almanacs and each year Hope refused Time, although she eagerly received his almanac. She was slow to age. Finally, however, her hair turned white and her face was a map of wrinkles; only her heart was green, like Time's. Both their hearts were green, eternally green. Time found her ancient but hardy, with an eternal smile on her lips, and asked her again to marry him. At first she refused; then she said, " 'All right, we are both old, the marriage won't last long.' " Old Time, however, took her to an infinite blue space where "the soul of one, gave the other's soul the kiss of eternity. All creation trembled with a shiver of delight." The green youthfulness of men's hearts became still more green and youthful. Henceforth Hope collaborated with Time in his almanacs. Each year she brightened the pages with cheerful prophecies, pictures, and anecdotes, and tied a green ribbon to each almanac.[105]

Natividade, we are told, was green with youthful hopes and her soul a clear blue with confidence. She inherited this hopeful nature, this belief in her destiny, from her father and to an even greater extent from her grandfather:[106] daughter of the Empire, she was still more the child of the older, Colonial Brazil. Her grandfather lived to be eighty-four.

> At that age he sincerely believed that all the delightful things of this world, from his morning coffee to his peaceful dreams, had been specially invented for him alone. The best cook on earth had been born in China for the unique purpose of leaving family, country, mother tongue, religion, everything, to come and cook him cutlets and make his tea for him. The stars gave *his* nights a splendid appearance, the moonlight too, and the rain, if it rained,

was to give him a rest from the sun. There he is now in the
São Francisco Xavier cemetery. If anyone could hear the
voice of the dead within their graves, you would hear him
shouting that it is time to close the gate and let no one else
in now that he is resting there for all eternity. He died sky
blue; if he had lived to be a hundred he would not have
had any other color.[107]

Like her grandfather, like the Hope of the apologue, Natividade was hardy, almost ageless: she was "eternal summer," and she was solid flesh. At forty she had the queenly
elegance of thirty.

> Her waist persisted in getting no bigger, the hips and
> bosom were the original upholstery.
> There are those regions in which spring is confused
> with autumn, as in our land, where the two seasons differ
> only in temperature. In her, not even in temperature. Fall
> had the heat of summer. At forty she was the same green
> lady with the very same sky blue soul.[108]

Flora's beauty had promised to be "long-lasting" like
Natividade's and "possessed of a life that might be great,"
but the ephemeral republic never blossomed into summer.
Even the old Brazil, spirit of illusory hopes, daughter of
Portugal, was not given "the kiss of eternity." She died.
"She should have lived much longer" (here we feel the
Machadean irony), but she was cut off in one of the city's
frequent epidemics.[109] Her belief in the predicted greatness
of her sons (Ayres tells us with dramatic irony) was "an illusion."[110] This society was not to fulfill its destiny. Brazil
was always to pursue, never to achieve its glorious future.
The old Brazil was dead. There was no reason to expect
anything of her sons: the frivolous bickering between political factions that were essentially alike would continue.
Ayres was left, however, and he too believed in the future,
he too believed in time,[111] and he kept forever young with
his European springs of wisdom.[112] We feel that Brazil will

live: *it* will not die between its past and future, as the republic died; it will perdure as long as Ayres does, and *he* shows no signs of buckling at the knees. As the novel ends, the flower of youth is still fresh in his buttonhole.[113] Brazil will continue to look forward to its future.

Thus, the story is incomplete, just as Braz Cubas's life was an unfinished book, as every man's life, as every people's history is incomplete, although life, history, time, go on. All men are destined never to fulfill the destiny they are capable of fulfilling: every soul is *"mal nata."*

Machado de Assis did not leave the matter there, however. The book had a sequel—*Ayres's Memorial*—because Machado de Assis was also Brazilian: he believed in Brazil's future and he believed in civilization's advance, for all its backward steps.

CHAPTER SIXTEEN

AYRES'S ODYSSEY

In *Esau and Jacob* the character Ayres, like the other personages, was in one sense an abstraction—of culture, intellectualism, enlightened good sense, reason. Although his roots were in Brazilian soil, he was not fiercely nationalist. He made a brief try for Brazil's love, failed, became her loyal servant, and carried a torch for her all his life;[1] but he had affairs with Spanish women and other Europeans.[2] He was, in his own words, "a bachelor by nature,"[3] recalling the ancient Greek belief that wisdom was an old maid— Athena. This intellectual, Ayres, in old age, wished he had sired the twins (the new political factions) because he loved their mother. "If they had been *his* sons they would not have disagreed."[4] He felt a special affinity for Flora (the republic) and wished he had been *her* father; then she would have endured.[5]

In the sequel to *Esau and Jacob*, *Ayres's Memorial*, Ayres is no longer an abstraction: he is a man but he is still a part of Assis's universal theme, the heart's struggle to attain love, and of the Dantean thesis that man does have a capacity for evolving and improving.

The events of *Ayres's Memorial* take place during the final two years of emancipation, 1888–1889, which was a part of the longer period that served as backdrop to *Esau and Jacob*. But *Ayres's Memorial* is not an allegory; it is not a living age preserved by Machadean magic. It is the personages, few in number, who dominate the scene, and they would be at home in any age. Ayres is there, and his sister, the faithful widow Rita. None of the others are out of *Esau and Jacob*; and, although they are in the same walks of life, their hearts are different, or in a different place. There is a self-made banker, but he is honest and kindly, concerned for all about him, and a banker's wife who does not belong to the social whirl. She is a homebody, a mother by nature who has neither chick nor child; she mothers strays. There is a benevolent plantation mistress. There is a breaking up of latifundia, the stubborn Portuguese blood persisting into modern Brazil, but in the cause of good—a golden age of the heart. The corrupting foreign influence that pervaded *Esau and Jacob* is nowhere present. "Home" is a theme that is begun on the first page with its first sentence.

> 1888—January 9
> Well, today marks a year since I returned from Europe for good. What reminded me of the date was that as I sat drinking my coffee I heard a broom peddler crying his wares in the street: "Brooms for sale! Dusters! Come buy dusters!" I have heard the cry other mornings but this time it brought to mind the day my ship touched port, and, I, pensioned off, came home to my own land, my own Rua do Cattete, my own language. Yes, it was the same cry I heard a year ago, in 1887; perhaps it was the same throat.

Later Ayres calls attention to the fact that he has not deliberately written a novel in his *Memorial*, as he did in *Esau and Jacob*; he has written only jottings in a diary. He never addresses a reader, as he frequently did in *Esau and Jacob*. Sometimes he addresses himself, "Old diplomat,"[6] "My dear old Ayres, old bumblehead."[7] Sometimes he addresses the paper in his notebook.[8] This exclusiveness gives us the feeling of reading over a person's shoulder secret thoughts not intended for our eyes. There seems no reason why we

should not piece together the young lovers' story that gradually unfolds from the diary's pages. It would seem that all
might read of the devotion between the old Darby-and-Joan
couple who foster young love and the lovers. Yet somehow
this twofold tale comes to us filtered not only through
Ayres's judicious observation and wit but also through his
emotions and imagination, so that we seem to be viewing a
revelation from within—we seem to have so entered Ayres's
being through his diary that we dream his dreams and see
his visions, and see *his* story—his own story—as it comes out
in hints and secret confessions to the paper in his notebook.
It is a continuation of his soul's journey, which was started
in *Esau and Jacob*, but *there* one got no more than brief
glimpses.

In *Esau and Jacob* Ayres, along with the rest of Brazil's
society, had come under foreign influence. It was not only
his affairs with foreign women, his predilection for foreign
authors—Homer, Xenophon, Horace, Fielding, and Dante,
and his addiction to European spring waters. In his first
paragraph of *Esau and Jacob* he introduced an English note
that from then on subtly vibrates through his whole story,
in that novel and in its sequel, *Ayres's Memorial*. "An old
Englishman [he wrote] who had wandered widely over
other lands confided to me many years ago in London that
all he really knew of London was his club, and it was all he
needed to know—of the metropolis and of the world." Brazilians, Portuguese, all Latins perhaps, tend to associate the
English, Anglo-Saxons, with a coldness, a dryness, an im-
passive logic and detachment such as that represented by
Ayres's Englishman.

Ayres himself partook of those qualities with his dry
humor, his nil admirari attitude, his classical education,
his measured manner of speaking; and he was definitely
Englished by Machado de Assis in at least two other ways—
first, by his name. An old and respected Portuguese name,

Ayres is also an easily recognized English name, and it may very well be for its Anglo-Saxon connotation that Assis chose to confer it on the old diplomat. The flower in his buttonhole, which serves to symbolize Brazil's eternal youth and hopefulness, strange as it may seem to us, was undoubtedly of English origin. It was not customary, it appears, for Brazilian and Portuguese gentlemen of the period to wear a boutonnière. When Luiza's maid (in the Queiroz novel) remarked Cousin Bazilio's foreign look she cited as conclusive evidence of this foreignness, that he had a bunch of flowers in his buttonhole.[9] In his column for May 14, 1893, Assis associated a flower in the lapel with British statesmen.

> Long live the flower. Gladstone never speaks in the House of Commons without wearing some on his morning coat; his great rival, now dead, [Disraeli] had the same vice. Imagine the effect on us, of Rio Branco or Itaborahy discussing fiscal matters with a rose on their chest and tell me if we are not a sad nation.[10]

In the same column Assis asserted his belief that the English govern themselves by the past, present, and future— that is, they are a wise, energetic nation with a controlled imagination. Again we are reminded of Ayres's character as portrayed in *Esau and Jacob*, and of his narrative attempts to reconcile the past, present, and future of Brazil in that novel.

It is not long before *memorialist* Ayres brings up the English. In the entries for the first day, January 9, 1888, his diary relates that his sister Rita invited him to visit the family burial plot in order to give thanks on the first anniversary of his return home. During the visit to the cemetery he noticed a beautiful young woman dressed in black, standing as if in prayer before a grave a short distance away. She brought to mind beautiful ladies he had known in Rome. His sister told him a story of romantic young love—

of Eduardo and Fidelia, whom Ayres likens to Romeo and
Juliet. Their fathers—one a wealthy planter, the other a
lawyer—were deadly political enemies in the province of
Parahyba. There was the love at first sight, occurring at the
theater. There followed the tyrannical actions of Baron
Santa Pia (Capulet), who "preferred to see his daughter
dead at his feet or mad rather than have his blood mixed
with that of the Noronhas (Montagues)." "Lady Capulet"
at first sided with her husband. Fidelia (Juliet), locked in
her room, wept endlessly and staged a hunger strike while
the servants sympathized. Campos, Baron Santa Pia's brother, like Prince Escalus of Verona, tried to conciliate the two
families, et cetera. But the outcome was different from that
of *Romeo and Juliet* because the passions of the principals
were not snuffed out in shortlived violence: they persisted
with sturdy Portuguese stubbornness. In this instance, Lady
Capulet, concerned for her daughter's health, persuaded
her lord to allow his daughter to marry her Romeo. He did,
but with the command never to darken his door again.
Eduardo (Romeo) was likewise disowned by his father. The
happiness of the young couple was brief, however. Eduardo
died of natural causes within a year. Fidelia, Rita further
informed Ayres, had daily tended Eduardo's grave for more
than two years.

"That doesn't mean she won't marry again," retorted
Ayres.

Rita, the faithful widow, replied that Fidelia would never
remarry, and she challenged her brother to just try and see
if he could win her hand. When Ayres protested his age—
sixty-two, Rita said *that* was no obstacle because he looked
to be no more than thirty; nevertheless she wagered he
could not persuade the widow Noronha to marry him.

Perhaps Ayres was put in mind of Juliet and Shakespeare
by two gravediggers he and Rita had passed on the way to
their family plot: these two dug and talked straight out of

Hamlet.[11] Then on January 20, Ayres wrote in his diary:

> Spent the day leafing through books, in particular, re-read some Shelley, and also some Thackeray. One consoled me for the other: the other freed me from the former's spell. Thus does genius complete genius, and the mind learn the various languages of the mind.

When he next saw Fidelia it was a line of Shelley that occurred to him.

Her mother dead and her father still unreconciled to her, Fidelia was living with her uncle, Campos, who happened to be a former schoolmate of Ayres's. She was also a kind of foster daughter to the banker Aguiar and his wife Carmo, at whose house she passed much of her time. Ayres's curiosity about the widow caused him to renew old acquaintance with both Campos and Aguiar. At his first meeting with her (at Aguiar's house) he found her beauty and charm exceeding expectation. After setting down each separate detail in his diary, he concludes:

> After the first few seconds of inspection, there is what I thought of her person. I did not immediately think in prose, but in verse as it happened, in a line of Shelley, whom I had been rereading at home, as I mentioned above, a verse from one of his stanzas of 1821:
>
> > *I can give not what men call love.*
>
> Just so I quoted it to myself in English; but then, right after, I repeated the poet's confession in our prose and with a close of my own composition: "I cannot give what men call love . . . and it's a pity!"[12]

It is this line of English poetry that launches Ayres on his odyssey; his diary is the odyssey's log. The odyssey is, in brief, to finish the poem, to end it with Shelley's "close," and without Portuguese comment. Shelley ends the poem as follows:

> I can give not what men call love,
>   But wilt thou accept not
> The worship the heart lifts above
>   And the Heavens reject not,—
> The desire of the moth for the star,
>   Of the night for the morrow,
> The devotion to something afar
>   From the sphere of our sorrow?[13]

Ayres and his poem are comparable to *Dom Casmurro*'s hero Santiago and his sonnet. Santiago never succeeded in filling in the missing lines of his sonnet—never succeeded in tying together the two ends of his life—he himself, he told us, was missing: that is he strayed from the path and never arrived at his promised destiny.[14] Ayres reached the end of *his* "poem": and his *memorial* to the event is a comedy with a happy ending.

In a prose fragment, Shelley defined love as

that powerful attraction towards all that we conceive, or fear or hope beyond ourselves. . . . We are born into the world and there is something within us which from the instant that we live, more and more thirsts after its likeness. . . . We dimly see within our intellectual nature a miniature as it were of our entire self, yet deprived of all that we condemn or despise; the ideal prototype of everything excellent or lovely that we are capable of conceiving as belonging to the nature of man . . . the meeting with an understanding capable of clearly estimating our own; an imagination which should enter into and seize upon the subtle and delicate peculiarities which we have delighted to cherish and unfold in secret; with a frame whose nerves, like the chords of two exquisite lyres, strung to the accompaniment of one delightful voice, vibrate with the vibrations of our own; and of a combination of all these in such proportion as the type within demands; this is the invisible and unattainable point to which love tends; and to attain which, it urges forth the powers of man to arrest the faintest shadow of that without the possession of which there is no rest nor respite to the heart over which it rules. . . . So soon as this want or power is dead, man becomes the living sepulchre of himself, and what yet survives is the mere husk of what once he was.[15]

Not only does Shelley's essay remind one of Assis's first letter to Carolina (quoted in chap. 4), but its last sentence epitomizes the theme of his novels in general, that love is the true manifestation of life, and that lack-love or self-love must be equated with death. In particular it describes the fate of both Felix, *Resurrection*'s hero, and of Dom Casmurro. Felix's heart "rose from the dead for a few days" then sank back into its tomb forever.[16] Santiago compared himself to a corpse that had been embalmed and painted by the undertaker.[17] Ayres, at the beginning of his diary on "January 9, 1888," found himself in a somewhat similar situation, but, as it turned out, he was not beyond resuscitation. His coldness, however, is thoroughly established in the graveyard scene—by his skepticism toward Fidelia's "eternal" devotion to her dead husband. Later he smiled incredulously at Rita's romantic account of Fidelia and her Eduardo,[18] and he included all conjugal love in his cynical doubts, in his reply, which follows.

> From what you tell me, while I was over there abroad representing Brazil, Brazil was turning into an Abraham's bosom. You, the Aguiar couple, the Noronha couple, all the married couples in short were becoming models of everlasting bliss.[19]

The graveyard, I believe, is intended to stand as a symbol for both Fidelia and Ayres—not for Rita, however. Rita's black tresses (sexual love) had been buried with her husband's body, but her heart was not entombed. True to her husband's memory and to her vow never to remarry, she still had love and trust to lavish on the living: on her brother, on all married couples, on young lovers, even on business associates.[20] Fidelia's heart *was* entombed (as we are to learn), and Ayres evidently regarded his own as dead. On a later page of the diary where he describes his insensibility and the well-preserved cadavers in his psyche he remarks, "As I reread those last few lines I get the feeling that I am a gravedigger."[21] We already knew from *Esau and Jacob*, and he repeats the fact for us, that *he* married for the sake of his career, and, like Santiago, buried his wife in the old country and forgot her.[22] Like both Felix and Santiago he had been a philanderer. He was "a bachelor by nature," he says. He never had a child and never felt the lack of one.[23]

Still, even though he tries to convey the impression that his heart was a tomb, his capacity for love was *not* dead. Rather, his years of diplomacy abroad had been a banishment from love, banishment from home. Among the changing seasons of those colder climes he had longed for the warmth, "the eternal summer" of his native Rio de Janeiro, for the warm tones of his native tongue, in which, presumably, one could not lie or deceive.[24]

The final stage of his homeward voyage began on his diary's first page when he discovered "new original life" in his native Portuguese. Next, piqued by curiosity and doubt about his countrywoman Fidelia and her show of devotion to her dead husband's memory, he fell under the spell of her physical charms. Sexual desire soon gave way to aesthetic appreciation of her beauty, he says.[25] Later, what he calls his "aesthetic tendencies" became an admiration for her mind and spirit and a trusting belief in her "heart," a longing for her happiness—a disinterested love for her that embraced all those who loved her or wished her well.[26] Thus Ayres arrived at his destination—at the end of his poem. A trace of the physical attraction to Fidelia persisted almost to the end, but even at its strongest it was nine-tenths unsubstantial dream and laughter. When he first quoted the line of Shelley to himself (at the Aguiars' anniversary dinner) with his own "close," "I cannot give what men call love . . . and it's a pity," he added:

> This confession did not lessen my cheerfulness. Thus, when Dona Carmo took my arm, I went along as to a wedding feast. Aguiar gave his arm to Fidelia, and seated himself between her and his wife. I set down these details with no other purpose than to explain how the man and wife, as they sat facing each other, were between their friend Fidelia and me—so that *we* could hear the beating of their two hearts—a pardonable hyperbole, which only means that in both of us, in me at least, there reverberated those twenty-five years of harmony and mutual solace.[27]

Not only did Ayres's heart continue to beat ever more steadily in that measured rhythm, there occurred true resurrections of dead hearts—Fidelia's, Tristão's, Cesaria's. And it was through Aguiar and Carmo that the changes took place. The old couple's love for each other spilled over in love for their foster children, Fidelia and Tristão—to their regret they had no children of their own.[28] Ayres, too, and all the others, even dumb animals[29] came within the circle of their love's radiant warmth. It was Carmo's maternal affection that first drew the young widow from her exclusive devotion to the dead. Finally Fidelia's whole heart came alive: this is symbolized by her return to her music, which she had abandoned when her husband Eduardo died. (Music, in Assis's symbolic language, is always love of one form or another.) When her uncle heard her playing the piano at seven o'clock in the morning, he exclaimed, "What resurrection is this?"[30] There was the other foster child, Tristão, whom Ayres called the Aguiars' resurrected son, "the son that died and came back to life."[31] A further indication of Tristão's initial coldness is the gratuitous detail that he came from Portugal on the "English packet."[32] Campos, Rita, and the rest all felt the warmth emanating

from the Aguiars—even the wickedly witty Cesaria. As
Cousin Justina of *Dom Casmurro* incarnated in living flesh
Santiago's meaner side, so Cesaria, a more charming, sophisticated Justina, gives voice to Ayres's cynicism and distrust with her sarcastic shafts at Fidelia's love and at her
professed indifference to worldly goods. But finally Cesaria
too was won over, and Ayres hymned the "god of love" in
his *Memorial* after he had described the event.

> The sweetness and enthusiasm with which she addressed
> [Fidelia] compensated in great part for the evil she had
> spoken of her, and in another way confirmed an old idea
> of mine . . . about the co-ownership of the world. In this
> instance, God triumphed over the devil with a smile so
> sweet and gentle as to make one forget the existence of
> His vile partner.[33]

Cesaria's husband, however, remained unregenerate, "a
man who would kick a messenger who brought him word he
had won the grand prize in the sweepstakes."[34]

The persons undergoing the changes of heart affected one
another, but they affected Ayres especially, and it was
Fidelia's "resurrection" that had the most powerful effect
upon him. His "return to love" might almost be said to
parallel hers. But *all* those miracles of regeneration were,
for him, waystations—magic islands where he put into port
for repose and refreshment and to wait for favoring winds.
The Aguiars' hearth was the court of Alcinous and his
queen, Arete, on the island of Scheria, where Ulysses was
loaded with gifts and sped on the final leg of his homeward
voyage. In *Esau and Jacob* Ayres compared himself to
Ulysses at the court of Alcinous[35] and intimated he had
passed his life abroad telling lies.[36] His philandering practices, hinted at in his *Memorial*, were well established in
the earlier novel.[37] We were also told he had a special love
for his own land, and it happened he was tired of other
places.[38] In the *Memorial* he talks of unfurling the sails of

his sagacity[39] and refers to his diary as "vagabondage"[40]—for his doubts, like adverse winds, frequently carried him off course. Old diplomatic habits would persist—tricks of the trade: he would fall back on a special smile he had, and a look of intense interest, for extracting information. At times he was not above invoking the "Muse of Diplomacy," that is, the goddess of Guile and Persuasion. He had Ulysses' doubting skepticism and that wily Greek's power of changing his manner to suit the occasion.

He did not easily rid himself of his cynical doubts: he doubted the widow Fidelia's devotion to the dead Noronha, and then her new love for Tristão. He doubted the unselfishness of Carmo's love for Fidelia and Tristão. He doubted Tristão's sincerity. He suspected a flirtation between Fidelia and Osorio. He looked with disapproval upon Aguiar's sentimentality over a dead dog as being out of keeping with a banker's duties. He indulged in cruel delight over old Noronha's sarcastic letter to his son. He could not help but laugh when Cesaria called Fidelia a "dead body,"[41] even though he had come to believe first that her dead husband, Noronha, was fixed eternally in her heart, and finally under the power of his own love he came to recognize the sincerity of her love for Tristão also, because the later love was a "resurrection" of the former love.

> The dead stay in the cemetery, and there they have the love of the living, along with their flowers and remembrances. This will happen even to Fidelia when she goes there. This is what has happened to Noronha, who is there. The question is not to actually break this bond but to keep life's law from destroying what properly belongs to life *and* death. I believe in Fidelia's "two" loves: I have come to believe that they form one continuous, unbroken love.
>
> When I was an active member of the diplomatic corps I did not believe so many things could be all stuck up together. I was suspicious and distrustful. But if I retired

it was for the very purpose of believing in the sincerity of others. Let the fellows who are still in active service do the distrusting.[42]

Retirement gradually restored him to his original nature.[43] He repented his old diplomatic training and reproved its methods of suspicion and deceit.[44] "Mend that tongue, old diplomat," he writes.[45] He quelled his doubts. He reconciled himself with "our land,"[46] that is, Brazil the home of love. He came to have a father's love not only for the Aguiars' foster children Tristão and Fidelia but for all children—he who had never felt the want of a child. And in this love he himself became "young."

> It seems I have acquired from the Aguiars a taste for children, or a fondness for them, which is a more elegant expression. Walking just now along the Rua da Glória, I came upon seven children, boys and girls, of various size, who went abreast, hand in hand, in a line. Their age, their laughter and liveliness drew my attention and I stopped on the sidewalk to watch them. They were all so full of grace and seemed such friends that I began to laugh with pleasure. The story would have ended there, had it not been for what one of them said—a little girl who saw me as I stood laughing and said to her companions, "Look at that big boy laughing and smiling at us."
>
> The words showed me what a child's eyes are. Me, with this great white moustache and gray hair, they called me a big boy! Most likely they give this name to a person's height without asking for his birth certificate.
>
> I let the children go by as I made the reflection. They went, jumping, stopping, pulling to the right and to the left, sometimes breaking the line, then joining hands again. I do not know where they separated and scattered. I do know that after ten minutes I saw nothing of them; but I saw other children, alone or in pairs. Some of them carried bundles or baskets that pressed down on their heads or were heavy upon their backs. Perhaps it is due

to having carried nothing in childhood that I now have
the boyish aspect that the other children saw in me. No,
no, it was not that. Each age gives its own aspect to things.
Childhood naturally sees "green." These children, too,
if I laughed, might find that "the big boy was laughing
and smiling at them." But I went along in serious mood,
thinking—perhaps pitying their weariness. They, not see-
ing that my white hair ought to have appeared black to
them, said nothing; they went silently on their way, and
I on mine.[47]

A few minutes later, during his nap before dinner, Ayres
dreamed:

All the children of the world—with burdens or without them—made a great circle around me and danced a
dance that was so joyous that I almost burst with laughter.
They all spoke of "this big boy that laughs so much."

Tristão had already confirmed the little girl's words the
month before when he told Ayres, "A spirit like yours, sir,
never grows old."[48] Ayres had come to have a child's belief
in the love and good intentions of others—Aguiar, Carmo,
Fidelia, Tristão, yes, and Cesaria. He had come to understand even his servant José's rather dishonest and devious
way of "loving the boss."[49] He no longer looked with suspicion upon a banker who shed tears over the last illness and
death of a pet dog.

On the last page of his diary Ayres intimates that he has
come to know love—in its essence. He found it, not in the
young lovers but in the old ones. He saw it and recognized
it in an expression on the faces of the couple, Aguiar and
Carmo, and in the attitude of their bodies, where there appeared "the solace of their memory of themselves." Ayres's
words are reminiscent of the anniversary dinner a year and
a half before, when "the happiness of those twenty-five years
of harmony and solace" that he heard in their beating hearts
reverberated in his own. His odyssey was over: he, Brazilian

Ulysses, had come home to *his* heart and regained his patrimony—love. He had reached the end of Shelley's poem, he had something better to give than "what men call love." It was not to Fidelia that he offered it, however, but to Carmo and Aguiar.

Not only does Ayres's *Memorial* bring to a conclusion the "odyssey" he began in *Esau and Jacob*, it ends that novel in another way. Flora has here become the hardy Fidelia, who resembles Flora in many ways but is not fragile. Fidelia will persist: she is gentle but determined, energetic, capable of decisive action, and she is the "spirit of order."[50] She succeeded in what Flora attempted; she reconciled the past and the future. On the eve of marrying Tristão, she placed flowers on her former husband's grave. "I imagined her," writes Ayres, "before the dead husband as if he were the future husband, making of the two a single man belonging to the present."[51] Noronha had been a Brazilian who traveled about Europe; Tristão was Brazilian-born but a naturalized Portuguese. The "home" at the end of Ayres's voyage is of Portuguese origin. There is a simple old-fashioned quality about the personages portrayed. The corrupting foreign atmosphere that pervaded *Esau and Jacob* is nowhere evident. And under the influence of "home," the English flower in Ayres's lapel—like Maeterlinck's bluebird—has changed color and become a Luso-Brazilian perennial.

CHAPTER SEVENTEEN

ASSIS'S ODYSSEY OR QUEEN CAROLINE'S HEAD

As mentioned in the preceding chapter, Ayres ostensibly kept his diary for his own amusement; but perhaps it was written for the reading pleasure of one other person, namely, Machado de Assis—who might be called Ayres's alter ego, or, vice versa, Ayres was more likely his. Some readers have identified Assis with the personage Ayres.[1] Although complete identification is not plausible, Assis probably loved this character and shared many of his opinions and feelings. There is, however, a character in the book whom Machado de Assis positively identified in letters to friends as his wife Carolina:[2] that is, the banker Aguiar's good wife Carmo—affectionate, motherly, kindly, the darling of old and young, loving her husband as much after twenty-five years "as on that first day."[3] This portrait Ayres repeats with countless variations on page after page of his *memorial*. For the ordinary reader there is perhaps a little too much Carmo; for the daydreaming widower Assis there would no doubt never be enough.

Such a conclusion is justified, I believe, by a curious phenomenon in the manuscript of *Ayres's Memorial* as well as by the novel's title and epigraph. Assis's harping on his loneliness in letters to friends during the last four years may also be taken as corroborative evidence. Carolina died October 20, 1904.[4] After that date, his letters, which had al-

ways been full of enthusiastic literary plans and discoveries,
with little mention of himself, are seldom free from the sorrowful note of complaint that permeates the following excerpt from a letter written to Joaquim Nabuco at the Brazilian Embassy in London, November 20, 1904.

> My dear Nabuco,
>   So far away, in other surroundings, you received the
> news of my great misfortune, and you straightway sent
> your sympathy by telegram, and the only word* with
> which I thanked you is the same one that I now send. She
> is gone, the better part of my life; and here I am alone
> in the world. The solitude does not trouble me, rather
> I am grateful for it because it is a means of living with her,
> of hearing her, of feeling the thousand little attentions
> that this companion of thirty-five years of married life
> showed me; but there is no imagination that does not
> wake, and the waking increases the emptiness. We were
> old, and I thought to die before her. She would have had
> relatives to console her. I have none. I have only friends,
> and truly they are of the best; but life has scattered them
> in space, in interests and in the different careers that each
> pursues. Here I remain, then, in the same house with its
> familiar furnishings. Everything reminds me of my sweet
> and gentle Carolina.

The strange thing about the *Memorial*'s manuscript—[5]
written entirely in Assis's hand—is this. The names of the
two main female characters, Carmo and Fidelia, were constantly written one for the other, then crossed out and corrected. No less than ninety-eight times Fidelia was first
written, then crossed and Carmo written above or below
the line. Conversely, Carmo was crossed eighty-eight times
and Fidelia written in its stead. The less important and less
lovable character, Cesaria—she of the witty tongue—is confused with Fidelia at least six times. The only confusion in

* *Obrigado, thank you.*

the names of male characters, on the other hand, is: Aguiar is wrongly written for Ayres once, crossed and corrected, and for Tristão once. Also once "o moço" (the young man), that is, Tristão, is crossed and corrected to Aguiar.

Some have thought that Machado de Assis was an old man completely broken in health and spirit[6]—an opinion not borne out by the facts. *Ayres's Memorial* was published in July, 1908.[7] It was written during the preceding year.[8] Assis's activity for several years before, even during the year of his death—his heavy responsibilities as comptroller for his Ministry, his personal correspondence, and his correspondence, speeches, and other tasks as president of the Academy of Letters—would seem to preclude the supposition that he was a feeble old man in his dotage.

The testimony of friends as to the keenness of his intellect and memory right up to the end must also be taken into consideration. Oliveira Lima, in his memorial speech in Paris, April 3, 1909, said, "His death agony was cruel but short, and up to the last moment he kept the litheness of spirit and mind that was his dominant quality and of which his style was the image." He did not die, said Lima, from progressive hardening of the arteries of the intelligence and sensibility (The physical cause of Assis's death was given as arteriosclerosis.), but "fathered beautiful books right up to the last." Mário de Alencar wrote (in 1910) that even during his final illness his mind still had all the strength of youth, and that he was planning to write another book.[9] Letters to friends written within two months, and even within the month, of his death bear the usual stamp of vigor.

Finally there is the testimony of his own hand. Correspondence for the Ministry, to his friends and colleagues, to his publisher, and for the Academy, as well as the printer's copy of *Ayres's Memorial*, are in his own hand—the writing as good as it ever was, even though *he* has a way of saying it is worse, adding however, "It was always terrible."[10] Certainly the manuscript of *Ayres's Memorial*, written in 1907, the year before he died, is extremely legible, as are letters written during the same period; and none of the writing differs noticeably from that of previous years.

The confusion is apparently not just a confusion of names. If it were, why would there not be a comparable confusion among names of male characters? Besides, in a number of instances it is seen to be not a simple confusion of names that occurs but rather of persons. "Carmo," for example, is corrected not to "Fidelia" but to "a viuva" (the widow), five times; and to "a moça" (the girl or young woman), twice—both of whom of course *are* Fidelia. The cause of the confusion, I believe, is this: both Fidelia and Carmo are portraits of Carolina at different ages, under different conditions, showing forth different aspects of the original. Assis acknowledged Carmo—that is, when pressed by his friends—as a portrait of his dead wife. Ayres dreamed, awake and asleep, of Fidelia playing the piano, appearing to him and conversing with him, promising to marry him . . . and he had urges to hug her, kiss her hand, and so on. These, I believe, were Machado's dreams of the *young* Carolina. It might be noted that twenty-three times Assis wrote the diminuitive D. Carmelita, crossed it and wrote Fidelia, crossed Fidelia and wrote Carmo. Once, Carmelita is corrected to Fidelia alone. Another interesting slip of the pen occurs in conjunction with the one instance in which Assis wrote Tristão for Aguiar (mentioned above): he had first written "D. Fidelia e Tristão" (Dona Fidelia and Tristão), then corrected it to "D. Carmo e Aguiar."

Even Cesaria's wit could be Carolina's. Carolina came of a witty family; her brother Faustino was a satiric poet; Miguel, in his letters to Machado, frequently displays sarcasm and a certain rough wit.[11] The name Cesaria suggests Carolina's middle name, Augusta,[12] or a combination of Carolina and Augusta. Apparently Assis had considered a less kind name for this character, Eulalia, because that name is written and corrected to Cesaria twelve times. Eulalia, meaning "kindly spoken," no doubt referred sarcastically to the lady's malicious tongue.

As Carmo represents the loving wife of many years, Fidelia would represent both the courted bride and the young widow in the event Machado had died young. Rita perhaps represents Carolina as widow if he had died at a more advanced age. There is no confusion over Rita's name, but Rita was a personage already established in *Esau and Jacob* as Ayres's sister, "saint of impossible situations," and symbol of old-style devoted widowhood. Her relationship is to Ayres rather than to the lonely devil Assis who at times crept into Ayres's body like some New Testament demon. Assis in letters to friends, as, for example, in the one to Nabuco quoted above, mentions conjuring up Carolina's presence in his lonely house. Ayres with his *memorial* does just that *for* Assis. The last three lines of the famous sonnet "*A Carolina*" seem to refer to the same mystical practice. I append the original with a verse translation by Ann Stanford.

A Carolina[13]

Querida, ao pé do leito derradeiro
Em que descansas dessa longa vida,
Aqui venho e virei, pobre querida,
Trazer-te o coração do companheiro.

Pulsa-lhe aquêle afecto verdadeiro
Que, a despeito de tôda a humana lida,
Fêz a nossa existência apetecida
E num recanto pôs um mundo inteiro.

Trago-te flôres,—restos arrancados
Da terra que nos viu passar unidos
E ora mortos nos deixa e separados.

Que eu, se tenho nos olhos malferidos
Pensamentos de vida formulados,
São pensamentos idos e vividos.

To Caroline

Beloved, to the marriage bed, the last
On which you rest from that far life,
I come, and I shall come, poor dearest,
To bring you the heart of a companion.

There beats in it true affection
Which in spite of all human troubles
Made our life worth desiring
And set a whole world in one dark corner.

I bring you flowers—remains torn by force
From the earth which watched us pass together
And now leaves us dead and apart.

And I, if my eyes, mortally wounded,
Hold thoughts rising up out of life
They are thoughts of what once lived and has ended.

The sonnet's second quatrain reminds one of Ayres when
he heard Carmo's and Aguiar's hearts beating and felt "those
twenty-five years of harmony and solace" reverberate in his
own breast.

Although neither Assis nor his friends specifically mentioned the fictional husband Aguiar, we must suppose that *he* bore some resemblance to Machado de Assis; so that from this character we can glean biographical details about the original and about the relationship that existed between that legendary couple the Assises.

Since Machado de Assis admitted Carmo to be a true life portrait of Carolina, we may (I suppose) assume that all her physical and spiritual attributes were actually those of his wife and that at least some of Aguiar's were also Machado's. In minor historical details there seem to be some irreconcilable divergencies between truth and fiction. Two of these differences are more apparent than real, however, and, if we take Fidelia as an aspect of Carolina, and Tristão as the young Machado, the rest tend to disappear.

Ayres's sketch of Carmo stresses the following traits: her fine mind, her affectionate nature and maternal type of love, "she is all motherly feeling," he says; her devotion to her husband, whom "she loves as much, or more, after twenty-five years as on that first day"; her interest in literature; her ability as interior decorator. She had a kind of architectural gift for arranging a house in such a manner that the eye was pleased and satisfied, and comfort assured. There is her religious devotion—sincere but unostentatious, her industry, cheerfulness, sociability with old and young, her gift for conversation and nice use of Portuguese, her youthful air, her bright eyes, and their gentle expression, her low voice and laugh that was "like no other," her smile that "showed the tips of her teeth."[14]

Aguiar's devotion to his wife is comparable to hers for him. And we find in Ayres's Aguiar, the unaffected cordiality, curiosity, but discreet manners, keenness of memory and observation, enthusiasm, and love of children ascribed to Assis by José Veríssimo, Mário de Alencar, and others.[15] We do not find, however, the asocial "timidity" constantly mentioned by most writers. Like his wife, Aguiar is sociable and hospitable, but a family man; he is all husband. He tells political experiences of 1859–1861 during his bachelor days, with apparent relish but without regrets. "He is not a man for public life: family is everything—his wife and now his foster son and daughter."[16] He is sentimental about dogs.[17] He is sensitive to word and look. His eyes reply to the expresson in his wife's, and the man and wife hold silent conversations with eyes alone and an occasional smile.[18] The two persons have become "one single being";[19] in particular "Aguiar is nothing without Carmo."[20] Their marriage is *"aconchego e união"* (sheltering warmth and oneness),[21] and it is symbolized by the "conversation chair" in which not only the fictional couple rocked back and forth facing each other but also the real Carolina and Machado.[22] All this reminds us of the sonnet and the letters to friends. Everything within and without the book points to the exclusive nature of the relationship between Machado and Carolina. The bluff Capistrano de Abreu, for example, in a letter to Francisco Ramos Paz (October 27, 1904), has the mystified air of one who has been left out of things. "Tomorrow [he writes] the Mass of the seventh day will be celebrated for Machado de Assis's wife. I saw her two or three times; I have no idea what she was like. I went to her funeral."[23] Apparently very few of Assis's friends knew her—only the very old friends: Paz, the Mendonças, Nabuco, Mário de Alencar, José Veríssimo.

We know of nothing really to contradict the characterization of our two couples—the Aguiars and the Assises; but what of their biographies—factual and fictional?

Aguiar married Carmo when he was a bookkeeper, and rose to be a banker. His wife, an only child, before marriage, lived with her mother, who came from Nova Friburgo, and father, who was a Swiss watchmaker from the same city. The marriage was "favored by everyone." Soon after the marriage Aguiar lost his position when his employer's business failed, and he worked at various jobs; Carmo weathered the hard times with cheerfulness, bolstered up her husband, made furnishings for their house with her own hands. Aguiar had a poetic flair which evinced itself in his conversation though he had never written anything. "If he had written," comments Ayres, "[Carmo] would have found him better than anyone." Aguiar liked to read but had little time for it; his wife read, and made resumés, analyses, and comments, which her husband absorbed and remembered, for he had a fine memory.[24]

It goes without saying, Machado de Assis had never been a bookkeeper, and he was never a banker. His wife Carolina was of foreign extraction but Portuguese not Swiss. Her father *had* been in the jewelry business, in Portugal, not Brazil. Far from being an only child she had three brothers and two sisters; and there is doubt that "*all* favored the marriage." The legend is that at least some of the brothers and sisters opposed;[25] and Assis's two letters to Carolina would seem to bear that out. The hard times following their marriage were real, as we have already seen.[26] Carmo's devotion in all its details may be presumed to be Carolina's devotion. It seems, too, that Carolina kept notes on her reading and that two of her notebooks are preserved in the Brazilian Academy of Letters.[27] We may assume that the real Carolina also had a keen interest in literature with a certain amount of critical ability and that her speech was chaste and elegant.[28] Ayres notes that if Aguiar "had written, Carmo would have found him better than anyone."[29] Since Assis *did* write, the natural conclusion is that Carolina found him "better than anyone." In a letter to José Veríssimo (February 4, 1905), Assis mentions that his "companion" always read his books when they came off the press. And in the first letter of courtship (quoted in chap. 4), he singles out her mind and heart—her idealism, sensitivity, and reason—as rare gifts. Along with Ayres, I believe Carolina found Assis's books "better than anyone's," perhaps because she understood them better than anyone.

The companionship of Assis and his Caroline is surely beyond doubt. And the Aguiars' hospitality and social life with its weekly "at homes,"[30] would appear to reflect that of the real couple to judge from Assis's correspondence. We know too that Assis played chess, won championships at it—if one can call a chess a social pastime, and that he sometimes danced the "Reel."[31]

The difference in the couple's ages has been altered: Aguiar is ten years Carmo's senior although Carolina was five years older than Machado. But perhaps she seemed younger to him—in spirit, experience, or even in physical stamina; for some reason he had expected to die before her.[32]

As for making Aguiar a bookkeeper, then banker—and a rich one at that, that is perhaps not so strange as it seems at first glance. Assis's duties as a bureaucrat had a good deal in common with Aguiar's as a banker. Aguiar's bank was deep in agriculture and all types of rural properties, especially the large plantations and ranches employing slaves.[33] And, of course, both the bookkeeper and the banker dealt with money and numerical figures. Machado de Assis had entered the Ministry of Agriculture, Commerce, and Public Works as an "amaneuensis," January 7, 1874, at the age of thirty-three, less than three years after his marriage. He rose to become director of the accounting division. This Ministry's functions were extensive. It had under its supervision, agriculture in all its phases—agricultural schools and institutes, agricultural colonies, agro-industries, sugar plantations, regulation of the big sugar mills and the whole industry, pest control, distribution of plants; mines and metal manufacture; hunting and fishing; botanical museums, art museums, public parks, and international expositions; all public works—street illumination, water control and supply, street and highway construction and maintenance, railroads, navigation, rivers, canals, harbors; all industries and their regulation; labor, including the enforcing of laws governing slaves. In short, this Ministry combined the functions now performed by five ministries, Machado de Assis was called upon to pass judgment, and make recommendations on violations of the various laws and regulations under the supervision of the Ministry—as for example the many servile laws leading up to the freeing of the slaves. Practically all the Empire's bills, that is, demands for payment—and later the Republic's—passed across his desk. He served the Ministry almost thirty-four years, under thirty-six ministers, from January 7, 1874 to June 1, 1908, three months before his death. At the time of the ministerial reorganization January 1, 1898, he was retired with full pay for not being a professional engineer as required by the regulations, but he was recalled to active service on November 15 of the same year.[34]

Thus, we see, banker Aguiar's and comptroller Assis's work had much in common. But what of their "wealth"? Aguiar owned "bank stock," "houses," and *"apólices"* in the amount of over two hundred contos (two hundred thousand milreis);[35] Assis did not own "houses," not even the house in which he had lived for twenty-four years; it belonged to Carolina's brother Miguel and his wife and to their heirs.[36] Apólices Assis *did* possess: they are listed in both his wills, not two hundred contos' worth, however. The 1898 will lists eight; the 1906, twelve.[37] With this word "apólice," I have an idea we are participating in a household joke—as perhaps "Machadinho is a capitalist he owns an apólice." At least, Assis, in his writings, used this word as a symbol for wealth and with comic overtones. For example, Braz Cubas, in describing the eulogy made by one of his friends at his funeral, exclaims, "No, I don't regret the twenty apólices I left him in my will."[38] Ayres also possessed some few apólices, but presumably nothing like Aguiar's hundreds.[39]

To return to Carmo and Carolina, why does Ayres specifically mention that *all* Carmo's family approved the match. I have suggested that Fidelia is the young Carolina—and Fidelia did, like Juliet, marry in opposition to her family's commands," just as, it is thought, Carolina married Machado in opposition to her family's wishes. The young Fidelia, although a vigorous spirit, has many attributes of the old Carmo, so that Ayres notes their harmony as they talk together: "in spite of the white hair and the black, they appear to be sisters."[40] His description of Fidelia's dress—dark colors, high neck, long sleeves, simple jewels—is a description of Dona Carolina's appearance in her photographs.[41]

If Fidelia represents the young Carolina, then the young lover Tristão, who wins the widow Fidelia's hand for a second marriage, represents the young Machado. As his namesake of story came out of a strange land to charm away Queen Isolde from her husband King Marc, so this modern Tristan stole away Fidelia from her dead Noronha. In one of the two letters to Carolina,[42] Machado tells her that one cause of his attraction to her is that she has "suffered"—which may mean that she had some attachment to the dead or to old memories. Here then we would have, with a slight geographical adjustment: Isolde (Carolina) landed on Tristan's (Machado's) Brazilian soil, and he charmed her away from her sufferings in the land of Portugal. Ayres, at least, if not Aguiar, looks upon the course of Tristão's love of the widow with the amused indulgence of an old man looking back on his own youth.[43] Perhaps Ayres not only dreamed Machado's dreams for him, but also served as his memory; and when Ayres felt the Aguiar couple's happiness and his own heart beating in sympathetic tempo, it was Assis looking back on his life with Carolina. Ayres, as we have seen, made a spiritual voyage that brought him home to his birthright. In true Portuguese style, however, this latter-day Ulysses was pushed to safe harbor mainly by women: Rita, sisterly love; Fidelia, conjugal and young love; and Carmo, who combined all woman's affection, maternal, wifely, filial, sisterly, and the innocent grace of young love—although Campos, Aguiar, Tristão, and Osorio were not without their effect.

There was a stowaway on Ayres's ship—one Machado de Assis. He too associated himself and *his* voyage with Ulysses. The epigraph—Machado de Assis's epigraph—to this novel consists of two short quotations from two medieval Portuguese love poems, which, taken together, form a single thought or message.

> Em Lixboa, sobre lo mar,
> Barcas novas mandey lavrar . . .
> > *Cantiga de* Joham Zorro.

> Para veer meu amigo
> Que talhou preyto comigo,
> Alá vou, madre.
> Para veer meu amado
> Que mig'a preyto talhado,
> Alá vou, madre.
> > *Cantiga d'el-rei* Dom Denis.

In Lisbon by the sea, I ordered new ships built . . .

To see my friend (lover), who promised me a tryst, I am off, mother. To see my beloved, who keeps tryst with me, I am off, mother.

"Lisbon," as Assis himself had once mentioned, "was, for Brazil, all Europe."[44] In his preface to the book published before *Ayres's Memorial, Relics from an Old House,* he had addressed his "leitor amigo," "dear reader" or "friend reader." The *Memorial's* double epigraph, then, may mean nothing more than: with this new book published in Europe (actually in Paris), I visit my reading public.

Lisbon, however, has other meanings, other connotations. For example, Lisbon has been called "the permanent capital of the Lusitanian world," by a modern Portuguese writer, who explains, "Without Lisbon it would not have been possible to create a true national literature."[45] If Lisbon represented the Portuguese Muse to Machado de Assis, the meaning of the epigraph—with its talk of sea and shipbuilding and lovers voyaging to keep tryst—might be somewhat as follows.

I built a ship out of poetic Portuguese (this book), in which I am carried by the sea (love) to keep tryst with my true public, my true friend, who understands me *and* my works, to my beloved Carolina.[46]

An interpretation not at all discordant with the facts, for we have seen from Assis's letters and from the sonnet "To Caroline" that he communed, in imagination, with his dead wife.

But where does Ulysses come into *this* voyage? Ulysses is a hero dear to the Portuguese heart. According to an ancient, and well-discredited, tradition, Lisbon was founded by that wayward Greek, from whom it took its name, formerly spelled, Olyssipo. Ayres himself alluded to the old tradition with a line from the *Lusiads*. As he stood on the sands in Rio de Janeiro, the sea coming and going along the shore seemed to beckon him to set sail for the harbor of famed Ulysses' city.[47]

The Portuguese word *memorial* of this novel's title, as already mentioned, has more than one meaning. It means notebook or memorandum book, and Ayres kept such a book or diary. It means memorial or monument, and Ayres's memorial, in that sense, commemorates his successful struggle—his odyssey—to regain love. But the word *memorial* also means "a petitionary letter containing an exposition

of fact and circumstances and soliciting attention to them."
In this sense the word has been used of Ulysses' petition to
Alcinous. As pointed out above, Ayres compared himself
to Ulysses at the court of Alcinous. Indeed, Assis's friend
and colleague Araripe Júnior had written in 1898 a long
article entitled, "Ulysses and the Modern World," in which
Ulysses is represented as a symbol of "the civilizing genius
of the Mediterranean race." Ulysses (says Araripe) civilized
men through the influence of language, through eloquence
applied to social betterment, through his experience of life,
his good sense, and a witty, ingenious deference to natural
forces. He was a civilizing force that resulted in an infinite
sympathy for man . . . leading to the feeling for humanity
and world brotherhood that distinguishes the modern age.[48]

Not only does Araripe's portrait of the diplomatic Ulysses
fit our Ayres, the author (Araripe) dwells admiringly and
at length on Ulysses' *"memorial,"* that is, the elaborate and
artfully eloquent plea that he made to Alcinous and his
court for help with a ship to carry him home to Ithaca.

The word *memorial* in this sense, it seems to me, applies
to Assis's situation: perhaps with a double significance.
Ayres's diary serves as Assis's *memorial* that will take him
home to Carolina, in spirit—and also in death. At the time
he composed this book he said it would be his last. It is possible that he later changed his mind and planned another
novel, as Mário de Alencar reported.

Sorrowful or not, Machado de Assis, as he demonstrated
over and over again, could not resist witty word-play. I
believe there is still another meaning in the title *Memorial
de Ayres*—a joke on himself in an allusion to David Copperfield's mad friend Mr. Dick, who also attempted to compose
a memorial. Mr. Dick could not keep King Charles the
First's head out of his Memorial no matter how hard he
tried or how many pens he blunted. Senhor Assis's aman-
uensis Ayres could not keep out of *his* memorial the femi-

nine of Charles—Caroline. She turned up in all his women. Mr. Dick asked David how the trouble could have got out of *Charles's* head into *his*.[49] Ayres, the level-headed Ulysses-like man wrote, "What! I can't leave off writing the *Memorial*. Here I am again with the pen in my hand. Truly, it gives a certain pleasure to pour out on paper the things that want to come out of the head by way of memory and reflection."[50]

EPILOGUE

CHAPTER EIGHTEEN

BIOGRAPHY
AND AUTOBIOGRAPHY

It might be noted that Ayres expends very little wit and humor on Carmo, whereas he holds all the other characters (including himself) up to ridicule. Certainly he does not spare Carmo's husband, the banker Aguiar. We have seen that Ayres had reservations about a banker who was sentimental over dogs. On another occasion he interrupted Aguiar's melancholy over a human being with a financial question that immediately changed the sentimentalist back into "a bank president" all milreis and mortgages.[1] It is to be supposed that, as the husband of Carmo, who stands for Carolina, Aguiar was intended by Assis as a portrait of himself; and, although not a government employee, Aguiar does have about him a certain bureaucratic dryness.

There is no doubt that Machado de Assis had a soft spot in his heart for civil servants. They are always honest in his stories, usually efficient, and not infrequently ridiculous. We know, too, that he prided himself on his own fine record at the Ministry. His treatment of Ayres, who *was* a public servant, is so sympathetic that some among Assis's contemporaries identified him with Assis himself.[2] Identification of Assis with any of his novels' protagonists, however, presents great, basic difficulties. There is nothing, for example, to show that Assis had ever been, like Ayres, "a bachelor at heart." It is apparent that he regarded his Cubas, Ayres, and the others, as pieces of erring humanity for whom he felt sympathy but with whom he could not identify himself completely. Minor characters are another matter. There is Aguiar, for instance, whose identity with himself he admitted by implication. Are there others? Do we have reason to believe that he sometimes inserted himself into the skin of rather unimportant characters, just as a director of a play will undertake a minor role along with the other actors?

I have already set forth elsewhere reasons for believing that the anonymous author of *The Panegyric of Saint Monica* was Dom Casmurro's sarcastic portrait of his creator Machado de Assis.[3] In spite of his pitiable literary pretensions, the *Panegyric's* author was a courteous, helpful, and efficient civil servant. Another minor character in *Dom Casmurro* was the government employee Padua who never reached the top of the bureaucratic ladder, although, like Machado de Assis, he had once been "Interim Administrator" for a few months.[4] Padua's consuming hobby as bird-fancier may perhaps reflect civil servant Assis's avocation of imprisoning ideas in gilded prose and verse. One of the most delightfully humorous figures in *Esau and Jacob* is Flora's "third" suitor, the young government employee Gouvêa, who wrote poetry on the side and had difficulty with his love letters—which came out either in the heavy style of government reports or in an overdone, high-flown poetic style all filled with thee's and thou's. Finally he caught a bad cold as he watched in the rain outside Flora's window, because the poet in him refused to put up the bureaucrat's umbrella.[5]

Not all Assis's civil servants are readily identifiable with their creator but they are all treated with a special sympathy —like the hopeful young clerk of "Animal Game,"[6] who was always expecting a promotion or to win the grand prize in a lottery; or like the more serious figure Luiz Garcia of the novel *Yayá Garcia*. There is one man, however, not strictly a public servant yet working for the government, who has more the quality of an autobiographical figure than any of Assis's other personages. It is Theophilo of the novel *Quincas Borba*, who, with his wife Fernanda, forms a vignette that seems a study for the full-length portrait of Carmo and Aguiar. Theophilo was an honest, hardworking member of the Chamber of Deputies, efficient, and consecrated to the public good. His morning routine was suspiciously like J. M. Machado de Assis's. He rose early, read five or six newspapers, wrote ten letters, and set the books straight on their shelves before his wife was up.[7] Everything in his study was in order, papers carefully filed, reports, budgets, speeches bound in semiannual volumes for easy reference: "all dry, exact, administrative."[8] There he spent long hours doing not only his own work but that of six colleagues also. "For what?" he gloomily asked his wife. He found consolation in doing a good job, she answered. And when he despaired over the administration's ingratitude and neglect, she told him that sooner or later he would be acclaimed, sooner or later he would receive his reward— almost the very words of Carolina's brother Miguel to the discouraged Machado.[9]

Fernanda had been born in a "port" city—not Porto, Portugal, Carolina's birthplace, but Porto Alegre, Brazil, "Joyful Port." She was jolly, expansive, full of life-strength and enthusiasm; she loved to help those less strong than herself.[10] Her love extended even to animals, to Rubião's dog, Quincas Borba.

> When Dona Fernanda stopped petting him . . . he remained looking at her, and she at him, so fixedly, so earnestly, that they seemed to penetrate one within the heart of the other. Universal sympathy, which was that lady's essential soul, forgot the man's troubles in her contemplation of this darkly enigmatic yet prosaic wretchedness. She extended to the animal a part of herself, enveloping

him, holding him in a spell. Thus the pity that his owner's madness had aroused in her was now shared by the dog, as if man and dog belonged to the same species.[11]

To her husband she was a loyal, adoring wife.[12] And he had no other mistress but his work.[13] Fernanda was not jealous of that mistress: with her own hands she dusted the papers and the "books he loved so much that he seemed to her to love them more than he did his wife."[14] She had the power with her love, her kisses and cheerful arguments to drive out his mood of black anger and despair over a misprint in a speech.

> He was a man of talent, of worth and serious accomplishment, but at that moment all the great works, the most formidable problems, the most decisive battles, the most important revolutions, the sun and the moon, and all the constellations, all the beasts of the animal kingdom, and all the generations of man were of less weight than that substitution of a u for an i.[15]

We know from Assis's correspondence that the pain caused him by misprints was intense.[16] And there is an apocryphal story that he once got down on his knees to Garnier, his publisher, to beg him to remove a comma.[17]

In a larger sense, Assis was all his personages, or, rather, they were all a part of him. He often hinted that his real life was in his books, as, for example, in his foreword to the 1907 edition of *Hand and Glove*.

> The thirty-odd years that separate the appearance of this little novel from its present reissue explain the differences in composition and in the temper of the author. If he would not write the story in this way today, it is certain that this is the way he wrote it back in those days; and, after all, everything can serve to define the same person. . . .
>
> He has altered nothing, only corrected typographical

errors, made changes in spelling,[18] and eliminated about fifteen lines.

Or, again, in his foreword to *Relics from an Old House:*

> Many a time, a house has its relics, souvenirs of one day or another, of sadness that has passed, of felicity lost. Suppose the master of the house conceives the idea of airing the relics and exhibiting them for your amusement and mine. Not all will be interesting—not a few, boring; but if the master uses discretion he can pick out a dozen or so that deserve to be displayed.
>
> Call my life a house, give the name of relics to the unpublished and published bits that are here displayed—ideas, stories, criticisms, dialogues—and you will find the book and its title explained.

In both these forewords, he rings a change on the idea running through *Posthumous Memoirs of Braz Cubas*—that a man's life is a series of editions, each a revision of the one before. Assis's actual books represent these various stages of his life. And the foreword to *Hand and Glove* suggests that he considered the later "editions," that is, his later books, improvements on the earlier ones. This is what I have tried to show in the foregoing study: that his novels constitute a history of his spiritual life and growth. Furthermore, each novel was an artistic experiment never repeated, which in one respect or another represented an advance over its immediate predecessor. That is not to say, of course, that the last novel was the "best" or the "greatest" or the "most powerful." It was, however, a new triumph in its limpid Portuguese, its narrative style, and its delicate humor. And the novel Assis was planning to write when he died would no doubt have added another incomparable "edition" to the incomplete book of his life.

In spite of Machado de Assis's desire to be known not as a man born of such and such parents, who lived in Rio de

Janeiro during a specified number of years, but as a man living in a series of artistic works, he died and was buried in a somewhat different capacity.

From his earliest years, as we have seen, he had been joining literary groups and projects,[19] perhaps with the idea that one of them would lead to a permanent national literary foundation. If so, they were disappointingly abortive until 1895, when José Veríssimo revived the defunct *Revista Brasileira* for the third time.[20] Its editorial room became the meeting place of a rather large circle of writers—such men as Machado de Assis, Veríssimo, Taunay, Joaquim Nabuco, Graça Aranha, João Ribeiro—who gathered in the afternoons to discuss matters of literature. On July 19, 1896, a monthly *Revista* dinner was initiated. In the last part of that year, a member of the group, Lúcio de Mendonça, suggested they form a Brazilian academy of letters. The idea was approved, Machado de Assis elected president, and the inaugural session of the Academia Brasileira de Letras held on June 20, 1897.

In opening that first session,[21] Machado de Assis defined the purpose of the Academy: to maintain Brazil's literary identity—the same ideal he had put forth thirty-nine years before in his article, "The Past, Present, and Future of Literature."[22]

It was not all smooth going for the young Academy, but Assis saw it through its difficult days, energetically interceding with the government time and again in his effort to obtain recognition and a permanent residence for it. At last, on August 11, 1905, he wrote Nabuco, "The Academy is finally housed and upholstered; it only remains for it to live."[23]

During those last years after Carolina's death, he devoted the time left over from his writing and his work at the Ministry to the Brazilian Academy of Letters. And the Academy honored him. In the spring of 1905 Nabuco sent a branch from the oak growing on Tasso's grave to Graça Aranha with the suggestion that the Academy present it to Machado in a fittingly symbolic ceremony.[24] On August 10, the oak branch was presented as homage to "the incomparable representative of Brazil's culture and her greatest poet."[25] In describing the ceremony to Nabuco, Assis wrote, "What the Academy did for me yesterday more than compensates for the labor of my entire life."[26]

On September 30, he wrote to Nabuco:

"You must already know of my portrait, which my friends of the Academy had painted by Henrique Bernardelli and is now in the annual exposition of the School of Fine Arts. The artist, to perpetuate your generous remembrance, copied on the canvas . . . the branch from Tasso's oak. The branch itself, with your letter to Graça, I still keep in my sitting room, in a box that rests below the picture of you which you sent me from London last year. Nothing is missing, unless it be the eyes of my dear old wife, who, like me, would be grateful for this two-fold remembrance of a friend. . . . The Academy will continue its work more assiduously now that it has a house and furniture.

The next to his last letter to Nabuco, June 28, 1908, concerning the latter's studies on Camoens, concludes:

On the 21st I completed my sixty-ninth year; I am entering the ranks of the septuagenarians. It is a wonder to me how I have been able to live till now, especially after the blow[27] that I received, and in the midst of the solitude in which I have remained, for all that friends do to relieve it with acts of kindness. A few days ago Victor[28] told me about a recent photograph of you. I still have hanging up there the one you sent me from London three years ago: it is superb; it hangs on the wall above the box that holds the branch of Tasso's oak. I have already made arrangements for the box and the branch, along with the two letters which accompany it, to be deposited in the Academy when I die.

His final letter to Nabuco, August 1, 1908, is still full of the Academy:

> The Academy goes along; we meet on Saturdays. . . . Your idea (of electing) José Rodrigues is good. . . . There is no vacant chair but who knows if mine will not be vacant.

Machado de Assis remained the Academy's devoted president, from its inception in 1897 till his death, September 29, 1908.[29] He died in Rio de Janeiro, as he had prophesied,[30] and in the house in which he had lived for twenty-four years. Tasso's oak went to the Academy.

Most of his other possessions, and they were not many—some household goods, his library, and the "apólices"—were willed to the daughter of Carolina's niece.[31] His literary properties, that is, his then collected works, belonged to his publisher Garnier.[32] Shortly before he died, it was said,[33] he entrusted to two old friends a box containing the letters he and Carolina had exchanged before their marriage and other mementoes, with the request that the box and its contents be burned. Although his request is thought to have been duly executed, somehow the two letters from Machado to Carolina (quoted in chap. 4) escaped burning.

By provision of his will, his own, human, remains were deposited in the same grave with his wife's, in the São João Baptista cemetery, and his name and dates (nothing besides) inscribed beneath hers—"J. M. Machado de Assis, 1839–1908.[34] The obsequies, however, had not been private. Even before death, in his last hours, the world began to take over.[35] It was as "illustrious man of letters," and president of Brazil's National Academy of Letters that Machado de Assis died and was buried.

His body lay in state at the Academy, amid all the pomp of black velvet, gold embroidered, great gold candle stands, a silver crucifix, and six silver candlesticks. It had been prepared for burial by the writers Afrânio Peixoto and Alfredo de Andrade, and a death mask taken by the sculptor Rodolfo Bernardelli. The Brazilian government paid him the homage of a state funeral, with the president of the Republic, two ministers of state, and the elite of the literary and social world attending. Condolences were received by the Academy from officialdom in various parts of Brazil, Europe, and the United States.[36]

And what was this man's "occupation" as given on his death certificate? "Civil servant."[37] Just that and nothing more. And, although buried as Brazil's laureate, the fact remained that *Ayres's Memorial*, his last work, went almost unnoted by the critics.[38]

Another ironic stroke that would have made Assis smile was what happened to the plaque on his house—the rented house at 18 Rua Cosme Velho, in which he had lived the last twenty-four years of his life, and where he had composed *Quincas Borba, Dom Casmurro, Esau and Jacob*, and *Ayres's Memorial*. After his death, members of the Academy wanted to purchase the house and keep it as a shrine, but they could not raise the money.[39] A compromise was made. On the first anniversary of Assis's death, the Brazilian Academy of Letters placed a bronze commemorative plaque on the house. In the space of a few years, however, the house was demolished and the plaque returned to the Academy.[40]

The same has not happened to Assis's *Old House*,[41] the spiritual house or life he left us in his works. That splendid piece of architecture stands forth more handsome with the passing years. Time, the same *time* that demolished 18 Cosme Velho, Assis's "invisible chemist," has brightened it with his merciless detergents and by the same token has dissolved away a crumbling rubble of edifices that obscured the view, so that the *Old House* looks down in shining eminence upon the Rua do Ouvidor, where Rumor, "mouth on ear," goes her busy way.

NOTES

NOTES

Unless otherwise indicated, writings of Machado de Assis mentioned in the text and in the notes of this study may be found in Machado de Assis, *Obra Completa*, ed. Afrânio Coutinho (Rio de Janeiro: José Aguilar, 1959). For full and accurate information on the publication of Assis's various works, one may consult J. Galante de Sousa, *Bibliografia de Machado de Assis* (Rio: Instituto Nacional do Livro, 1955).

CHAPTER 1.

1. The novels published in English are: *Memórias Posthumas de Braz Cubas*, under the title *The Posthumous Memoirs of Braz Cubas*, trans. William L. Grossman (São Paulo [1951]); under the title *Epitaph of a Small Winner*, trans. William L. Grossman (New York: Noonday Press, 1952); under the title *Posthumous Reminiscences of Braz Cubas*, trans. E. Percy Ellis (Rio: Instituto Nacional do Livro, 1955). *Dom Casmurro*, trans. Helen Caldwell (New York: Noonday Press, 1953); 2d ed.; Berkeley and Los Angeles: University of California Press, 1966). *Quincas Borba*, under the title *Philosopher or Dog ?*, trans. Clotilde Wilson (New York: Noonday Press, 1954). *Esaú e Jacob*, under the title *Esau and Jacob*, trans. Helen Caldwell (Berkeley and Los Angeles: University of California Press, 1965). *A Mão e a Luva*, under the title *The Hand and the Glove*, trans. Albert I. Bagby, Jr., is scheduled for publication in English by University of Kentucky Press in 1970.

An English translation of three of the short stories, "O Enfermeiro," "Viver," and "A Cartomante," will be found in Isaac Goldberg, *Brazilian Tales* (Boston: Four Seas, 1921), under the titles "The Attendant's Confession," "Life," and "The Fortune-Teller."

Machado de Assis, *The Psychiatrist and Other Stories*, trans. William L. Grossman and Helen Caldwell (Berkeley and Los Angeles: University of California Press, 1963) contains: "O Alienista," "Uns

Braços," "O Espelho," "A Causa Secreta," "O Caso da Vara," "Jôgo do Bicho," "Missa do Galo," "Pai Contra Mãe," "Teoria do Medalhão," "Umas Férias," "Noite de Almirante," and "Verba Testamentária," under the titles "The Psychiatrist," "A Woman's Arms," "The Looking Glass," "The Secret Heart," "The Rod of Justice," "The Animal Game," "Midnight Mass," "Father versus Mother," "Education of a Stuffed Shirt," "The Holiday," "Admiral's Night," and "Final Request."

2. As in his 1907 foreword to *A Mão e a Luva*, or in his foreword to *Reliquias de Casa Velha*; he frequently alludes to his devotion to the literary art in his journalism and in his correspondence, for example: "A Semana," *Gazeta de Notícias* (Rio), Dec. 27, 1896; "O Velho Senado," *Revista Brazileira*, XIV (June, 1898), 257–271 (reprinted in *Páginas Recolhidas*); letter to Afrânio Peixoto, July 24, 1908; letter to Carlos Magalhães de Azeredo, April 2, 1895, quoted by Lúcia Miguel Pereira, *Machado de Assis: Estudo Crítico e Biográfico* (5th ed.; Rio: José Olympio, 1955), pp. 220–221, and May 26, 1895, quoted by Josué Montello, *O Presidente Machado de Assis* (São Paulo: Martins, 1961), p. 135 (uncollected letters in the possession of the Brazilian Academy of letters). His friend and colleague Araripe Júnior, in an article published 1895, confirms the idea that Machado de Assis's real life was in his writing, *Obra Crítica de Araripe Júnior* (Rio: Ministério da Educação e Cultura/Casa de Rui Barbosa), III (1963), 5–6.

On the need for a factual and complete biography of Machado de Assis, something which does not exist to date, see J. Galante de Sousa, "Cronologia de Machado de Assis," *Revista do Livro*, III (Sept., 1958), 141.

3. For this portrait, see in particular the following articles by friends: Mário de Alencar, "Machado de Assis: Páginas de Saudade," *Almanaque Brasileiro Garnier* (Rio, 1911), pp. 203–216; José Veríssimo, "Machado de Assis: Impressões e Reminiscências," *Revista do Livro*, II (March, 1957), 151–163 (article reprinted from *Jornal do Commercio* [Rio], Oct. 29, 1908); Araripe Júnior, "Machado de Assis," *Jornal do Commercio* (Rio), Oct. 4, 1908, reprinted in *Obra Crítica de Araripe Júnior*, IV (1966) 279–284. Assis's correspondence, for the most part addressed to friends, betrays his warm friendliness, good taste, courtesy, and loyalty. In addition to his correspondence in the Aguilar edition, the large body of uncollected letters to Magalhães de Azeredo is liberally quoted by Montello, *O Presidente*, pp. 127–184, and by Luiz Viana Filho, *A Vida de Machado de Assis* (São Paulo: Martins, 1965), pp. 141–280. We find the same man reflected in his friends' letters to him, as in Machado de Assis, *Correspondência* (Rio: Jackson, 1938): *Euclydes da Cunha a Seus Amigos*, ed. Francisco Venâncio Filho (São Paulo: Companhia Editora Nacional, 1938); and Graça Aranha, *Machado de Assis e Joaquim Nabuco: Commentários e Notas*

à *Correspondência entre Estes Dous Escriptores* (São Paulo: Monteiro Lobato, 1923). For the dog Graziela, see chap. 17 of the present study. For his social life, see chap. 3. He himself testifies to his fondness for tea, "A Semana," Oct. 28, 1894, in Machado de Assis, *A Semana* vol. II (Rio: Jackson, 1938); for music, "A Semana," July 5, 1896, *ibid.*, vol. III. He came in third in a chess tournament, April, 1880: see Sousa, "Cronologia," pp. 155–156. For his social dancing, see letter of Miguel de Novaes, Jan. 21, 1883, "Cartas de Miguel de Novaes a Machado de Assis," *Estado de São Paulo* (Suplemento Literário, p. 2), June 20, 1964; cf. Viana, *Vida*, p. 127. The latter also recounts the talks over tea and cookies, pp. 164–167.

4. According to João Ribeiro, for example, as quoted by R. Magalhães Júnior, *Machado de Assis Desconhecido* (Rio: Civilização Brasileira, 1955), pp. 289–290. Cf. Graciliano Ramos, "Os Amigos de Machado de Assis," *Revista do Brasil* (June, 1939), pp. 86–88; Paulo Barreto, *O Momento Literário* (Rio: Garnier, n.d.), pp. 320–322. Mário R. Martins, *A Evolução da Literatura Brasileira*, II (Rio: Jornal do Brazil, 1945), 107–109, relates this and other items of the legend.

5. Araripe, *Obra Crítica*, II (1960), 294–296.

6. Pereira, *Machado de Assis: Estudo Crítico*, pp. 144–149, 155–156.

7. E.g., *ibid.*, p. 248; José Lins do Rego, *Conferências no Prata* (Rio: C.E.B., 1946), pp. 81–105; Corrêa Pinto, *Machado de Assis* (Rio: Irmãos Pongetti, 1958). Cf. R. Magalhães Júnior, *Machado de Assis, Funcionário Público* (Rio: Ministério da Viação e Obras Públicas, Serviço de Documentação, 1958), p. 21.

8. Araripe, *Obra Crítica*, II: 296; Renato de Mendonça, "Três Prosadores Maiores," *Revista Brasileira*, V (Dec., 1945), 55; Peregrino Júnior, "A Timidez de Machado de Assis e a de Amiel," *Revista Brasileira*, I (Sept., 1941), 129–139. Mário Matos, *Machado de Assis: O Homem e a Obra: Os Personagens Explicam o Autor* (São Paulo: Companhia Editora Nacional, 1939), p. 59; H. Pereira da Silva, *A Megalomania Literária de Machado de Assis* (Rio: Aurora, 1949). Pereira attempted with her *Machado de Assis* to trace in Assis's characters the influence of his acute consciousness of his Negro blood and humble origins, and also the effect of his epilepsy. Modesto de Abreu, "Infância e Adolescência de Machado de Assis," in *Machado de Assis Conferências, Federação das Academias de Letras do Brasil* (Rio: Briguiet, 1939), condemns such practices on pp. 16–17, and on p. 32 lists sixteen writers by name who followed them. Barreto Filho, *Introdução a Machado de Assis* (Rio: Agir, 1947), pp. 98–100, effectively disproves the psychoanalytical "timidity" theory. For further condemnation of this type of literary criticism, see Franklin de Oliveira, "O Artista em sua Narração, a Fortuna Crítica de Machado de Assis: 1912–1958," *Revista do Livro*, III (Sept., 1958), 61–69.

9. Matos, *Machado de Assis*, pp. 14–15, 115; Óthon Costa, "Machado

de Assis Epiléptico," in his *Conceitos e Afirmações* (Rio: Pongetti [1939]), pp. 73–86; Clodomir Vianna Moog, Heróis da Decadência (Porto Alegre: Globo, 1939), pp. 208–209; Peregrino Júnior, *Doença e Constituição de Machado de Assis* (Rio: Olympio, 1938); Hermínio de Brito Conde, *A Tragédia Ocular de Machado de Assis* (Rio: A Noite [1942]).

Assis himself appears not to have mentioned suffering from epilepsy, in his correspondence or elsewhere, until after his wife's death. What is taken as an allusion to the disease occurs in a letter to Mário de Alencar, Aug. 29, 1908. There are also extant some accounts, written in his hand, of seizures—in *Exposição Machado de Assis* (Rio: Ministério da Educação e Saude, 1939), p. 137. Lúcia Miguel Pereira placed the composition of the notes within the years 1905–1906 (*Machado de Assis*, p. 263, n. 238). There seems to be no exact information, however, as to when the first attacks occurred, nor how frequent and severe they were.

For the supposed effect of Assis's stuttering on his style: Sylvio Romero, *Machado de Assis* (2d ed.; Rio: Olympio, 1936), pp. 54–55; letter of Medeiros e Albuquerque to Alfredo Pujol, from Syracuse, Jan. 31, 1916, in Alfredo Pujol, *Machado de Assis* (São Paulo: Levi, 1917), pp. 347–349; also Afrânio Peixoto, quoted by Pereira, p. 290, n. 256. Assis's friends reported that he stuttered only very slightly, e.g., Veríssimo, "Machado de Assis: Impressões e Reminiscências," p. 154.

10. Matos, *Machado de Assis*, p. 18; Pereira, *Machado de Assis*, pp. 176–177; Magalhães, *Machado de Assis Desconhecido*, pp. 50, 282–288.

11. E.g., Veríssimo, "Machado de Assis: Impressões," pp. 154, 156, 158, 162; Mário de Alencar, *Alguns Escriptos* (Rio: Garnier, 1910), p. 33; letter of Veríssimo to Alencar quoted by Viana, *Vida*, p. 208; Alfredo Pujol, *Machado de Assis*, p. 60; Olívio Montenegro, *O Romance Brasileiro* (Rio: Olympio, 1938), pp. 105 ff.; R. Magalhães Júnior, *Ao Redor de Machado de Assis* (Rio: Civilização Brasileira, 1958), pp. 227–228 (quotation from a column by Artur Azevedo upon the appearance of *Dom Casmurro*); letter of Assis to Azeredo, March 19, 1900, about public's surprise, quoted by Viana, *Vida*, p. 196; cf. letter of Assis to Alencar, Feb. 8, 1908. That he was not entirely secretive about his work is indicated by letters from Miguel de Novaes, July 21 and Nov. 2, 1882, "Cartas de Miguel de Novaes," and by Assis's letters to Azeredo quoted by Montello, *O Presidente*, pp. 158, 166. Montello, *O Presidente*, p. 162, and Viana, *Vida*, p. 183, cite letters to Azeredo (Dec. 25, 1897 and Sept. 9, 1898, respectively) which also appear to contain allusion to his epilepsy.

12. J. Galante de Sousa, *Bibliografia* (Rio: Instituto Nacional do Livro, 1955), pp. 305–306, is of the opinion that "A Palmeira" was composed before "Ella," his first published poem.

13. "A Semana," Aug. 13, 1893, *A Semana*, vol. I. Unless otherwise

noted, foreign passages quoted in English are translations made by the author of this study.

14. "A Semana," Dec. 6, 1896, *A Semana*, vol. III.
15. Gastão Cruls, *Aparência do Rio de Janeiro* (Rio: Olympio, 1952), pp. 337–339.
16. "A Semana," Aug. 13, 1893, *A Semana*, vol. I.
17. Machado de Assis, *Chronica*, vol. I (Rio: Jackson, 1937).
18. *Ibid*, vol. II.
19. In *Contos Fluminenses*, vol. II (Rio: Jackson, 1937).
20. *Resurrection*, chap. xviii.
21. "A Semana," Dec. 6, 1896, *A Semana*, vol. III.
22. Agrippino Grieco, *Machado de Assis* (Rio: Olympio, 1959), pp. 170–171. A transcription of the Santos article will be found in Gondin da Fonseca, *Machado de Assis e o Hipopótamo* (2d ed.; São Paulo: Fulgor, 1960), pp. 247–255.
23. Pereira, *Machado de Assis*, pp. 28–44, 124.
24. *Ibid.*, p. 124.
25. In particular, Magalhães, *Machado de Assis, Funcionário Público*; *Machado de Assis Desconhecido*; *Ao Redor de Machado de Assis*. Cf. Astrojildo Pereira, *Machado de Assis* (Rio: Livraria São José, 1959), pp. 13–112.
26. E.g., the publication of uncollected writings of Machado de Assis through the efforts and research of R. Magalhães Júnior, J. Galante de Sousa, and Eugenio Gomes; and Carlos Magalhães de Azeredo's gift to the Brazilian Academy of Assis's letters to him.
27. Magalhães, *Ao Redor*, p. 212; Machado de Assis, *Poesia e Prosa*, ed. J. Galante de Sousa (Rio: Civilização Brasileira, 1957), pp. 154–157. For Sylvio Romero, see chap. 12 of this study.
28. Sousa, "Cronologia," p. 141.
29. Alencar, "Machado de Assis," pp. 203–216; Veríssimo, "Machado de Assis: Impressões e Reminiscências," pp. 151–163. Sousa, *Fontes para o Estudo de Machado de Assis* (Rio: Instituto Nacional do Livro, 1958), lists 97 publications on Machado de Assis for the single year following his death.
30. José Veríssimo, *História da Literatura Brasileira* (3d ed.; Rio: Olympio, 1954), p. 344. Mário de Alencar wrote Veríssimo, Feb. 6, 1915, that he once heard the Baron de Vasconcellos say he had known Machado de Assis's mother and that she was a colored woman (unpublished letter quoted by Viana, *Vida*, p. 12).
31. See above, nn. 8 and 9. At the age of twenty-four, Machado de Assis referred to himself as a "timid and fearful author," in a letter to Quintino Bocayuva, 1863.
32. Eloy Pontes, *A Vida Contradictória de Machado de Assis* (Rio: Olympio, 1939), p. 255, identifies Assis with Braz Cubas, Quincas Borba, Luiz Garcia, Dom Casmurro, Aguiar, and Ayres. Miguel Pe-

reira, *Machado de Assis*, pp. 149–150, 156–165, 170, 205–206, 248–249, 272, identifies him with Guiomar, Helena, Estella, Luiz Garcia, Braz Cubas, Rubião, Ayres, and Flora. Constantino Paleólogo, *Machado Pöe e Dostoievski* (Rio: Revista Branca, 1950), pp. 99–151, identifies him with Flora, as does Augusto Meyer, *Machado de Assis* (Rio: Simões, 1952), "Flora," pp. 39–43. Meyer also identifies Assis with Dom Casmurro, À *Sombra da Estante* (Rio: Olympio, 1947), pp. 51–58.
33. E.g., Miguel Pereira, *Machado de Assis*, pp. 176–177 (Capitu), 273–276 (Fidelia).
34. See above n. 9, on Romero.
35. Letter to Veríssimo, April 21, 1908, about publication of correspondence. For refusal to write memoirs, Veríssimo, "Machado de Assis: Impressões e Reminiscências," p. 158.
36. Grieco, *Machado de Assis*, pp. 247–248.
37. *Esau and Jacob*, chap. lxxviii.

CHAPTER 2.

1. *Exposição Machado de Assis* (Rio: Ministério da Educação e Saúde, 1939), p. 21; J. Galante de Sousa, "Cronologia de Machado de Assis," *Revista do Livro*, III (Sept. 1958), 142.
2. Sousa, *ibid.*
3. *Ibid.*, pp. 142–143, transcribes documents (1) and (2). Documents (3) through (6) are transcribed and described by Gondin da Fonseca, *Machado de Assis e o Hipopótamo* (2d ed.; São Paulo: Fulgor, 1960), pp. 257–264. Fonseca's later discoveries and conclusions are evaluated by R. Magalhães Júnior, "Quem Era a Mãe de Machado de Assis," *Jornal do Commercio* (Rio), May 29, 1960, 2. Caderno, pp. 1–2.
4. Ernesto Cybrão, quoted by Alfredo Pujol, *Machado de Assis* (São Paulo: Levi, 1917), p. 33.
5. Luiz Viana Filho, *A Vida de Machado de Assis* (São Paulo: Martins, 1965), pp. 54–55, who cites the 4th ed. of Fonseca's work.

CHAPTER 3.

1. In addition, during the spring and summer of 1870, he translated all or the greater part of Dickens's *Oliver Twist* for the *Jornal da Tarde*: see J. Galante de Sousa, *Bibliografia de Machado de Assis* (Rio: Instituto Nacional do Livro, 1955), pp. 452–453.
2. It is not a translation; there are only a few phrases taken from the original French, and the idea is somewhat different. Champcenetz concentrates on the (bad) nature of women; Assis, on the differences between the *tolos* and the *homens de espirito*.
3. "O Jornal e o Livro," *Correio Mercantil* (Rio), Jan. 10 and 12, 1859, reprinted in Machado de Assis, *Poesia e Prosa*, ed. J. Galante de Sousa (São Paulo: Civilização Brasileira, 1957), pp. 85–102. For Assis's

financial difficulties during these years, see also Luiz Viana Filho, *A Vida de Machado de Assis* São Paulo: Martins, 1965), pp. 66–67.

4. "História de Quinze Dias," *Illustração Brazileira*, Aug. 1, 1876, in Aguilar edition of the *Obra*; "A Semana," *Gazeta de Notícias* (Rio), April 22, 1894, in Machado de Assis, *A Semana*, vol. II (Rio: Jackson, 1938).

5. The activities listed on this and the following pages were assembled from: Sousa, *Bibliografia*; Sousa, "Cronologia de Machado de Assis," *Revista do Livro*, III (Sept., 1958), 141–181; R. Magalhães Júnior, *Machado de Assis Desconhecido* (Rio: Civilização Brasileira, 1955); Magalhães, *Machado de Assis, Funcionário Público* (Rio: Ministério da Viação e Obras Públicas, 1958); *Obra Crítica de Araripe Júnior* (Rio: Ministério da Educação e Cultura/Casa de Rui Barbosa), III (1963), 5–9; Lúcia Miguel Pereira, *Machado de Assis* (5th ed.; Rio: Olympio, 1955).

6. Sousa, *Bibliografia*, p. 172 and items 140, 141, 144, 149, 150, 151, 154, 155, 161, 164, 174, 185, 193, 200, 208, 209; a 17th "parecer," of 1870, is described, p. 703. The first 16 are published in *Revista do Livro*, I (June, 1956), 178–192; notes and discussion—J. Galante de Sousa, "Machado de Assis, Censor Dramático," *Revista do Livro*, I (Dec., 1956), 83–92.

7. "História de Quinze Dias," *Illustração Brazileira*, July 15, 1877, in Machado de Assis, *Chronicas*, vol. III (Rio: Jackson, 1938).

8. Assis's numerous readings and recitations are surprising in view of Veríssimo's statement that his stuttering interfered with his speaking in public, that his voice was so soft as not to be heard beyond a few feet, and that he gave only "two or three little speeches in his whole life." "Machado de Assis: Impressões e Reminiscências," *Revistas do Livro*, II (March, 1957), 154–155.

9. Note by Afrânio Coutinho, in Machado de Assis, *Obra Completa*, III (Rio: Aguilar, 1959), 1046.

10. For Castello Branco's opinion of Machado de Assis, see Graça Aranha, *Machado de Assis e Joaquim Nabuco* (São Paulo: Monteiro Lobata, 1923), p. 17; *Dispersos de Camilo*, ed. Júlio Dias da Costa, IV (Coimbra: Imprensa da Universidade, 1924–1929), 546.

11. "Ao Acaso," *Diário do Rio de Janeiro*, Jan. 31, 1865, in Machado de Assis, *Chronicas*, vol. II.

12. "O Velho Senado," *Revista Brasileira*, XIV (June, 1898), 257–271, reprinted in *Páginas Recolhidas*; "Pedro Luiz," *A Illustração*, Oct. 5, 1884, reprinted in the Aguilar edition of the *Obra*, III: 1021–1022.

13. Magalhães, *Machado de Assis Desconhecido*, p. 76.

14. "Ao Acaso" (see above, n. 11), Jan. 3, 1865. Cf. the same column, Sept. 11, 1864; also Sousa, *Bibliografia*, p. 382: Assis wrote the notice on the debut of his own play *The Apple of Discord*.

15. E.g., Viana, *Vida*, pp. 164–167.
16. *Obra Crítica de Araripe Júnior*, II: 295–296, reprinted from *Gazeta de Notícias*, Jan. 16, 1892.
17. "Versos a Corinna," in *Chrysalidas*.
18. Letter to Magalhães de Azeredo, April 2, 1895, in Josué Montello, *O Presidente Machado de Assis* (São Paulo: Martins, 1961), p. 135.

CHAPTER 4.

1. Information on the Novaes family was obtained from Sanches de Frias, *Memórias Literárias: Apreciações e Críticas* (Lisbon, 1907 [Typ. da Empresa Literária e Typográfica, Porto, April, 1907]), pp. 266–396.
2. The year is easily obtained from the information given on the month and weekdays in the text of the letters.
The initials M, A, and F evidently stand for Miguel, Adelaide, and Faustino.
3. A copy is printed in J. Galante de Sousa, "Cronologia de Machado de Assis," *Revista do Livro*, III (Sept. 1958), 150–151.
4. Especially in the correspondence with Joaquim Nabuco and with Salvador de Mendonça.
5. In Josué Montello, *O Presidente Machado de Assis* (São Paulo: Martins, 1961), p. 132; *ibid.*, p. 176, letter to Azeredo, Oct. 20, 1903, Assis mentions that he and his wife are both ill and both frail.
6. Letters of Nov. 2, 1881, Nov. 2, 1882, June 22, and Sept. 16, 1884, "Cartas de Miguel de Novaes a Machado de Assis," *Estado de São Paulo* (Suplemento Literário, pp. 2–3), June 20, 1964.
Miguel married the Count de São Mamede's widow, Nov. 15, 1876. See Sousa, "Cronologia," p. 154. He and his family moved to Portugal.

CHAPTER 5.

1. "Idéias Vagas—A Comédia Moderna," *Marmota Fluminense*, Sept. 4 and 6, 1856. For discussion of Assis's ideas about the theater and its relation to his fiction, see J. Galante de Sousa, "Machado de Assis, Censor Dramático," *Revista do Livro*, I (Dec., 1956), 83–92. Cf. Joel Pontes, *Machado de Assis e o Teatro* (São Paulo: Campanha Nacional do Teatro, Ministério da Educação e Cultura, 1960).
2. J. Galante de Sousa, *Bibliografia de Machado de Assis* (Rio: Instituto Nacional do Livro, 1955), item 31, dated Sept. 24, 1857.
3. *Gabriella*, performed in São Paulo, Sept. 20, 1862; lost. Sousa, *Bibliografia*, item 158.
4. In *Obra Completa*, Aguilar edition, "Epistolário," 1.

CHAPTER 6.

1. *Resurreicão*/Romance/por/Machado de Assis/Rio de Janeiro/
B. L. Garnier/Livreiro Editor do Instituto/69, Rua do Ouvidor, 69
[1872].
2. Chap. xv.
3. Chap. ix.
4. Chap. ii.
5. Chap. i.
6. Chap. ix.
7. Chap. i.

CHAPTER 7.

1. *A Mão e a Luva*/por/Machado de Assis/Rio de Janeiro/Editores,
Gomes de Oliveira & C./Typographia do Globo—Ourives, 51/1874.
Previously published in installments in *O Globo* (Rio), Sept.–Nov.,
1874.
2. *Hand and Glove*, chap. xv.
3. *Ibid.*
4. *Ibid.*, chap. i.
5. *Ibid.*, chap. x.
6. *Ibid.*, chap. xv.
7. *Ibid.*, chap. xii.
8. *Ibid.*, chap. iv.
9. *All's Well That Ends Well*, I. i. 212–215. All Shakespeare refer-
ences are to *Arden Shakespeare*, ed. R. H. Case (2d ed.; London:
Methuen, 1909–1944).
10. Cf. Clifford Leech, "The Theme of Ambition in 'All's Well That
Ends Well,' " *English Literary History*, XXI (1954), 17–29.

CHAPTER 8.

1. *Helena*/por/Machado de Assis /Rio de Janeiro/B. L. Garnier/
Livreiro-Editor do Instituto Historico Brasileiro/65 Rua do Ouvidor/
1876.
Published in installments in *O Globo* (Rio), Aug.–Sept., 1876.
2. Diário do Rio de Janeiro, Aug. 24, 1863, in Machado de Assis,
Crítica Literária (Rio: Jackson, 1937). Cf. Machado de Assis, *Adelaide
Ristori Folhetins* (Rio: Academia Brasileira de Letras, 1955), p. 56, "In
modern times the law that rules tragic action is moral freedom."
3. "Her father bequeathed her to me." (I.iii.96.)
4. In Machado de Assis, *A Semana*, vol. II (Rio: Jackson, 1938).

5. *Posthumous Memoirs of Braz Cubas* (*Epitaph of a Small Winner*), chap. xv.
6. *Helena*, chap. xii.
7. *Ibid.*, chap. ii.
8. *Ibid.*, chap. iv.
9. E.g., he burns the letter Helena gave him to deliver to Mendonça, chap. xix.
10. *Ibid.*, chap. xx.
11. *Ibid.*, chap. xxiii.
12. *Ibid.*, chap. xxiv.
13. *Ibid.*, chap. xxi.
14. *Ibid.*, chap. i.
15. *Ibid.*, chap. xii.
16. *Ibid.*, chap. xiv.
17. *Ibid.*
18. Albert Cook, *The Dark Voyage and the Golden Mean* (Cambridge: Harvard University Press, 1949), p. 47.

CHAPTER 9.

1. *Yayá Garcia*/por/Machado de Assis/Rio de Janeiro/G. Vianna & C., Editores/Typ. do *Cruzeiro*/1878.
Published in installments in *O Cruzeiro* (Rio), Jan.–Mar., 1878.
2. *Yayá Garcia*, chap. i.
3. *Ibid.*, chap. vi.
4. *Ibid.*, chap. xiv.
5. *Ibid.*, chap. xvii. Cf. "No Alto," *Ocidentais*, the last poem.
6. *Yayá Garcia*, chap. xv.
7. Cf. *ibid.*, chap. v, in which Jorge draws "estrelas" (stars) on the ground with his sword or seeks them in the sky.
8. *Contos Fluminenses.* Cf. Galante de Sousa, *Bibliografia de Machado de Assis* (Rio: Instituto Nacional do Livro, 1955), item 394.
9. *Yayá Garcia*, chap. iv.
10. "Qual dos Dous," in Machado de Assis, *Histórias Românticas* (Rio: Jackson, 1938). Cf. the short story "Conversão de um Avaro," *Contos Fluminenses*, vol. II (Rio: Jackson, 1938).
11. "O Primo Bazilio, Romance do Sr. Eça de Queiroz," *O Cruzeiro* (Rio), Apr. 16 and 30, 1878.
12. E.g., "Notas Semanaes," *O Cruzeiro*, Aug. 4, 1878; *Esau and Jacob*, chap. lxiv.
13. *Yayá Garcia*, chap. i.
14. *Ibid.*, chap. ii.
15. *Ibid.*, chap. i.

CHAPTER 10.

1. *Memorias Posthumas*/de/Braz Cubas/por/Machado de Assis/Rio de Janeiro/Typographia Nacional/1881.
Published in installments in *Revista Brasileira*, III–VI (Rio), Mar.–Dec., 1880.

2. Braz's dedication to the worm is omitted in *Epitaph of a Small Winner* and in Ellis's translation.

3. Eugenio Gomes noted the allusion in his *Espelho Contra Espelho* (São Paulo: Instituto Progresso Editorial, 1949), p. 67.

4. Laurence Sterne, *The Life and Opinions of Tristram Shandy Gentleman*, Bk. I, chap. 22.

5. *Posthumous Memoirs*, chap. vi. Cf. chaps. cxxv and cxxvi, where Braz again illustrates the advantage of his narrative method for making transitions.
Machado de Assis frequently satirized what he termed the *ab ovo* style of composition, e.g., in the short stories "Cão de Lata ao Rabo" and "Identidade," and best of all in his column on Dr. Capelli's remedies for prostitution, "A Semana," Oct. 21, 1894, in *A Semana*, vol. II (Rio: Jackson, 1938).

6. E.g., "História de Quinze Dias," Nov. 15, 1876, in Machado de Assis, *Chronicas*, vol. III (Rio: Jackson, 1938).

7. *Posthumous Memoirs*, chap. iii.

8. *Gil Blas*, Bk. 12, chap. 3.

9. *Posthumous Memoirs*, chap. xi.

10. *Tristram Shandy*, Bk. V, chap. 16.

11. *Posthumous Memoirs*, chap. liii, trans. William L. Grossman, *Epitaph of a Small Winner*.

12. *Posthumous Memoirs*, chap. cxxv.

13. *Ibid.*, chap. cxxvi.
The sinister "slave-trading" note is introduced in the first pages of the novel, in the conversation at the banquet of chap. xii.
Cotrim's daughter Sara died a few months after Dona Eulalia. Did she too die of yellow fever? The epidemic continued and increased in 1850.
For an account of the epidemic of 1849–1850, and the slave ship theory, see James C. Fletcher and D. P. Kidder, *Brazil and the Brazilians* (Boston: Little, Brown, 1866), p. 609.

14. *Posthumous Memoirs*, chap. clx.
For a discussion of the ideal picaro, see G. Reynier, *Le Roman Réaliste au XVII Siècle* (Paris: Hachette, 1914), pp. 19–55.

15. *Posthumous Memoirs*, chap. xxxviii.

16. *Ibid.*, chap. cxxxi.

17. *Ibid.*, chap. xlviii.

18. *Ibid.*, chap. xci.

19. Cf. R. Magalhães Júnior, *Machado de Assis Desconhecido* (Rio: Civilização Brasileira, 1955), p. 201.

20. E.g., Clodomir Vianna Moog, *Heróis da Decadência* (Rio: Guanabara, 1934), pp. 198–199 (Leibnitz); William L. Grossman, "Translator's Introduction," *Epitaph of a Small Winner*, p. 14 (Nietzsche); Barreto Filho, *Introdução a Machado de Assis* (Rio: Agir, 1947), pp. 104, 136–137 (evolution and Positivism).

21. Chap. 9 of the present study.

22. For an account of Positivism in Brazil, see João Cruz Costa, *A History of Ideas in Brazil*, trans. Suzette Macedo (Berkeley and Los Angeles: University of California Press, 1964), pp. 82–228, and *passim*.

23. E.g., "A Semana," Dec. 4, 1892, in Machado de Assis, *A Semana*, vol I (Rio: Jackson, 1938); or Oct. 21, 1894 in vol. II.

24. *Posthumous Memoirs*, chap. cxvii.

25. *Ibid.*, chap. cxlii.

26. *Ibid.*, chap. xci.

27. *Ibid.*, chap. cix.

28. *Ibid.*, chap. cxvii.

29. *Ibid.*, chap. clvii.

30. *Ibid.*, chap. vii.

31. *Ibid.*, chap. cxxiii.

32. *Ibid.*, chap. cxvii.

33. *Ibid.*, chap. cxvii, trans. William L. Grossman, *Epitaph of a Small Winner*.

34. *Posthumous Memoirs*, chap. xlii.

35. Ibid., chap. cxliv. See also chap. lxii, where Braz says the reason for Virgilia's existence was to soothe his spirit.

36. *Ibid.*, chap. xlii.

CHAPTER 11.

1. *Posthumous Memoirs*, chap. cxli.

2. *Ibid.*, chap. xxv.

3. Edward Dowden and H. N. Hudson, quoted in *A New Variorum Edition of Shakespeare, As You Like It*, ed. Horace Howard Furness (New York: Lippincott, 1890), pp. 414, 416. Dowden adds that Jaques died but came to life again as Laurence Sterne.

4. *As You Like It*, II.vii.65–66.

5. See Machado de Assis, *Memórias Póstumas de Brás Cubas*, ed. Comissão Machado de Assis (Rio: Instituto Nacional do Livro, 1960), p. 111, *apparatus criticus*.

The quotation is *As You Like It*, III.ii.273–274.

6. *As You Like It*, I.i.1–75.

7. *Ibid.*, IV.i.17–19.

8. *Ibid.*, IV.i.30–35.

9. J. Galante de Sousa, *Bibliografia de Machado de Assis* (Rio: Instituto Nacional do Livro, 1955), pp. 74–75, explains the confusion about the early editions and Assis's "Foreword to the Third Edition." The publication in the *Revista Brasileira* (1880) was treated as the first edition; the first publication in book form (1881) as the second, although it was not so labeled. The second edition in book form (1896) was labeled "third edition." No extant copies of this third edition have been found by Sousa to contain a foreword by Assis; but the "fourth edition" (1899) contains a "Foreword to the Third Edition," signed "Machado de Assis." Evidently he wrote the foreword for the third edition, although, it would seem, it did not appear in that edition.

10. This foreword does not appear in the Grossman translation, *Epitaph of a Small Winner.*

11. *As You Like It,* IV.i.23, "rich eyes and poor hands."

12. *Posthumous Memoirs,* chap. cxli.

13. *As You Like It,* II.i.31–66; *Posthumous Memoirs,* chap. cxxxvii.

14. See his letter to Afrânio Peixoto, July 24 [1908]; to Magalhães de Azeredo, May 26, 1895, quoted in Josué Montello, *O Presidente Machado de Assis* (São Paulo: Martins, 1961), pp. 134–135; cf. his prefatory letter to *Harmonias Errantes* by Francisco de Castro, Aug. 4, 1878, *Obra Completa,* III (Aguilar), 924–925—"Aponto-lhe o melhor de mestres, o estudo; e a melhor de disciplinas, o trabalho"; and letter to Azeredo, Sept. 3, 1895, quoted by Luiz Viana Filho, *A Vida de Machado de Assis* (São Paulo: Martins, 1965), p. 14—"Quem lhe fala, trabalhou muito."

15. *As You Like It,* II.vii.58–61.

16. *Tristram Shandy,* Bk. IV, chap. 22. Cf. *ibid.,* chap. 32.

17. *Exposição Machado de Assis* (Rio: Ministério da Educação e Saude, 1939), p. 178, and photographic reproduction, preceding p. 179; Sousa, *Bibliografia,* p. 698.

The fact that ten years elapsed between the date on which Assis had undertaken to deliver his MS and the first publication date of *Memórias Posthumas de Braz Cubas,* is nothing to the point. There is abundant evidence that he carried ideas for novels in mind over long periods of time. For example, an early sketch for *Esau and Jacob* appeared in print almost ten years before its novel—"Orai por Êle!" in *Almanaque da Gazeta de Noticias* for 1895, pp. 17–19, reprinted in Machado de Assis, *Contos Esparsos,* ed. R. Magalhães Júnior (Rio: Civilização Brasileira, 1956), pp. 275–277.

18. Reprinted in the collections, Machado de Assis, *Contos Avulsos* and *Contos Esquecidos,* ed. R. Magalhães Júnior (Rio: Civilização Brasileira, 1956), pp. 31–47 and 147–173, respectively.

19. It might be noted that a Licentiate Garcia, a young man suffering from an interesting form of insanity, appears in Assis's "Psychia-

trist" (*O Alienista*), which was published the year after *Posthumous Memoirs*. The recognized founder of Braz's family was Licentiate Luiz Cubas, who had studied at the university of Coimbra. Braz is not called "Licentiate," but he too had a degree from Coimbra.

20. E.g., Man as a vehicle (carriage), *Tristram Shandy*, Bk. IV, chap. 8, is elaborated upon by Quincas's philosophy, where he becomes vehicle, coachman, and passenger (*Posthumous Memoirs*, chap. cxvii). Uncle Toby whistles Lillibullero when in a tight spot; Braz whistles an air from *Norma*.

21. *Tristram Shandy*, Bk. IV, chap. 4.

22. *Ibid.*, Bk. II, chap. 12.

23. *Posthumous Memoirs*, chap. ciii.

24. See, for example, John Traugott, *Tristram Shandy's World: Sterne's Philosophical Rhetoric* (Berkeley and Los Angeles: University of California Press, 1954).

25. *Posthumous Memoirs*, chap. xxvi; cf. Virgil, *Aeneid* IV.279–282.

26. *Quincas Borba*, chap. lxxxii.

27. *Don Quixote*, Pt. II, chap. 48, "traidor y atrevido Eneas"; *Resurrection*, chap. ii, "prófugo Dardânio."

28. *Posthumous Memoirs*, chap. xxxv.

29. *Ibid.*, chap. xxxi.

30. Camoens, *Lusiads*, II.23.

31. Virgil, *Aeneid* IV.401–415.

32. *Ibid.*, VI.

33. *Posthumous Memoirs*, chap. vii.

34. *Ibid.*, chap. xxvi.

35. Dante, *Purgatoria*, canto xxx, line 49.

36. *Posthumous Memoirs*, chap. cliii.

37. *Ibid.*, chap. xxvii. Cf. chaps. vi and xxxviii, whose title is "The Fourth Edition."

38. Dante, *Inferno*, canto xxxii.

39. *Quincas Borba*, chap. clix.

40. *Posthumous Memoirs*, chap. ii. Cf. letter of Capistrano de Abreu to Assis, Jan. 10, 1881, *Correspondência de Capistrano de Abreu*, ed. J. H. Rodrigues, I (Rio: Instituto Nacional do Livro, 1954), 49, "esfíngico X." Cf. Eugenio Gomes, *Prata de Casa* (Rio: A Noite [1953]), p. 81, "a lépida idéia transforma-se na imagem petrificada de uma esfinge."

41. *Posthumous Memoirs*, chap. lix.

42. Machado de Assis, *Adelaide Ristori Folhetins* (Rio: Academia Brasileira de Letras, 1955), p. 35.

43. *Posthumous Memoirs*, chap. cxxxvii.

44. Cervantes, *Don Quixote*, Pt. I, chaps. 47–48.

45. In a review of *O Culto do Dever*, by J. M. de Macedo, *Diário do*

Rio de Janeiro, Jan. 16, 1866, reprinted in Machado de Assis, *Crítica Literária* (Rio: Jackson, 1938).

46. "História de Quinze Dias," Jan 1, 1877, in Machado de Assis, *Chronicas,* vol. III (Rio: Jackson, 1938).

47. Cervantes, *Don Quixote,* Pt. I, chaps. 10, 15, 17, 25.

48. *Posthumous Memoirs,* chap. cv; *Don Quixote,* Pt. I, chap. 21.

49. E.g., *Don Quixote,* Pt. I, "Prologue"; Pt. II, chap. 23, title of II, chap. 70. Of course these mannerisms were adopted by Fielding and Sterne, both of whom Assis flattered with his imitation.

50. *Ibid.,* Pt. I, chap. 25.

51. *Posthumous Memoirs,* chap. cliii.

52. *Ibid.,* chap. xv.

53. *Ibid.,* chaps. lii, cix; *Don Quixote,* Pt. II, chap. 5.

54. *Posthumous Memoirs,* chaps. cix and cxv.

55. Cervantes, *Don Quixote,* Pt. II, chap. 34; *Posthumous Memoirs,* chaps. iii and xliv.

56. *Posthumous Memoirs,* chap. cxxix.

57. E.g., *ibid.,* chaps. i, v, vii (life itself); xix (storm); xix, xxiii (death agony); xxxvii (greed); cxxi (cockfight); cxli (dogfight); cxxv (plague).

58. *As You Like It,* V.iv.149–196.

59. *Posthumous Memoirs,* chap. viii.

60. *Ibid.,* chap. xxv.

61. See above, n. 14.

62. Letter to Magalhães de Azeredo, Dec. 25, 1897, quoted by Josué Montello, *O Presidente Machado de Assis* (São Paulo: Martins, 1961), p. 163. Cf. letter to Salvador de Mendonça, Aug. 29, 1903, and letter to José Veríssimo, Jan. 5, 1900.

63. "A Semana," Feb. 28, 1897. Cf. José Veríssimo, "Machado de Assis: Impressões e Reminiscências," in *Revista do Livro,* II (March, 1957), 156.

64. See above, n. 9.

65. *Posthumous Memoirs,* chap. cxviii ("Imagina, por exemplo, que eu não tinha nascido," continuou o Quincas Borba. "É positivo que não teria agora o prazer de conversar contigo . . ."); chap. cxxii (". . . cheguei a atribuir a Nhan-loló a intenção positiva de separar, no meu espírito, a sua causa da causa do pai."). Cf. "Notas Semanais," July 7, 1878 (Se o mau éxito cênico do *Primo Basilio* nada prova contra o livro e o autor do drama, é positivo tambem que nada prova contra a escola realista e seus sectários.)

66. See John Stuart Mill, *Auguste Comte and Positivism* (Ann Arbor: University of Michigan Press, 1961), pp. 63–65.

67. E.g., "A Semana," Apr. 22, 1894, in *A Semana,* vol. II (Rio: Jackson, 1938).

68. "Eça de Queiroz: *O Primo Bazilio,*" O Cruzeiro (Rio), Apr. 16 and 30, 1878.

69. *Posthumous Memoirs*, chap. lxv ("um hospital concentrado").
Cf. chaps. lxxxviii and lxxxix. See also, Eugenio Gomes, *Machado de Assis* (Rio: Livraria São José, 1958), pp. 84–90.

70. *Posthumous Memoirs*, chap. cix. It might be noted that the word Braz uses for mire, "lama," was the word used by Camillo Castello Branco to characterize the Naturalist School, for example in the title, *Volcões de Lama* (volcanos of mire).

71. *Posthumous Memoirs*, chap. lxxvii.

72. *Ibid.*, chaps. lxi and lxii.

CHAPTER 12.

1. Machado de Assis, *Epitaph of a Small Winner*, trans. and introd. William L. Grossman (New York: Monday, 1952). Mr. Grossman had published his translation in São Paulo, Brazil, 1951, under the title *Posthumous Memoirs of Braz Cubas*.

2. Machado de Assis, *Memórias Póstumas de Brás Cubas*, ed. Comissão Machado de Assis (Rio: Instituto Nacional do Livro, 1960), pp. 16–17.

3. *Ibid.* See also Assis's criticism of *O Primo Bazilio*, by Eça de Queiroz.

4. E.g., in "O Instincto de Nacionalidade," *O Novo Mundo* (New York), March 24, 1873; "*O Primo Bazilio*," *O Cruzeiro* (Rio), April 16 and 30, 1878; "A Nova Geração," *Revista Brasileira*, II (Rio), Dec. 1, 1879.

5. "A Nova Geração."

6. *Ibid.*

7. "*O Primo Bazilio.*"

8. *Ibid.*

9. *Memórias Póstumas*, ed. Comissão Machado de Assis, pp. 16–17; Lúcia Miguel Pereira, *Prosa de Ficção de 1870 a 1920* (Rio: Olympio, 1950) (*História da Literatura Brasileira sob a Direção de Álvaro Lins*, v. 12), p. 27. Aluísio de Azevedo himself, however, acknowledged Assis's superiority: see Luiz Viana Filho, *A Vida de Machado de Assis* (São Paulo: Martins, 1965), pp. 129–130.

10. "A Nova Geraçao."

11. Assis wrote in the foreword: "Capistrano de Abreu, in his notice on the publication of the book, put this question: 'Are *The Posthumous Memoirs of Braz Cubas* a novel?' "

12. Capistrano de Abreu, "*Memórias Posthumas de Braz Cubas*," in "Livros e Letras," *Gazeta de Notícias*, Jan. 30, 1881, reprinted in *Dom Casmurro* (Rio), July 19, 1941, p. 4, in the article, "Capistrano de Abreu Crítico Literário," by J. A. Pinto do Carmo. Cf. J. Galante de Sousa, *Fontes para o Estudo de Machada de Assis* (Rio: Instituto Nacional do Livro, 1958), item 93.

13. "Cartas de Miguel de Novaes a Machado de Assis," *Estado de São Paulo* (Suplemento Literário, pp. 2–3), June 20, 1964.

14. Letter to Magalhães de Azeredo, May 26, 1895, quoted by Josué Montello, *O Presidente Machado de Assis* (São Paulo: Martins, 1961), pp. 134–135.

15. See his correspondence, literary criticism, and columns, *passim*.

16. Quoted in R. Magalhães Júnior, *Machado de Assis Desconhecido* (Rio: Civilização Brasileira, 1955), p. 250.

17. Letter of Nov. 13, 1876.

18. Letter to Magalhães de Azeredo, Oct., 1905, in Montello, *O Presidente Machado de Assis*, p. 182.

19. *Ibid.*, p. 184; letter written to Azeredo in 1908.

20. Letter to Joaquim Nabuco, Aug. 1, 1908. See also letters to José Veríssimo, July 19, 1908, and to Mário de Alencar, Wednesday [July 30], [1908], and Aug. 1, 1908, in which he expresses gratitude for his friends' praise.

21. *Quincas Borba* came out in 91 semimonthly installments in *A Estação*—the first appearing, June 15, 1886; the last, Sept. 15, 1891. (See Sousa, *Bibliografia de Machado de Assis* [Rio: Instituto Nacional do Livro, 1955], item 821.) For the paucity of reviews, see Sousa, *Fontes para o Estudo de Machado de Assis* (Rio: Instituto Nacional do Livro, 1958), p. 29.

22. Sylvio Romero, *Machado de Assis, Estudo Comparativo de Literatura Brasileira* (Rio: Laemmert, 1897).

23. Nelson Werneck Sodré, *O Naturalismo no Brasil* (Rio: Civilização Brasileira, 1965), pp. 156–157.

24. Araripe, "Romero Polemista," in *Obra Crítica de Araripe Júnior*, III: 330–332. Cf. Sousa, *Fontes*, items 50, 91, 102.

25. Araripe, "Romero Polemista."

26. Romero, *Machado de Assis*, (2d. ed.; Rio: Olympio, 1936), p. 140.

27. *Ibid.*, pp. 55, 93, 121, 123, 127.

28. *Ibid.*, p. 141.

29. Labieno, "*Machado de Assis—Estudo Comparativo* por Sylvio Romero," *Jornal do Commercio* (Rio), Jan. 25 and 30, Feb. 7 and 11, 1898.

30. E.g., Magalhães de Azeredo, "Machado de Assis," *Revista Moderna* I (Paris, Nov. 5, 1897), 269–271; Eloy, o Heroe [Pseud. of Artur Azevedo], "Croniqueta," *A Estação* (Rio), Dec. 15, 1897.

31. Letter to Pereira, Feb. 19, 1898; letter to Veríssimo, Dec. 1, 1897; for uncollected letters to Azeredo, now in the Brazilian Academy of Letters, see Montello, *O Presidente*, pp. 155, 157, 159–160.

32. Letter to Azeredo, Feb. 2, 1898, in Montello, *O Presidente*, p. 159.

33. José Veríssimo, "Machado de Assis: Impressões e Reminiscên-

cias," *Revista do Livro*, II (March, 1957), 151 (article reprinted from *Jornal do Commercio* [Rio], Oct. 29, 1908).

34. *Ibid.*, pp. 151–152, 156; Clovis Beviláqua, *Epochas e Individualidades* (2d. ed.; Rio: Garnier, n.d.), pp. 68–69; cf. Lúcia Miguel Pereira, *Prosa de Ficção* (Rio: Olympio, 1950), pp. 167–178.

35. Manoel Cardozo, "The Transition," in *Brazil*, ed. Lawrence F. Hill (Berkeley and Los Angeles, University of California Press, 1947), chap. ii; *A Documentary History of Brazil*, ed. E. Bradford Burns (New York: Knopf, 1966), pp. 186–193; Jonathas Serrano, *História do Brasil* (Rio: Briguiet, 1931), pp. 304–463.

36. Letter to Veríssimo, Feb. 16, 1901.

37. Beviláqua, *Epochas*, pp. 68–69.

38. Pereira, *Prosa de Ficção*, p. 125.

39. Sodré, *O Naturalismo*, pp. 165–166.

40. See chap. 1, n. 2.

41. "História de Quinze Dias," *Illustração Brazileira*, Feb. 1, 1877, July 1, 1877, in Machado de Assis, *Chronicas*, vol. III (Rio: Jackson, 1938).

42. "A Semana," Mar. 11, 1894, in Machado de Assis, *A Semana*, vol. II (Rio: Jackson, 1938).

43. E.g., in his review *"Un Cuento Endemoniado e La Mujer Misteriosa por Guilherme Malta,"* July 2, 1872, in Machado de Assis, *Crítica Literária* (Rio: Jackson, 1938).

44. *Posthumous Memoirs of Braz Cubas*, chap. lxxii.

45. "A Semana," Aug. 19, 1894, in *A Semana*, vol. II (Jackson). Cf. Viana, *Vida*, p. 196 and letter to Azeredo, Nov. 5, 1900, there quoted.

46. A letter to Assis from Miguel de Novaes, "Cartas de Miguel de Novaes," Aug. 19, 1887, indicates that at the request of Machado he had been exploring the possibility of publication in Portugal in order to secure a wider and perhaps more sophisticated public for Assis's books: Assis's publisher Garnier had refused to publish them in Portugal. Garnier also refused to permit translation into other languages: see correspondence, *Exposição Machado de Assis* (Rio: Ministério da Educação e Saude, 1939), pp. 198–199.

CHAPTER 13.

1. Machado de Assis/*Quincas Borba*/Rio de Janeiro/B. L. Garnier, Livreiro-Editor/71, Rua do Ouvidor,/1891.

Published in 91 installments in *A Estação* (Rio), June 15, 1886–Sept. 15, 1891.

2. *Posthumous Memoirs of Braz Cubas*, chap. cxvii; and cxxvi.

3. *Quincas Borba*, chap. vi. Cf. R. Magalhães Júnior, *Machado de Assis Desconhecido* (Rio: Civilização Brasileira, 1955), pp. 201–203.

4. *Quincas Borba*, chap. vi.

5. See Machado de Assis, "Commentários da Semana," *Diário do Rio de Janeiro*, Nov. 1, 1861, in Machado de Assis, *Chronicas*, vol. I (Rio: Jackson, 1938); "Gazeta de Hollanda," *Gazeta de Noticias* (Rio), Dec. 6, 1886, in *Chronicas*, vol. IV. Cf. Magalhães, *Machado de Assis Desconhecido*, pp. 201–203.

It might be noted that Assis possessed the following French translations: Darwin, *La Descendance de l'Homme et la Sélection Sexuelle* (1873), in 2 vols., *L'Origine des Espèces au Moyen de la Sélection Naturelle ou la Lutte pour l'Existence dans la Nature* (1876); Huxley, *Physographie: Introduction a l'Étude de la Nature* (1882); Spencer, *Introduction à la Science Sociale* (1878), L'Individu contre l'État (1888), *Principes de Sociologie*, vol. I (1878), vol. II (1879), *Principes de Biologie* (1878); A. R. Wallace, *La Selection Naturelle: Essais* (1872). See Jean-Michel Massa, "La Bibliothèque de Machado de Assis," *Revista do Livro*, VI (March–June, 1961), 223–224.

6. *Quincas Borba*, chap. vi.

7. *Ibid.*, chaps. v, xiv. As for Borba's book in 91 parts, curiously enough *Quincas Borba* came out in 91 parts.

8. *Ibid.*, chap. xiv.

9. *Ibid.*, chap. xviii.

10. *Ibid.*, chap. xv.

11. *Ibid.*, chap. v (Borba); vii, xv, xxviii (Rubião); xxviii (the dog).

12. *Ibid.*, chap. vii.

13. *Ibid.*, chaps. xlix, lxix, lxxix, cxxxiii.

14. See John Stuart Mill, *Auguste Comte and Positivism* (Ann Arbor: University of Michigan Press, 1961), p. 137.

15. *Quincas Borba*, chaps. xvi, xxviii, cxcvii.

16. It is mentioned that Rubião's French cook liked the dog, but nothing is said of the dog liking Jean, chap. xxviii.

17. "A Semana," Feb. 25, 1894, Machado de Assis, *A Semana*, vol. II (Rio: Jackson, 1938).

18. *Quincas Borba*, chaps. x through xiii.

19. *Ibid.*, chap. iii.

20. *Ibid.*, chap. xxviii.

21. *Ibid.*, chap. lxxx.

22. *Ibid.*, chap. lxxxii. Cf. chap. clxxix.

23. Massa, "La Bibliothèque," p. 202, item 5. Cf. *Posthumous Memoirs*, chap. viii, in which Folly wants a corner of Braz's garret. Assis wrote a piece entitled "Praise of Vanity," a kind of imitation of Erasmus's "Praise of Folly." It appeared in *O Cruzeiro* (Rio), May 28, 1878, and is reprinted in Machado de Assis, *Obra Completa*, III (Aguilar), 1011–1015.

The Greek names of Folly's train are: *Philautia, Kolakia, Hedone, Misoponia, Komos, Tryphe, Anoia, Lethe, Negretos hypnos*.

24. *Quincas Borba*, chap. cxlv.

25. See the article "desfolhada," in *Grande Enciclopédia Portuguesa e Brasileira* (Lisbon and Rio de Janeiro: Editorial Enciclopédia, 1945).

26. E.g., *Quincas Borba*, chaps. iv, vi.

27. *Ibid.*, chap. xxi.

28. *Ibid.*, chap. xcix.

29. *Ibid.*, lix.

30. *Ibid.*, chaps. ii, x, xxviii.

31. Cervantes, *Don Quixote*, Pt. I, chap. 15.

32. Miguel de Unamuno, *The Life of Don Quixote and Sancho*, trans. Homer P. Earle (New York: Knopf, 1927), p. 36.

33. *Quincas Borba*, chap. vi. Assis also associates Quincas Borba with Don Quixote by the extraordinary thinness of his legs, chap. v. One of Assis's frequent comparisons was "as thin as Don Quixote"; see, for example, the short story "Almas Agradecidas," in Machado de Assis, *Histórias Românticas* (Rio: Jackson, 1938), or "Elógio da Vaidade," cited above.

34. Cervantes, *Don Quixote*, Pt. I, chap. 16. Even in *Don Quixote*, the knight and the squire have much in common: in Pt. II, chap. 2, the priest remarks that the pair of them seem to be cast in one mold.

35. *Quincas Borba*, chap. cxliii. Fielding's Sophia also fell off her horse: once Tom caught her and broke his arm, another time her skirts flew up and made the bystanders laugh. N.B., in chaps. cxii and cxiii, Machado de Assis frankly pays his respects to Fielding.

36. *Ibid.*, chap. lxxx.

37. E.g., Rubião's French and Spanish servants, and his dream of a marriage feast (chap. lxxxi) with Bohemian glass, Hungarian china, Sèvres vases.

38. Rubião's dream (chap. cix), in which the horses kept increasing in number. Cf. chap. clii, when he actually rode off with Sophia in her carriage and was fascinated by the sound of the horses' hooves. There are many horses in *Quincas Borba*, but they are all one—egoistic sexual appetite. Sophia beat hers with her riding crop, and he threw her (chap. cxliii).

39. *Quincas Borba*, chaps. clxx–clxxiii. Cf. Maria Benedicta's own words, chap. cxvii, "I love him as I love God in heaven."

40. E.g., *ibid.*, chap. cxxix.

41. *Ibid.*, chap. cxxxii.

42. *Ibid.*, chap. clxxxviii. Cf. the present study, chap. 18.

43. *Quincas Borba*, chaps. lvi, lix. Cf. chap. lxxx, lxxxii.

44. *Ibid.*, chap. cxcv.

45. Which Don Quixote thought to be Malbrino's golden helmet, *Don Quixote*, I, chap. 21; *Quincas Borba*, chap. cc.

46. *Quincas Borba*, chap. cxcvii.

47. As Napoleon III, emperor of the Franco-Prussian War, Rubião

had won the "Battle of Solferino" (chap. cxlv), a Pyrrhic victory. It is interesting to note that potatoes were one of the three main crops, if not the main crop, of Hanover, Prussia: see "Hanover," in *The Columbia-Viking Desk Encyclopedia*; and "Prussia" in the *Grande Enciclopédia*, cited above.

48. For example, in *Esau and Jacob*, chap. vi, where Natividade's name shone among the chief stars in the society columns.

49. *Quincas Borba*, chap. xl. Cf. *Posthumous Memoirs of Braz Cubas*, chap. xcix, in which Braz, seated in a crowded theater, isolates himself from the crowd by going to the "moon." "The world of the moon," writes Braz, "that luminous, secret attic in the brain—what else is it but the disdainful affirmation of our spiritual liberty?"

50. Cf. Barreto Filho, *Introdução a Machado de Assis* (Rio: Agir, 1947), p. 162.

CHAPTER 14.

1. Argument and annotation have been omitted, for the most part, from this chapter. For detailed discussion of *Dom Casmurro*, the reader is referred to Helen Caldwell, *The Brazilian Othello of Machado de Assis: A Study of Dom Casmurro* (Berkeley and Los Angeles: University of California Press, 1960). In the years since that book's publication I have found no reason to radically alter the views there expressed, but, on the contrary, have discovered a good deal of corroborative evidence. Hence it seemed better not to repeat what I said, as well as I could, in that rather fully documented monograph.

2. *Dom Casmurro*/por Machado de Assis/da Academia Brazileira/ H. Garnier, Livreiro-Editor/71, Rua Moreira Cezar, 71/Rio de Janeiro/6, Rue des Saints-Pères, 6/Pariz.

The printing of *Dom Casmurro* had been finished in France by Dec. 5, 1899; but the copies did not reach Rio de Janeiro until some time after Feb. 12, 1900. (See the correspondence of Assis and his publisher between the dates, Dec. 5, 1899 and Feb. 12, 1900 in *Exposição Machado de Assis* [Rio: Ministério da Educação e Saude, 1939], pp. 201–203.) Thus the date of publication is variously given as 1899 and 1900.

3. *Quincas Borba*, chaps. xxviii, xl. Cf. chaps. iii with its busts of Mephistopheles and Faust; and the repetition of the word "devil" (diabo) in connection with Sophia and Rubião and also with the city, e.g., in chaps. xl, xlv, l, li, lxviii, xcix, cxviii, xlii.

4. Richard B. Sewell, *The Vision of Tragedy* (New Haven and London: Yale University Press, 1959), p. 7.

5. *Quincas Borba*, chaps. xvi, cxxxiii.

6. His mental capacity is first indicated in chaps. iv through xii.

7. The feminine form *dona* is freely used as a prefix to a woman's name without any implication of noble blood.

8. Machado de Assis, *Adelaide Ristori* (Rio: Academia Brasileira de Letras, 1955), pp. 35, 56 in particular.

9. See for example, Assis's introduction to *Resurrection*.

10. *Quincas Borba*, chap. xlvii.

11. *Ibid.*, chap. cix.

12. *Ibid.*, chap. xl.

CHAPTER 15.

1. "Sobre *Dom Casmurro*," Jornal do Commercio (Rio), Mar. 19, 1900. When this review was republished in José Veríssimo, *Estudos de Literatura Brazileira*, Terceira Série (Rio and Paris: H. Garnier, 1903), pp. 33–45, it was given the title "Um Irmão de Braz Cubas" (A Brother of Braz Cubas).

Cf. Graça Aranha's comment on Joaquim Nabuco's letter informing Machado de Assis that he had read *Dom Casmurro*: "É singular [writes Aranha] não haver uma palavra de julgamento da obra." Graça Aranha, *Machado de Assis e Joaquim Nabuco* (São Paulo: Monteiro Lobato, 1923), pp. 47–48.

2. *Posthumous Memoirs of Braz Cubas*, chap. xi.

3. Helen Caldwell, *The Brazilian Othello of Machado de Assis* (Berkeley and Los Angeles: University of California Press, 1960); see in particular chaps. 6, 7, 10.

4. Machado de Assis/(da Academia Brasileira)/*Esaú*/e/*Jacob*/H. Garnier, Livreiro-Editor/71, Rua do Ouvidor, 71/Rio de Janeiro/ 6, Rue des Saints-Pères, 6/Paris/1904.

Machado de Assis/Da Academia Brasileira/*Memorial de Ayres*/ H. Garnier, Livreiro-Editor/7, Rua do Ouvidor, 7/Rio de Janeiro /6, Rue des Saints-Pères, 6/Paris [1908].

5. José Veríssimo, "Vida Literária—*Esaú e Jacob* o Ultimo Livro do Sr. Machado de Assis," *Kosmos* (Rio, Dec., 1904). Republished in José Veríssimo, *Estudos de Literatura Brazileira*, Sexta Série, pp. 215–222.

6. *Quincas Borba*, chaps. iii, x, xxi.

7. *Ibid.*, chap. xlvii. The episode is drenched with a certain morbidity, and there runs through it, over and over, the symbol of the horse.

8. Caldwell, *Brazilian Othello*, pp. 26–28.

9. Cf. Assis's criticism of Eça de Queiroz's *O Primo Bazilio*, in which he states, "Aesthetic truth is perfectly autonomous."

10. *Hand and Glove*, chap. iii.

11. "Foreword to the Third Edition." See this study, p. 112.

12. Caldwell, *The Brazilian Othello*, pp. 150–160.

13. *Esau and Jacob*, chap. xiii.

14. "*O Primo Bazilio.*"

15. *Quincas Borba*, chap. cliii; cf. the similar scene where Braz's Virgilia arrives at the cottage, see this study, chap. 11 and n. 71.

16. *Esau and Jacob*, chap. civ.

17. *Ibid.*, chap. lxxxiii.

18. Tom Jones, Bk. II, chap. 1 and Bk. III, chap. 1. Sterne followed the same method: see *Tristram Shandy*, Bk. II, chap. 11, where Shandy says writing is like conversation, a well-bred author will not talk all the time but will leave the reader something to imagine.

19. *Hand and Glove*, chap. xi.

20. *Quincas Borba*, chap. cvi.

21. *Posthumous Memoirs*, chap. xiii.

22. *Ibid.*, chap. cxxvi.

23. *Dom Casmurro*, chap. lix.

24. *Esau and Jacob*, chap. lv.

25. *Ibid.*, chap. v. N.B. this was also a favorite injunction of Cervantes's.

26. *Ibid.*, chap. xxiii.

27. See chap. 11, n. 45.

28. *Esau and Jacob*, chap. xiii.

29. *Yayá Garcia*, chap. i, "Time the invisible chemist." See this study, chap. 9. Cf. *Esau and Jacob*, chap. xxii: "Time is an invisible web."

30. Dante, *Inferno*, canto v, lines 4–12. *Esau and Jacob*, chap. lxxxiv. Santos, like Dante's damned souls pours out a "secret confession."

31. Ps. 54:10, 12. Cf. Assis, "A Semana," Aug. 16, 1896, on the Philistines taking over the city of Rio de Janeiro.

32. Ps. 54:8.

33. Dante, *Paradiso*, canto viii, lines 115–118. See William Warren Vernon, *Readings on the Paradiso of Dante*, I (2d ed.; London: Methuen, 1909), 275; *Esau and Jacob*, chap. xxxiii.

34. Exposição Machado de Assis (Rio: Ministério da Educação e Saúde, 1939), p. 192, item 13, contract with H. Garnier, dated July 18, 1903, for the rights to *Último*; p. 205, item 35, letter from Assis to Garnier, dated Nov. 9, 1903, enclosing the proofs of *Último*; pp. 192–193, item 14, contract with H. Garnier, dated Apr. 15, 1904, in which the title *Último is changed to Esaü e Jacob*. Cf. J. Galante de Sousa, *Bibliografia de Machado de Assis*, pp. 176, 684–685, and item 1253.

35. Gen. 25:21–26.

36. Dante, *Paradiso*, canto xxxii, lines 61 ff.; xx, 130–138; xxi, 83–99; viii, 121–148. Cf. Paul's Epistle to the Romans 9:10–15; Karl Vossler, *Mediaeval Culture An Introduction to Dante and his Times*, I (New York: Ungar, 1958), 39, 47, 66–67, 121 ff.; Vernon, *Readings*, II:484–492.

37. *Esau and Jacob*, chaps. xxix, xxxi.

38. *A Bíblia Sagrada contendo o Velho e o Novo Testamento*, traduzida em Portuguez Segundo a Vulgata Latina por António Pereira de Figueiredo (Londres: Officina de Harrison e Filhos, 1866). See Jean-Michel Massa, "La Bibliothèque de Machado de Assis," *Revista do Livro*, VI (Mar.–June, 1961), 206. Cf. *Esau and Jacob*, chap. ciii, in which Nobrega is termed that "grandee of the last years of the century."

39. See in particular the short story "A Cartomante" ("The Fortune-Teller"). Cf. "História de Quinze Dias," *Illustração Brazileira* (Oct., 1, 1876), in Machado de Assis, *Chronicas*, vol. III (Rio: Jackson, 1938).

40. Cf. *Esau and Jacob*. chap. xxii; *Dom Casmurro*, chap. cxviii.

41. Dante, *Purgatorio*, canto i, lines 22–24; iii, 3.

42. *Ibid.*, iv, 88–96; Virgil, *Aeneid* VI. 126–129.

43. See Gastão Cruls, *Aparência do Rio de Janeiro* (Rio: Olympio, 1952), pp. 61–68.

44. *Esau and Jacob*, chap. ii.

45. *Ibid.*, chap. xv.

46. *Ibid.*, chap. lxxxi.

47. *Ibid.*, chap. iv.

48. *Ibid.*, chap. lxxv.

49. *Ibid.*, chap. xix.

50. In particular *ibid.*, chap. xxxi. Cf. Eugenio Gomes, *Machado de Assis* (Rio: Livraria São José, 1958), pp. 183–205.

51. E.g., *Esau and Jacob*, chap. lxxxiii.

52. *Ibid.*, chap. cvi.

53. *Ibid.*, chap. xxxv.

54. *Ibid.*, chap. xxxi.

55. *Ibid.*

56. *Ibid.*

57. *Esau and Jacob*, chap. xcix.

58. *Ibid.*, chap. c.

59. *Ibid.*, chap. lxxxiv.

60. E.g., *Ibid.*, chaps. xxxii, xxxiv, liii, lxxxvii, xcviii.

61. *Ibid.*, chap. xxxi.

62. *Ibid.*

63. See, for example, Pedro Calmon, *História da Civilização Brasileira* (4th ed.; São Paulo: Editora Nacional, 1940), pp. 296–347.

64. *Esau and Jacob*, chap. cvii.

65. *Ibid.*, chap. cviii.

66. *Ibid.*, chaps. lxxxiv, cx.

67. *Ibid.*, chap. xci.

68. *Ibid.*, chap. cx. Cf. "A Semana," June 5, 1892, in Machado de

Assis, *A Semana*, vol. I (Rio: Jackson, 1938). See also, R. Magalhães Júnior, *Ao Redor de Machado de Assis* (Rio: Civilização Brasileira, 1958), pp. 212–214.

69. *Esau and Jacob*, chaps. xlvii and liii.
70. *Ibid.*, chap. lxvi.
71. *Ibid.*, chaps. lxii–lxiii.
72. *Ibid.*, chap. xci.
73. *Ibid.*, chap. xc.
74. *Ibid.*, chap. xxxvi; cf. chap. xlviii, in which the ball for the Chilean officers is called a Venetian dream.
75. *Ibid.*, chap. cvii.
76. *Ibid.*
77. *Ibid.*, chaps. liii, l.
78. *Ibid.*, chaps. xlix, lxii, lxiii.
79. *Ibid.*, chap. lxxii.
80. *Ibid.*, chap. ciii.
81. *Ibid.*, chaps. cxvi–cxvii.
82. *Ibid.*, chaps. l, xi.
83. *Ibid.*, chap. xix.
84. *Ibid.*, chap. xxiii. The second man, although he went up as well as down the same street (i.e., marched backward in time), "one day turned the corner of Life and dropped dead in Death Square."
85. *Ibid.*, chap. lxix. The "present hour" was anarchy—"no real government."
86. Cf. Dante: the damned souls in Hell know only the past and future, not the present (*Inferno*, x, 97 ff.).
87. As, for example, those reproduced in R. Magalhães Júnior, *Deodoro A Espada Contra o Império* (São Paulo: Editora Nacional, 1957), *passim*.
88. *Esau and Jacob*, chap. lxxxvii.
89. *Ibid.*, chap. lxx.
90. E.g., "Metafísica das Rosas," *Gazeta Literária* (Rio), Dec. 1, 1883, in Machado de Assis, *Obra*, III (Aguilar) 1017–1019.
91. *Esau and Jacob*, chap. lvi. In respect to Perpetua, it might be remarked that Deodoro rallied his Paraguayan war veterans for the coup that established the Republic. In this novel, the "army" is sterile.
92. *Ibid.*, chap. lxxxiii.
93. *Ibid.*, chap. xlviii.
94. *Ibid.*, chap. lx.
95. *Ibid.*, chap. xli.
96. E.g., "A Semana," April 19, 1896, Machado de Assis, *A Semana*, vol. III (Rio: Jackson, 1938).
97. *Esau and Jacob*, chap. lxiii.
98. In addition to the play on the adjective (perpetual), St. Per-

petua was St. Augustine's sister, and St. Augustine seems to have been associated in Assis's mind with Brazilian men: cf. Caldwell, *Brazilian Othello*, pp. 150–160.

99. *Esau and Jacob*, chap. xv.

100. *Ibid.*, chaps. i, ii.

101. Luís da Câmara Cascudo, *Dicionário do Folclore Brasileiro* (Rio: Instituto Nacional do Livro, 1954), article "arruda."

102. *Esau and Jacob*, chap. cx.

103. José Leite de Vasconcellos, *Antroponimia Portuguesa* (Lisbon: Imprensa Nacional, 1928), p. 473.

104. *Esau and Jacob*, chap. xci.

105. "Como se Inventaram os Almanaques," *Almanaque das Fluminenses 1890* (Rio: Lombaerts), republished in Machado de Assis, *Contos Avulsos*, ed. R. Magalhães Júnior (Rio: Civilização Brasileira, 1956), pp. 249–253.

106. *Esau and Jacob*, chap. xci.

107. *Ibid.*, chap. xix.

108. *Ibid.* Eugenio Gomes, *Machado de Assis*, pp. 39, 185, finds in Natividade the symbol of a fecund Nature and identifies her with Cybele.

109. Assis frequently expressed bitterness in his journalistic columns about the poor sanitary conditions of his native city, and especially about its epidemics: e.g., "História de Quinze Dias," Feb. 1, Apr. 1, Apr. 15, 1877, in which he discussed yellow fever, burying alive, and dirty water pipes respectively. These columns are republished in Machado de Assis, *Chronicas*, vol. III (Rio: Jackson, 1938). Cf. discussion of Eulalia's death, chap. 10 of the present study.

110. *Esau and Jacob*, chap. cxviii.

111. *Ibid.*, chap. cxv.

112. *Ibid.*, chap. cxvi.

113. *Ibid.*, last sentence of the book.

CHAPTER 16.

1. *Esau and Jacob*, chap. xii.

2. E.g., *ibid.*, chaps. xxxii, xl.

3. *Ibid.*, chap. xii.

4. *Ibid.*, chap. xlii.

5. *Ibid.*, chap. lxxxvii.

6. *Ayres's Memorial*, entry for *September 3*, 1888.

7. Ibid., *August 10*, and *October 17*, 1888.

8. E.g., *ibid.*, *April 8, 12* and *June 16*, 1888.

9. Eça de Queiroz, *O Primo Bazilio*, chap. iii ("um ramo").

10. "A Semana," *Gazeta de Noticias.*

11. Cf. Eugenio Gomes, *Espelho Contra Espelho*, (São Paulo: Instituto Progresso Editorial, 1949), p. 22.

12. *Memorial, January 25*, 1888.

13. To ——, 1821.

14. Cf. Helen Caldwell, *The Brazilian Othello of Machado de Assis* (Berkeley and Los Angeles: University of California Press, 1960), chap. 8.

15. "On Love."

16. *Resurrection*, chap. xxiv.

17. *Dom Casmurro*, chap. ii.

18. *Memorial, February 10*, 1888.

19. *Ibid., January 25*, 1888.

20. E.g., the auctioneer.

21. *Memorial*, September 30, 1888; cf. his coldness to others, *May 17* and *June 16*, 1888.

22. *Esau and Jacob*, chaps. xii, cxvi, xl; *Memorial, January 12*, 1888.

23. *Memorial, February 6*, 1888, *night*.

24. *Ibid., January 9* and *Last of May*, 1888; *February 13*, 1889.

25. *Ibid., June 30*, 1888. He repeats the statement in the entry of *September 22*.

26. *Ibid., April 8*, 1888.

27. *Ibid., January 25*, 1888.

28. *Ibid., February 4, February 6, night*, 1888.

29. *Ibid., August 4*, 1888.

30. *Ibid., August 31, six o'clock*, 1888. Cf. *July 31*, when Ayres wrote, "Tristão knows music . . . "; also *December 22*, where he says of the young lovers Fidelia and Tristão, "They let themselves follow the sound of that inner music, which was not new to her." *August 31*: Ayres wishes he were a musician.

31. *Ibid., August 27*, 1888.

32. *Ibid., July 1*, 1888.

33. *Ibid., March 26*, 1889. Note the gradual capitulations, as in entries for *August 21* and *October 29*, 1888. The word resurrection occurs frequently.

34. *Ibid., March 26*, 1889.

35. *Esau and Jacob*, chap. ciii.

36. *Ibid.*, chap. xli.

37. E.g., *ibid.*, chaps. xl, cxvi.

38. *Ibid.*, chap. xxxii. Cf. the end of *Quincas Borba*: Rubião's return home to Barbacena is called an "odyssey."

39. *Memorial, November 12*, 1888.

40. *Ibid., August 2*, 1888.

41. *Ibid., July 5*, 1888.

42. *Ibid., April 8*, 1889.

43. *Ibid., November 12, 1888.*
44. *Ibid., June 16, 1888.*
45. *Ibid., September 3, 1888.*
46. *Ibid., July 27, 1888.*
47. *Ibid., September 9, evening (tarde), 1888.*
48. *Ibid., August 4, 1888.*
49. *Ibid., October 17, 1888.*
50. *Ibid., July 2, 1888; cf. October 17, midnight.*
51. *Ibid., February 26, 10 o'clock at night, 1889.*

CHAPTER 17.

1. See chap. 1, n. 32. Even some of Assis's friends identified Ayres with him. See letter to Assis from Joaquim Nabuco, Hamilton, Mass., Sept. 3, 1908, Machado de Assis, *Correspondência* (Rio: Jackson, 1938).
2. Assis, *Correspondência* (Jackson), letters from Mário de Alencar to Assis, Dec. 16, 1907 and Feb. 20, 1908; Assis to Alencar, Feb. 8, 1908; letter from José Veríssimo, July 18, 1908, and Assis's reply, July 19, 1908.
3. *Ayres's Memorial, September 18,* 1888.
4. She died of a tumor of the intestine, Oct. 20, 1904, at the age of 69, according to the death certificate, which is reproduced in *Exposição Machado de Assis* (Rio: Ministério da Educação e Saude, 1939), p. 135.
5. The manuscript belongs to the Academia Brasileira de Letras, Rio de Janeiro.
6. E.g., Carmelo Virgilio, "Love and the 'Causa Secreta' in the Tales of Machado de Assis," *Hispania*, XLIX (Dec., 1966), 785.
7. J. Galante de Sousa, *Bibliografia Machado de Assis* (Rio: Instituto Nacional do Livro, 1955), pp. 41, 113.
8. Assis wrote Joaquim Nabuco, Feb. 7, 1907, that he was planning and sketching out a book; and on May 8, 1908, "Last year I wrote a book which must be already printed in France." Both letters are in Assis, *Correspondência* (Jackson). The title page of the manuscript bears the date 1907. See Sousa, *Bibliografia*, p. 177. Cf. n. 2, above: Alencar must have read the *Memorial* in printer's proof; Veríssimo, the book.
9. Oliveira Lima, "Machado de Assis et Son Œuvre Littéraire," in *Machado de Assis et Son Œuvre Littéraire*: avant-propos d'Anatole France (Paris: Michaud [1909]), p. 81. Mário de Alencar, "Advertência," in Machado de Assis, *A Semana*, ed. Mário de Alencar (Rio and Paris: Garnier [1914]); republished in Machado de Assis, *A Semana*, I (Rio: Jackson, 1938), 7–8. Cf. excerpt from *Gazeta de*

Noticias (Rio), Sept. 30, 1908, reprinted in *Revista do Livro*, III (Sept., 1958), 216.

10. See letter to Azeredo, Oct., 1905, in Josué Montello, *O Presidente Machado de Assis* (São Paulo: Martins, 1961), p. 182. Cf. Lúcia Miguel Pereira, *Machado de Assis*, (Rio: Olympio, 1955), p. 149. Photographic reproductions of Assis's handwriting at different periods of his life may be found in Sousa, *Bibliografia* at the end of the volume and in *Exposição Machado de Assis, passim*.

11. See chap. 4, n. 6. The same type of jocularity is present in Miguel's will, excerpts from which may be found in Sanches de Frias, *Memórias Literárias, Apreciações e Críticas* (Lisbon, 1907), pp. 380–381.

12. For possible connotations of the name Augusta, see Helen Caldwell, *The Brazilian Othello of Machado de Assis* (Berkeley and Los Angeles: University of California Press, 1960), pp. 50–52. Cesaria was the name of Crispim Soares's wife in the "Psychiatrist" (*O Alienista*)—from whom, though he had been married thirty years, he had never once been parted for a single day.

Carmo is named for the Virgin as Our Lady of Mt. Carmo (or Carmel) who, according to Leite de Vasconcellos, *Antroponimia* (Lisbon: Imprensa Nacional, 1928), p. 141, was patron of women in childbirth. Hence Dona Carmo's maternal quality is stressed throughout. Dante used the name Augusta for the Virgin, *Paradiso*, canto xxxii, line 119.

13. Machado de Assis, *Reliquias de Casa Velha* (Rio and Paris: Garnier, 1906): the sonnet serves as a dedication. The translation "To Caroline" will appear in Ann Stanford, *The Descent* (New York: Viking, 1970).

14. For the portraits of Carmo and Aguiar, see in particular *Ayres's Memorial, January 25, February 4, and October 6*, 1888. Note that in Carmo all ages mingle (*January 25*), as if there were more than one woman in Carmo. Cf. Filinto Almeida's account of the Assis couple, quoted by Luiz Viana Filho, *Vida de Machado de Assis* (São Paulo: Martins, 1965), p. 126.

15. See chap. 1 and n. 3.

16. *Memorial, August 3*, 1888.

17. *Ibid., August 4* and *September 18*, 1888. The literature on the Assises' dog Graziela is rather extensive, putting her in the class with Issa and Flush, for example: Lúcia Miguel Pereira, *Machado de Assis* (5th ed.; Rio: Olympio, 1955), pp. 173–174; letter from Miguel de Novaes to Assis, May 21, 1882, "Cartas de Miguel de Novaes a Machado de Assis," *Estado de São Paulo* (Suplemento Literário, pp. 2–3), June 20, 1964; Augusto Fragoso, "Achegas à Bibliografia Machadiana," *Revista do Livro*, III (Sept., 1958), 137–139.

18. *Memorial, January 25,* 1888.
19. *Ibid.*
20. *Memorial, October 6,* 1888.
21. *Ibid., Monday* (between *Saturday* and *February 4*), 1888.
22. *Ibid., September 18,* 1888. A description of the real chair will be found in *Gazeta de Notícias* (Rio), Sept. 30, 1908, reprinted in *Revista do Livro,* III (Sept., 1958), 217.
23. *Correspondência de Capistrano de Abreu* (Rio: Instituto Nacional do Livro), I (1954), 14.
24. *Memorial, February 4* and *September 18,* 1888.
25. Pereira, *Machado de Assis,* p. 112; cf. letters of Machado to Carolina, this study, chap. 4. Miguel's letters to Machado from 1881, however, are extremely friendly: see chap. 12 and n. 13.
26. See Assis's letter to Francisco Ramos Paz, chap. 4, this study.
27. Pereira, *Machado de Assis,* p. 254. On the basis of these notebooks, the testimony of *Ayres's Memorial,* and Carolina's general reputation for being "uma senhora inteligente e instruida," as Alfredo Pujol calls her (*Machado de Assis,* 1917, p. 57), Pereira would almost have her *writing* Assis's novels. As Magalhães Júnior has shown (*Machado de Assis Desconhecido,* pp. 262–279), this appears to be somewhat of an exaggeration. Assis wrote Veríssimo (Feb. 4, 1905) that she read the books, after publication, "which she saw me write." That seems to mean she was by and interested as he wrote them. In a letter to Azeredo, Apr. 2, 1895 (Montello, *O Presidente,* p. 132), Assis mentions that he dictated some half-dozen chapters of the *Posthumous Memoirs* to her when his eyes were troubling him.

For Assis's confidence in marriage as a boon to a literary man, see his letters congratulating friends on their marriages: to Salvador de Mendonça (Apr. 15, 1876), quoted this study, chap. 9; to Mário de Alencar (Jan. 10, 1895) in *Exposição Machado de Assis* (Rio: Ministério da Educação e Saude, 1939), p. 128, "Your father found in marriage another source of inspiration for Brazilian letters. Follow his example, which is one of the best."; to Azeredo (Jan. 12, 1896), quoted by Viana, *Vida,* p. 158, "You are going to marry, which is as much as to say you are going to be blessed."

28. It is likely that she is the subject of the poem "Quando Ela Fala" ("When She Speaks"). If so, she must have had a beautiful voice, intonation, and diction. N.B., both Carmo and Fidelia spoke in a low voice: *Memorial, September 3,* 1888.
29. *Ibid., September 18,* 1888.
30. *Ibid., March 2,* 1888.
31. See chap. 1, n. 3.
32. Letter to Nabuco quoted, p. 198.
33. *Memorial, June 16,* 1888.
34. For the details of Assis's career as a government employee, one

may consult: J. Galante de Sousa, "Cronologia de Machado de Assis," *Revista do Livro*, III (Sept., 1958), 141–181; R. Magalhães Júnior, *Machado de Assis Funcionário Público* (Rio: Ministério da Viação e Obras Públicas, 1958).

35. *Memorial, February 5*, 1888. Machado de Assis's "apolices" were government bonds: see below, n. 37.

36. Letter of Miguel de Novaes, July 22, 1891; and of his widow Rosa, Dec. 11, 1904, "Cartas de Miguel de Novaes a Machado de Assis," *Estado de São Paulo* (Suplemento Literário, pp. 2–3), June 20, 1964.

37. *Exposição Machado de Assis*, pp. 126–128 and 136–137: see also letter of Assis to the "Gerente do London Bank," July 21, 1908.

38. *Posthumous Memoirs*, chap. i.

39. *Memorial, July 2*, 1888.

40. *Ibid., September 3*, 1888.

41. *Ibid., May 15*, 1889: even Fidelia's wedding dress was dark in color, high-necked, with long sleeves and garnet buttons at the wrists.

42. Chap. 4, this study.

43. E.g., *Memorial, September 22*, 1888. Like Carmo and Aguiar, Tristão and Fidelia finally became one (*February 15*, 1889).

44. "A Semana," May 12, 1895, Assis, *A Semana*, vol. II (Jackson).

45. João de Castro Osório, *Cancioneiro de Lisboa* (Lisbon: Câmara Municipal, 1956), vol. I, "Introdução," p. 135; cf. *ibid.*, pp. 18, 133, 136–138, and *passim*.

46. Assis's friend Salvador de Mendonça seems to have interpreted the epigraph as addressed to Carolina, in his criticism "Memorial de Ayres," *Jornal do Commercio*, Sept. 6, 1908, republished in *Revista da Academia Brasileira de Letras*, IX (March, 1921), 49–54.

For Assis's use of the sea as a symbol for love, see Caldwell, *Brazilian Othello*, pp. 109–111.

47. *Memorial, Thursday* (between the dates *May 26* and *June 11*), 1889. The allusion is to Camoens, *Lusiads*, IV.84.

48. "Ulisses e O Mundo Moderno," in *Obra Critica de Araripe Júnior* (Rio: Casa de Rui Barbosa), III (1963), 345–366.

49. Charles Dickens, *David Copperfield*, chap. xiv.

50. *Memorial, August 24*, 1888.

CHAPTER 18.

1. *Ayres's Memorial, June 16*, 1888; cf. *ibid., September 9*.

2. E.g., Nabuco: see chap. 17.

3. Helen Caldwell, *The Brazilian Othello of Machado de Assis* (Berkeley and Los Angeles: University of California Press, 1960), pp. 150–160.

4. *Dom Casmurro*, chap. xvi, "The Interim Administrator." For

Assis's interim administration, see R. Magalhães Júnior, *Machado de Assis Funcionário Público* (Rio: Ministério da Viação e Obras Públicas, 1958), pp. 18 ff.

5. *Esau and Jacob*, chap. xcv, "The Third Party."

6. (*Jôgo do Bicho*) in Machado de Assis, *The Psychiatrist and Other Stories*, trans. William L. Grossman and Helen Caldwell (Berkeley and Los Angeles: University of California Press, 1963).

7. *Quincas Borba*, chap. cxciii. Cf. Mário de Alencar's account of Assis's habits, "Machado de Assis: Páginas de Saudade," *Almanaque Brasileiro Garnier* (Rio, 1911), pp. 203–216; see also Machado de Assis, "A Semana," Feb. 19, 1893 in Machado de Assis, *A Semana*, vol. I (Rio: Jackson, 1938).

8. *Quincas Borba*, chaps. clxxv and clxxviii.

9. *Ibid.*, chap. clxxv; cf. Miguel de Novaes's letter, chap. 12.

10. *Quincas Borba*, chap. cxviii.

11. *Ibid.*, chap. clxxxviii.

12. *Ibid.*, chap. cxcii.

13. *Ibid.*, chaps. clix, cxciii.

14. *Ibid.*, chap. clxxviii.

15. *Ibid.*, chap. cxix.

16. See, for example, the two letters to his publisher, Sept. 8, 1902 and July 10, 1903, *Exposição Machado de Assis* (Rio: Ministério da Educação e Saude, 1939), p. 204. Cf. letter of 1895 to Azeredo in Josué Montello, *O Presidente Machado de Assis* (São Paulo: Martins, 1961), p. 138.

17. Cf. Lúcia Miguel Pereira, *Machado de Assis* (5th ed.; Rio: Olympio, 1955), p. 222.

18. Necessitated by spelling reforms.

19. See chap. 3, this study; and for the years after 1870, J. Galante de Sousa, "Cronologia," *Revista do Livro*, III (1958), 141 ff.

20. *Exposição Machado de Assis*, p. 94, presents a brief history of the *Revista Brasileira* in its first three phases; and, pp. 94–96, a brief account of the beginnings of the Academy with a list of the founding members.

21. *Obra*, III (Aguilar), 935.

22. *Ibid.*, p. 799, "O Passado, O Presente e O Futuro da Literatura."

23. Assis's collected correspondence for the years (1897–1908). See also Luiz Viana Filho, *A Vida de Machado de Assis* (São Paulo: Martins, 1965), pp. 203–207, 221–222.

24. See Nabuco's letter to Aranha, April 12, 1905, in Graça Aranha, *Machado de Assis e Joaquim Nabuco* (São Paulo: Monteiro Lobato, 1923), p. 207.

25. *Ibid.*, pp. 207–215—the presentation speech by Aranha and poems by Alberto de Oliveira and Salvador de Mendonça, recited on the occasion.

26. This letter (Aug. 11, 1905) and the ones that follow appear with Aranha's annotations in the same work, pp. 156 ff.

27. Carolina's death, four years before.

28. Joaquim Nabuco's brother.

29. See above, n. 20.

30. Letter to José Veríssimo, Dec. 1, 1897, "I am a poor blighted fruit of the capital where I was born, live, and, I believe, shall die."

31. *Exposição Machado de Assis*, pp. 136–137.

32. *Ibid.*

33. Pereira, *Machado de Assis*, p. 112.

34. *Exposição Machado de Assis*, pp. 136–137.

35. Pereira, *Machado de Assis*, p. 285. Cf. Euclydes da Cunha, "A Última Visita," *Jornal do Commercio* (Rio), Sept. 30, 1908, in *Revista da Academia Brasileira de Letras*, XX (Mar., 1926), 222–225.

36. "A Morte de Machado de Assis," *Revista do Livro*, III (Sept., 1958), 213–218—account of Assis's death and funeral taken from *Gazeta de Noticias* (Rio), Sept. 30, 1908.

37. Sousa, "Cronologia," p. 168, reproduces the death certificate, according to which Assis died of arteriosclerosis. According to Alfredo Pujol, *Machado de Assis* (São Paulo: Levi, 1917), p. 341, he was suffering from cancer of the tongue. Lúcia Miguel Pereira, using information supplied by D. Sara Costa, Carolina's niece, names the same disease, *Machado de Assis*, p. 281. Alencar, "Machado de Assis: Páginas," p. 203, states that Assis did not know the nature of the terrible disease that was destroying him.

38. Alencar, "Machado de Assis: Páginas," p. 216. Cf. Sousa, *Fontes Para o Estudo de Machado de Assis* (Rio: Instituto Nacional do Livro, 1958) for the year 1908. Even in 1910 Capistrano de Abreu attempted to discourage Mário de Alencar from publishing Assis's uncollected works, on the ground that they were "very mediocre," letter of Jan. 20, 1910, *Correspondência de Capistrano de Abreu*, I (Rio: Instituto do Livro, 1954), 220.

39. Letter of Nabuco, Washington, Oct. 29, 1908, to Aranha, in Graça Aranha, *Machado de Assis e Joaquim Nabuco*, pp. 242–243.

40. Sousa, "Cronologia," p. 169. Pujol, *Machado de Assis*, pp. 359–363, transcribes Olavo Bilac's speech on the occasion, and also the legend on the plaque, which is as follows: "Machado de Assis, nascido nesta cidade a 21-6-1839, habitou esta casa 24 annos, nella escreveu a maior parte da sua obra e falleceu a 29-9-1908. A Academia Brazileira, da qual elle foi primeiro Presidente, collocou esta lapide a 28-9-1909.'

41. See chap. 1, this study.

INDEX